1 9 9 0

Fadwa Tuqan

# A Mountainous Journey

An Autobiography

Translated by Olive Kenny

Poetry translated by Naomi Shihab Nye
with the help of the editor

Editor: Salma Khadra Jayyusi

Graywolf Press

*A Mountainous Journey* is published by arrangement with The
Women's Press, London.

Originally published in Arabic as
*Rihla Jabaliyya, Rihla Sa'ba* by Dar al-Aswar, Acre, Jordan, 1985

Publication of this volume is made possible in part by grants from
the Minnesota State Arts Board. Graywolf Press is the recipient of a
McKnight Foundation Award administered by the Minnesota
State Arts Board and receives generous contributions from
corporations, foundations, and individuals, Graywolf Press is a
member agency of United Arts, Saint Paul.

Published by Graywolf Press, 2402 University Avenue, Suite 203,
Saint Paul, Minnesota 55114. All rights reserved.

ISBN 1-55597-138-5
9 8 7 6 5 4 3 2
First Printing, 1990

This anthology was prepared under PROTA, Project of
Translation from Arabic Literature, founded and directed by
Salma Khadra Jayyusi.

Typeset by AKM Associates (UK) Ltd, Southall, London
Printed and bound in Great Britain by BPCC Hazell Books,
Aylesbury, Bucks, England. Member of BPCC Ltd.

# Contents

*Fadwa Tuqan and Salma Khadra Jayyusi*

# Foreword:
# Mistress of the Two Gifts:
# Love and Pain

One of the most interesting phenomena about Palestinian writing today is the abundance of personal account literature. This must stem from the experience of uprootedness, from the fact that a good part of the present world tries to dislodge the Palestinians and to deny the tragic facts of their recent experience, which has directed much of the course of their own personal lives. By writing their own personal accounts,[1] Palestinians assert not only their own identity as eyewitnesses to Palestinian life and experience, but the identity of their own country: an Arab Palestine with roots that go deep into the past not simply as religious history of major significance to both Muslim and Christian Arabs in Palestine, but as an actual, cumulative life modified and shaped by the very fauna and flora of the land, its ecology, its customs and mores – the whole experience of the meeting of one human being with another in a certain place, with nature. These writings embody the conventions, saying, concepts, humour and creative illuminations of many generations of Palestinians and stand to testify to the rootedness of a society whose culture is ingrained in the consciousness of all Palestinians wherever they are – indeed they stand in defence of this society's integrity against the forces that try to smash and disintegrate it.

This aspect of Palestinian writing is intriguing and fascinating. It is a phenomenon of life in crisis, a call on the outside world to look in on the true, live experience of an afflicted people, to see their tragedy as it is actually experienced, to feel the pulse of their suffering, and of their pride and resistance. There is something vibrant with life, self-respect and self-reliance in these writings which can never fail to capture the affection and respect of the reader. The tone of self-pity, of victimisation, which can characterise 'siege' literature, is replaced by a voice of dignity, patience, and anguished confidence in the self and the future. The Palestinian has refused to be the absolute victim and neither cringes nor loses faith. Even in the gentle and refined tones of Fadwa Tuqan, Mai Sayigh and Laila al-Sa'ih, there is much resilience and fortitude that restores faith in the inevitability of justice and freedom. This literature usually reflects artistic control of the author over his or her work, and is capable of erecting bridges across gulfs of misunderstandings and prejudices. The message it imparts is humanising in the extreme.

When I selected Fadwa Tuqan's autobiography for translation under PROTA (Project of Translation from Arabic Literature, which I founded in 1980 for the dissemination of Arabic literature abroad), I did so for several reasons. The first is the book's importance as a testimony of Palestinian identity and rootedness, a rootedness many centuries old. The second is its great pathos as a work of literature that delineates, poignantly, the struggle of a gifted woman born into a very conservative society where women were kept in tragic isolation away from the male world of success, eminence and intellectual endeavour, but who succeeds in forging her way to fame despite unbelievable difficulties. And the third reason is the fact that its writer is one of the most famous poets in the Arab world today. Her experience as a poet, and the processes she had to go through in order to learn her craft, are important artistic testimonials to the way art prevails over strange and intractable odds. It is also a testimonial to the way political 'commitment' can prevail over a poet's natural preferences and tendencies. The private, intimate voice of Fadwa Tuqan which we knew for the greater part of her literary career, turned into a voice of sonorous protest, full of pride and anger, at the sight of her country falling again in the June War of 1967 into the grip of an occupation which threatens the very survival of Palestinian society and culture.

To Fadwa Tuqan the Palestinian, the woman and the poet, we then owe a triple homage: to her conquest of incredible odds, her unriching contribution to modern Arabic literature, her modesty and gentleness, her assertions and courage, and the great qualities of soul, heart and mind that have endeared her to so many. Revered at once by compatriot and enemy, she had in the late sixties a long meeting *alone* with President Jamal Abd al-Nasser, which extended for one hour and forty minutes (a dream of every Arab intellectual at the time), while, during the same period, one of the enemy's most prominent men, Moshe Dayan, sought to meet her more than once. And it was Dayan who said about her that one of her poems is enough to create ten fighters for the Palestine resistance. Chairman Yasir Arafat, a man proud of every Palestinian achievement, is known to have expressed his great appreciation of, and affection for her on many occasions.

Fadwa's struggle as a woman is discussed vividly by my colleague, Fedwa Malti-Douglas, in her introduction to this book. I would like to say a few words about Fadwa Tuqan's personality, life and work in general.

Fadwa writes a poetry of tenderness and transparency, stemming from the depth of her true experiences in life. Her *oeuvre* reflects not only the events of her life but also all her spiritual and emotional conflicts. The first poem I read by Fadwa was 'A Life'. I was then a young woman, going to university and already trying to direct my own life. The description of such an incarcerated existence rang strange in my ears. We had all had our share of repression and control over our lives, but never to this extent. That a young woman's life should be nothing but tears and unrequited longings seemed impossible to me. When I met Fadwa in the mid-fifties, I did not recognise in the quietly confident woman I saw the same weeping 'damsel' of impossible passions and repressed emotions. But time had been acting quickly on her, positively opening up her life to greater aspirations. By 1960 she had become a renowned poet, standing completely on her own, and despite her brother Ibrahim's lasting fame in Palestine and outside, her standing as a poet was quickly superseding his. It happened in the winter of 1960 that Fadwa, Nazik al-Mala'ika and I were staying in Beirut at the same time. Nazik had become, by that time, highly renowned, almost a legend in her own right. I myself had started publishing poetry and criticism in the mid-fifties, quickly gaining acceptance, a testimony to the fact that the Arab world, despite its repressive stance towards woman, was tolerant – even proud – of woman's creative achievement. Beirut, that city of elegance and style, of culture and poetry, of unbelievable hospitality and irrepressible enthusiasm, celebrated the presence in town of the three women poets with many parties and meetings. The celebrations tired Fadwa and Nazik very quickly. My own endurance stemmed from the training I had had as a diplomat's wife during the previous ten years or so. But it was Fadwa who first ran away home to Nablus, leaving me a note of apology for her sudden departure.

What we all remember about Fadwa the moment her name is mentioned is her elegiac voice. Arabic poetry has a tradition of women poets writing elegies on their loved ones. The famous pre-Islamic woman poet, al-Khansa', filled the annals of our literary history with her beautiful elegies on her brother Sakhr. In a way, at the beginning of her career, with her deep grief over the death of her brother Ibrahim, Fadwa represented to us the tradition of al-Khansa', until her love poems cut the umbilical cord with the classical poetess, and showed us a modern woman who was going to assert the freedom of the heart despite the most brutal repression she experienced.

The greatest role Fadwa Tuqan has played in modern Arabic poetry is her early liberation of the erotic. She paved the way to emotional veracity before men poets did. There is a tradition of erotic verse in Arabic not based on real experience, which came down to us over the centuries. Of course, not all erotic verse was conventionalised in this way. The Umayyad period (660–747), for example, abounded with the most sublime and authentic love poetry in any language. But although most of it was a poetry of experience and anguish, one of the era's greatest poets, Jarir (d.734), whose love poetry, especially his *nuniyya* poem, is still memorised by many Arabs for its captivating tenderness and shimmering beauty, said of himself, 'I have never been in love. Had I ever loved, I would have made the hag weep over her youth.' Jarir was admitting to the presence of literary traditions that could direct the semantics of the poem without an authentic basis in human experience.

When Fadwa came on the scene in the late forties. Arabic poetry was in need of emotional liberation. For anyone who knows the social atmosphere of Nablus, its vigilant watchfulness over the slightest deviation from traditional norms (in both personal and political experience), its jealous gossip and harsh expectations, Fadwa's mounting candour about her emotional life as portrayed in her verse remains an amazing feat of pioneering courage. There is something pure and innocent about her work, something captivating in its natural approach to major existential problems as she tried to find, in an era of search for national liberation, the meaning of individual freedom which must be the foundation of any collective freedom. She went straight to the roots of the problem of coercion and alienation – speaking neither shyly, nor boldly, but with stubborn decorum, befitting her refined nature. It is the poetry of a restless mind which recognises its own convictions. Her open-hearted address bridged the large gap between her times and those of classical women poets. One classical woman poet who comes to mind is Maysun of the Kalb tribe who decried her fate as Caliph Mu'awiya's (ruled 661–82) wife and denounced her urban surroundings in the great ruler's palace in favour of a tent buffeted by the winds and a life uncomplicated by palace conventions and spent in the company not of a 'violent king' but of a simple, unsophisticated cousin. The anguish and veracity of her famous short poem about this experience persuaded Mu'awiya to grant her her freedom. It is in this tradition of authentic simplicity that Fadwa wrote. In her verse, the single voice of the maligned young woman cast into a place of isolation and deprivation finds its moment of greatest triumph in her famous poem. 'I Found It!' In this poem the celebrant voice of a woman once made absent by the force of outmoded traditions and therefore lost to all causes, to all outer action, announces now her coming to freedom and self-realisation, to a joyful inner knowledge of her own worth. Following this triumphant self-assertion of her individuality, many women authors were to appear on the scene competing with each other for louder proclamations of emotional freedom. Eroticism became rampant in women's literature even at a time when the theme was dwindling considerably in men's works because of political involvement.

In her later love poetry, eros is completely liberated, and the poet expresses with no reserve the sensuous elation of body and soul. Such elation, seen in her poem, 'In The Flux', contains an ennobling message where love, desire, spiritual buoyancy and physical freedom are merged together. In her poetry sensuous expression is elegant yet never repressed, its delicacy stemming from her innate decorum, her gentle nature and her good breeding which could never give way to exhibitionism or vulgarity. The bold bravado and loud audacity of some later women writers in Arabic speaking about sexuality and love could never be shared by her.

In a poem I wrote to her at the death of her younger brother Nimr in 1963 I called her: 'Mistress of the two gifts: love and pain'. She is as eloquent in her praise of love as she is in her communion with death, and later on, when her political anger changed her into a poet of the Palestinian resistance, in her homage to the struggle of her people for freedom. A new phase of her career as poet began when she started holding her audiences spellbound as she read her poetry denouncing the evils of occupation.

A second volume of her life story is soon to be published. This recounts her life from 1967 up to the present and at the same time tells the history of the Israeli occupation of the West Bank as it was experienced by this sensitive, ardent and elegant poet. A woman with no inclination to preach, teach or pontificate, the riches of her life and experience cannot fail to set the example of final triumph and achievement to thousands of women all over the world.

Salma Khadra Jayyusi
*Director of PROTA*
*General Editor*

## Notes

1. Autobiography (Fadwa Tuqan's *A Mountainous Journey*; Hisham Sharabi's *Embers and Ashes*, 1978; Jabra Ibrahim Jabra's *The First Well*, 1987;); diaries (Khalil Sakakini's *Thus I am, Oh World*, 1955; Rashad Abu Shawar's *Ah Beirut!*, 1983); memoirs (Mahmud Darwish's *Diary of Ordinary Grief*, 1973 and *A Memory for Forgetfulness*, 1986; Mu'en Bseiso's *Palestinian Notebooks*, 1978; Mai Sayigh's *The Siege*, 1988; and Laila al-Sai'ih's *Roots That Do Not Depart*, 1984;) and reminiscences (Subhi Ghoshe's *Our Sun will Never set*, 1988; Yusuf Haykal's *Days of My Youth*, 1988; Nasir al-Din Nashashibi's *Do You Know my Beloved Jerusalem?*)

# Editor's Acknowledgments

My thanks go to Olive Kenny, the first translator, for her painstaking work on the translation, which she did with meticulous care and the empathy of a woman who deeply appreciates the struggle and tribulations of another woman. I would also like to thank Dr Ahdaf Suoef for her advice on points of style, and Dr Aida Bamia for volunteering her time to help me check the accuracy of the many Palestinian words and phrases with which only Palestinians are familiar. I must also express my gratitude to my colleague, Dr Fedwa Malti-Douglas, for her enthusiastic response to my request to write the introduction to this book, made with generosity and style. Her support for all PROTA works lends strength and added value to our efforts. No less supportive of PROTA is Naomi Shihab Nye. Her help on the Tuqan poems in this book and on other poetry prepared by PROTA has added flair and artistic value to the Project and I want to thank her very much. And above all, my thanks go to Fadwa Tuqan, the author, for her spontaneous help in answering my many questions, and for securing for us rare pictures of the old town in Nablus and many pictures of herself.

S.K.J.

# Introduction
# A Palestinian Female Voice
# against Tradition

The name of the Palestinian Fadwa Tuqan has long been associated with poetry. Her revolutionary, feminist auto- biography, *A Mountainous Journey* (in Arabic literally, 'A Mountainous Journey, A Difficult Journey'), will now permit her to stand alongside the leading writers in prose.

Fadwa Tuqan was born in 1917 to an influential land- owning family in Nablus in what is now the West Bank, a city whose rich history extends back to the ancient Near East. Nablus prides itself on its tradition of struggle and resistance, and for this its region was dubbed the 'Jabal an-Nar' (The Mountain of Fire). A twentieth-century leader in this domain was Fadwa's brother, the nationalist poet Ibrahim Tuqan, who takes pride of place in histories of the city and of the Palestinian struggle. It is also to him that Fadwa Tuqan owes her poetic training. The teacher can certainly be proud of his student, who now boasts several collections of poetry to her name. This critical education was supplemented by studies in England.

Fadwa Tuqan's earliest work was self-centred and emotion- ally directed. After the June 1967 War, however, her poetry showed a much deeper commitment to the Palestinian cause. Among her most celebrated collections are *Alone With The Days, I Found It, Give Us Love, In Front of the Locked Door* and *The Freedom Fighter and the Land.* Her autobiography was first published serially in 1978–9. Fadwa Tuqan now lives in Nablus.

**1**

*A Mountainous Journey*, clearly defined as an autobiography (and not as memoirs) on the cover of the book, enriches the Arabic autobiographical tradition, already many centuries long. There were numerous personalities in the Islamic Middle Ages who felt the narcissistic urge to bare their souls before what have now become centuries of readers. Names such as those of al-Ghazzali, Ibn Khaldun, Usama ibn Munqidh are but a few that can be gleaned from the rich literary tradition. But, interestingly enough, it is the male voice that dominates the classical or medieval genre.

In the modern period, autobiographies abound. The classics include *al-Ayyam* (*The Days*) by the twentieth-century blind Egyptian intellectual and moderniser, Taha Husayn. It is in the modern period as well that the female autobiographical voice joins that of the male. And this venture is not, as one might imagine, restricted to secular feminists, but also extends to women active in the Islamic movement. In the forefront of twentieth-century women who write of their own struggle stands without a doubt Huda Sha'rawi, the first to take off the veil in a dramatic public gesture at Cairo railway station in 1923. Important as well, as an account of religious struggle, is Zaynab al-Ghazzali's *Days from My Life*. Others whose works are of literary importance include Amina as-Sa'id, Wadad al-Maqdisi Qurtas, and, most recently, Sahar Khalifeh. It is in this perspective that Fadwa Tuqan's autobiography must be seen.

The first-person narrator of this life story is, without a doubt, clearly concerned with the political plight of the Palestinians. But Fadwa Tuqan's revolutionary autobiography is not an account of a political struggle. Hers is an often feminist vision which at times is not in agreement with the political one. Of course, the link between feminism and nationalism or between feminism and political consciousness is of crucial importance to any Arab or even Third-World feminist. Whether an individual gives precedence to one or to the other often determines the nature of that individual's feminism. This is a point of great controversy for Arab feminists. It must not be forgotten, however, that feminism

2

itself is a political statement. The problem is clearly posed in Fadwa Tuqan's autobiography.

The reader is alerted to her special vision in the opening lines of her saga.

> I emerged . . . into a world unprepared to accept me. My mother had tried to get rid of me during the first months of her pregnancy. Despite repeated attempts, she failed. (p. 12)

This beginning is strangely reminiscent of that presented by the first-person narrator of Nawal al-Sa'dawi's autobiographical novel, *Memoirs of a Female Physician*. Both acts of entry into the world become problematic events. But as-Sa'dawi's female narrator is in revolt against her femininity, and the narrative, with medicine playing a key role, becomes an eventual resolution of this conflict.

In Fadwa Tuqan's *Journey*, however, the opening declarations by the narrator are radical sunderings of several important processes. Traditionally, autobiographies (which are, after all, the story of one's life) start with the subject's family and continue to his or her birth, childhood, and so on. What Fadwa Tuqan's narrator does in this dramatic beginning is simply to break off sharply any relations with her family tradition. That on the one hand. On the other hand, and from a literary point of view, this is also an attack on the traditional autobiographical form itself, one of whose functions is the sanctification of family structures. This procedure on the narrator's part in a sense frees the female protagonist from any previous attachments and liberates her immediately from the psychological constraints of the traditional family.

More dramatically, this non-event, the aborted abortion, calls attention to the problematics of a woman's control over her own body and motherhood. Motherhood, a quasi-sacred activity and the life dream of virtually all Middle Eastern women – and, among the uneducated, their only access to status – is demystified and subverted. The repeated unsuccessful attempt to eliminate the foetus only adds failure

3

and impotence to the rejection of motherhood.

At the same time, other elements come into play to turn these few lines into a revolutionary vision. The attempted abortion also undercuts the heroine of the text herself. Her birth turns from what should normally be a joyous event into the opposite. In fact, it turns out that the exact birth date of the heroine is also a victim of forgetfulness. She does not know when she was born. When it was necessary for Fadwa to get a passport, her mother was able to link the birth to a concrete event, the death of her own cousin during a war. The narrator then tells her mother that she will take her birth date from the tomb of her cousin. A feminist reading dictates more than this mere birth/death connection. It is, in fact, the death of a male that permits the establishment of the birth of a female.

This relationship of conflict between mother and daughter only sets the stage for further complications. The mother figure, in fact, becomes almost an obsession with the narrator of *Journey*. In addition to the attempted abortion, the portrait drawn of the mother is generally quite negative. She is responsible for Fadwa's unbecoming clothing as a child, she gives her to someone else to take care of, when she combs Fadwa's hair she causes her pain, she punishes her inappropriately, and so on. This obsession with the mother goes so far as to cause Fadwa to have nightmares about her, even after her death.

But this problematic and bitter (the narrator's word) relationship with the mother does not go unnoticed by this self-aware narrator, who realises at a certain point that she must enumerate the mother's positive characteristics. However, this need only surfaces after the mother appears in the public bath. Here, without clothing, she 'appeared more beautiful and more attractive . . . In my eyes she looked like a fairy-tale houri' (p. 24). Houris are the maidens promised to believers in Paradise. The mother can be a positive figure, but only outside the confines of the family and when literally and figuratively denuded of her everyday attire. It is her public persona which permits this transformation. The

4

woman can be beautiful, the mother not.

Most eloquent perhaps is Fadwa's association of her feeling of nothingness with the mother. The narrator mentions that the mother always told her children anecdotes and entertaining stories about their childhood at which they would laugh. Fadwa invariably awaited her turn, which never came. And when she asked her mother to tell stories about her, she got nothing in response. She felt like a nonentity: 'I am nothing. I have no place in her memory' (p. 19). The nothingness is also non-existence in the Arabic (*lashay'iyya*), an interesting term given that the mother really did try to reduce the foetus to non-existence in the repeated but unsuccessful attempts at abortion.

Even more suggestive is the link to memory. Of all literary genres, it is perhaps autobiography that relies most on the act of memory. After all, the autobiographer relates past events and it is memory that permits their re-creation. This literary act of creation forms a clear parallel to the biological one. And this is where Fadwa Tuqan's subversive beginning links to her non-existence in her mother's memory. She becomes free to create her own life story, unencumbered by any ties, be they biological or sentimental.

The mother's desire to deny the act of procreation through the attempted abortion turns the birth into a literary absence which had to be retrieved by the protagonist. And one could argue that the creation of the autobiography represents this retrieval. The literary absence of the birth act is combined with the absence of the birth date and, most important, with the initial absence of a proper name for the protagonist. A name gives a character identity in a text and the first appearance of the subject's name in any autobiographical text permits the fusion between author, narrator and central character, fundamental to the autobiographical process.

The name Fadwa Tuqan surfaces for the first time in *Journey* in an interesting intertextual situation. After a boy gave her a flower in the street, Fadwa was forbidden to go to school. It was after this that her brother, Ibrahim, began teaching her poetry. She, a thirteen-year-old, then looks at

5

the cover of her study notebook and sees her bad hand-writing:

> Name – Fadwa Tuqan
> Class – (I crossed out this word, writing in its place:
> Teacher – Ibrahim Tuqan)
> Subject – Learning Poetry
> School – The House (p. 58).

It is here that, for the first time, the reader encounters the name Fadwa Tuqan. But, precisely because the name is presented on a document, the cover of the notebook, it takes on a different guise. It is a written text within another text, the autobiography, permitting it to stand on its own as an independent phenomenon, detached from the entity that is the central character. Further, since the name in its first appearance is directly associated with poetry, it means that the official persona to which it refers also becomes from that point on attached to, and defined through, poetry. A name is, of course, something an individual receives at birth. But the heroine's birth in *Journey* was already shown to be a literary absence. The acquisition of the name, concomitant as it is with the acquisition of poetry, signals a type of rebirth for the heroine.

But the appearance of the name and its association with verse is not sufficient in and of itself to set down the self-definition and identification of the character. For, if the actual name, i.e. Fadwa Tuqan, will define the character and the persona that is Fadwa Tuqan the female Palestinian poet, then its surfacing in the text is not sufficient.

Poetry plays a key role in this intricate game of identity. Fadwa studies poetry with her brother and has constantly to fight the claims that Ibrahim is actually the one responsible for her verse. Clearly, the ownership of the poetic voice is a major issue. After her brother's death, she resists her father's attempts to steer her to political poetry. *'How and with what right or logic does father ask me to compose political poetry, when I am shut up inside these walls? I don't sit with the men. I don't listen to their . . . discussions'* (p. 107). Her social situation does not encourage political awareness. 'Since I was not socially emancipated,' she muses, how could she fight with her pen 'for political, ideological or national freedom?' (p. 110). Since the autobiographical text ends with the June 1967 War, and since this event also marks the advent of Fadwa Tuqan's political poetry, it means that *Journey* de-emphasises the political in favour of the personal.

There is a tension, however, on the level of the subtext in the role of poetry in Fadwa's search for self. For the first lesson in poetry, Ibrahim, imbued with the classical Arabic literary tradition, chooses a poem from the medieval collection by the ninth-century neoclassical poet, Abu Tammam. The poem, we are told, is a poetess' eulogy (*ritha'*) of her brother. This choice is extremely important. The writing of *ritha'*, especially of male relatives (brothers or fathers, most often), was something found more suitable to the female poetic voice, from even before the birth of Islam. Thus Fadwa's initial relationship with poetry is the traditional female one. This crucial poem is also a literary foreshadowing of Fadwa's own later activity, when she writes a eulogy of her brother. Fadwa's attachment to the *ritha'* (elegiac verse) is an attachment to the high poetic culture.

Parallel with this, and in a subversive fashion, is another link made with the poetic tradition, and that is through the pen-name Dananeer, which Fadwa attaches to her earliest poetry. As the narrator herself explains, Dananeer was a slave girl of one of the famous eighth-century viziers of the Barmakid family. Slave girls in the Islamic Middle Ages were trained to compose and recite poetry as well as to entertain at social occasions where men were present. Treatises from the classical period on singing slave girls, such as that of the famous ninth-century *littérateur*, al-Jahiz, make it clear that singing slave girls were sex objects and great courtesans, whose singing and poetry had enormous seductive potential. Hence, the choice of this pen-name is rich in irony concerning the female poetic voice, especially considering that the Islamic Middle Ages did boast a few liberated female iconoclasts, such as the Andalusian royal poetess, Wallada.

7

A pen-name ties a character to an alternate reality. More importantly here, it raises a question about Fadwa Tuqan's right to poetic speech. It is only through identity with another established female poetic voice, the slave girl Dananeer, that the narrator feels she has a right to speak.

And a right to speak means control over discourse. This is a seminal question in *Journey*, one tied to the larger issue of the male versus the female voice. For example, the narrator resorts to travellers' accounts to describe the city of Nablus and its inhabitants. These travellers are men. And it is as men that they provide credence for what follows, material presented in the female narrator's voice. Or, when Fadwa received letters from her cousin in England in which he describes his educational adventures and discusses her own eventual trip to the west, the reader encounters direct quotations from the missives themselves. Fadwa, it is clear, answered her cousin's letters, but in this case her own letters are not quoted. Indeed, this intertextual presence of the male voice is disturbing.

These various textual ruses are, in fact, but small links in the larger chain used by the narrator to bemoan women's status in the Middle East. Not only does the reader encounter the familiar imagery of the Arab women's existence as prison (eloquently exploited by an earlier fiction writer, the Egyptian Ihsan Kamal) but *Journey* goes further. It is in England that she knows the joy of the prisoner escaping into space and light. The narrator minces no words in her harsh attack on women's existence. Women are 'faceless victims with no independent life' (p. 106), they are old at the age of twenty-five, they have no friends, and so on. Rather than a place in which one could find social or political consciousness, the house becomes 'a large coop filled with domesticated birds' to whom feed was thrown, which they would swallow without question (p. 110).

Fadwa Tuqan's articulate denunciation of women's status in the Arab world paints a harsh picture of the existence of many of her sisters. In this, she comes close to the position of the Egyptian feminist Nawal as-Sa'dawi and to that of the

Algerian artist and cartoonist, Kaci. Both these internationally known figures have been attacked for what is perceived as an incorrect portrayal of women's roles in the Middle East. Kaci and as-Sa'dawi are said by their detractors to be simply promulgating obviously false western notions about the Arab woman and not the true reality of her existence. In this debate, Fadwa Tuqan's autobiography makes a cutting statement. Are we to eliminate yet another testimony to the confining world of the Arab woman as simply western falsehood?

Fedwa Malti-Douglas
*University of Texas, Austin*

## Song of Becoming

They're only boys
who used to frolic and play
releasing in the western wind
their blue red green kites
the colour of the rainbow
jumping, whistling, exchanging spontaneous jokes
and laughter
fencing with branches, assuming the roles
of great heroes in history.

They've grown suddenly now
grown more than the years of a lifetime
grown, merged with a secret word of love
carried its letters like a Bible, or a Quran
read in whispers
They've grown more than the years of a lifetime
become the trees plunging deep into the earth
and soaring high towards the sun
They're now the voice that rejects
they're the dialectics of destruction and building anew
the anger burning on the fringes of a blocked horizon
invading classrooms, streets, city quarters
centring on the squares
and facing sullen tanks with a stream of stones.

With plain rejection they now shake the gallows of the dawn
assailing the night and its deluge
They've grown, grown more than the years of a lifetime
become the worshipped and the worshipper
When their torn limbs merged with the stuff of our earth,
they became a legend
They grew, and became the bridge
they grew, grew and became
larger than all poetry.

# A Mountainous Journey

**1**

Throughout my literary career I have shrunk within myself and shied away whenever confronted with questions concerning my private life and the factors that have directed and influenced it. I've always recognised that the reason for this shrinking and shying away may be that I have never been satisfied or happy with my life. Like a tree that has borne little fruit, I have always longed for greater achievement and wider horizons.

Why then should I write this book, laying bare some of the hidden recesses in an unsatisfactory life? With sincere humility, I say that, despite its meagre output, this life has not been without its stormy conflicts.

A seed does not see the light without first cleaving a difficult path through the earth. This story of mine is the story of the seed's battle against the hard rocky soil; a story of struggle, deprivation and enormous difficulties.

This story, I hope, may provide a ray of light that will shine upon wayfarers on arduous paths. I should like to add here that the struggle for self-fulfilment is sufficient to satisfy our hearts and give meaning and worth to our lives.

There is no shame in losing the battle. The main thing is not to give up and lay down our arms.

The powers of darkness, whether metaphysical, social or political, challenge us in order to destroy us. But, despite our weakness, we confront these powers with stubborn pride.

I have not completely removed the lid from my life's treasure chest. We are not obliged to dig out all our private affairs.

We feel it is best to keep certain matters, precious to us alone, concealed in some corner of our inner being away from probing eyes. We must keep the veil down over some aspects of the soul to safeguard it from debasement. The part I have laid bare is mainly the struggle I have just mentioned: how I succeeded, despite the limitations of my ability and my circumstances, in surmounting what would have been insurmountable without the will and the determination to pursue the noblest and best goals, and to give my life a higher meaning and value than seems to have been planned for it.

The iron mould the family cast us in and would not allow us to break, the time-worn rules difficult to overturn, the mindless traditions imprisoning the girl in a life of trivialities ... I yearned continually to escape from my time and place. The time was an age of subjection, repression and dissolution into nothingness; the place was the prison of the house.

Some come into this world to find the way smoothly paved before them; others arrive to find it thorny and rough.

Fate threw me on to a rough path and on it I began my journey up the mountain.

I carried the rock and endured the fatigue of the endless ascents and descents.

Great expectations and soaring dreams are not enough; even sheer will-power is not sufficient.

I realised that action is the obverse of the coin, the reverse being dream and will-power. I determined to do business with this two-sided coin: will and action.


2

I emerged from the darkness of the womb into a world unprepared to accept me. My mother had tried to get rid of me during the first months of her pregnancy. Despite repeated attempts, she failed.

Mother had ten pregnancies: she gave birth to five boys and five girls. She did not try to abort herself until my turn came.

I have listened to her relating this from my earliest childhood.

She was overcome with the burden of pregnancy, birth and nursing, for every two or two and a half years she presented the family with a newborn infant. Married at eleven, she was not yet fifteen when she bore her first son. This fertile soil – just like the soil of Palestine – continued to present Father regularly with sons and daughters.

Ahmad, Ibrahim, Bandar, Fataya, Yusuf, Rahmi... as far as Mother was concerned this was quite enough; it was time for her to take a break. However, under duress, she conceived number seven. When she wanted to rid herself of this number seven, it clung to her womb with the tenacity of a tree to the soil, as if it carried, within the mystery of its nature, a spirit of determination and challenge.

Angry at the attempted abortion, for the first time in their married life, Father would not speak to Mother for several days. In his view, wealth and sons were life's status symbols. He craved a fifth son.

My arrival dashed his hopes. He now had three girls along with the four boys. After me came Adeeba, Nimr, then Hanan, making up the ten.

Father and Mother, addicted to reading the historical novels of Jurjy Zaidan, fell in love with the heroine of *Aseerat al-Mutamahdi* (*Prisoner of the Mahdi Pretender*), and kept her name in mind to give to the first girl born to them afterwards.

The date of my birth vanished from their memories in the mists of time. Whenever I asked Mother. 'But Mother, at least in what season was it? What year?', she would reply, laughing: 'The day I was cooking *akkub* (globe thistle). That's the only birth certificate I have for you. I have forgotten the month and year. All I remember is that I began to feel labour pains while cleaning the spines from the stalks of *akkub*.'

**13**

*Akkub* is a spiny herb of the Compositae family growing in the Nablus mountains. Its season spans three months: February, March and April. Like all our people Mother dated events by relating them to outstanding occurrences. She would say: 'That happened the year of the big snowstorm, or the year of the grasshoppers, or the year of the earthquake', etc. This was a tradition followed by the previous generation and still in use in some Palestinian rural communities.

When, with my natural bent towards the metaphysical, I investigated the special characteristics attributed to those born under the various signs of the Zodiac covering these three months, I found that the characteristics ascribed to Pisces – from 20 February to 20 March – conform amazingly to my disposition and inclinations.

So I placed myself under the sign of Pisces.

We scoff at this nonsense, but we still feel secretly drawn towads it. Our minds always reject whatever lies outside our own scope, although this hankering after the unknown lies hidden within us.

In 1950 I had to apply for my first passport. 'I'll tell you where you can find a reliable clue to the year you were born,' said Mother. 'When my cousin, Kamil Asqalan, fell in action, I was seven months pregnant. I loved my cousin Kamil very dearly. I had no brothers; he was my brother. A horseman who dazzled the eyes, and whose towering height, handsome features, sharp wit, gentleness and charm over-whelmed everyone. The day of the tragedy I felt I was being consumed by fire. I went to wail and weep with his mother and sister. He was the only one they had. You were bumping and jumping from side to side in my belly. The women at the wake implored me to have mercy on the unborn, saying: "Have pity on this child in your womb. Fear God."'

I remembered what I had read about the environment of the foetus and how it directly affects the innate constitution of the human being – how the mother's health during

**14**

pregnancy, her physical activity, nutrition, and emotions all affect the child.

I felt sorry for myself, so, to dispel these feelings, I humoured her by replying: 'Tell me where I can find your cousin Kamil's grave. Than all I have to do is obtain my birth certificate from your cousin's gravestone.'

Laughing together over the irony, we agreed she should go with me the following day to the eastern cemetery where her cousin, Kamil Asqalan, the war martyr, lay at rest.

## 3

I arrived at a time when one world was in its death throes and another was about to be born: the Ottoman Empire was breathing its last; and Allied armies were continuing to open the way for a new western colonisation – 1917.

The British occupation of Palestine was completed in September of that year. In Nablus the British authorities arrested Father, banishing him to Egypt along with others aware of the dangers of western imperialism.

The Arab National Movement had arisen with the dawn of the twentieth century. In his book *The Roots of the Palestinian Question*, Dr Emile Touma says:

Egypt, Libya and North Africa were distributed amongst the colonizing states: Britain, Italy, France – and the Ottoman Arab States became targets of French and English greed.

With the growth of the National Movement, the Arabs had formed groups and secret societies in various provinces of the Ottoman Arab States, in a struggle to attain their rights.

In the first Arab Congress held in Paris in June 1913, the agenda had stated, very clearly, that the Arab National Movement saw that its path lay within the framework of the Ottoman Empire, not outside it. The leaders of the movement were convinced that this declaration would deter the European imperialists away from the Ottoman Arab States. (pp. 90-1)

Father supported this enlightened national trend, conscious of the dangers of western colonisation encroaching on the Arab States. His banishment along with other national patriots – Shaykh Rif'at Tuffaha, Sayf al-Din Tuqan, Fa'iq al-Anabtawi and others – was the first repressive action taken by the Mandatory Government in an endless chain of repression and suppression of freedom, paving the way for the realisation of the dangerous Zionist scheme, which became apparent to Palestinians with the Balfour Declaration.

## 4

During my childhood years the circumstances of our family life did not satisfy my psychological needs, any more than my material ones. If childhood is the decisive period, shaping one's character and determining what is important in a person's life, fortunately or unfortunately mine was not a happy pampered childhood.

I longed continually for a doll that would open and close its eyes. As a substitute for such a factory-made doll, I had dolls made from bits of rags and coloured scraps of cloth by my aunt, Imm Abdullah, or by our neighbour's daughter, Alya.

I was not happy with either the material or the style of my clothes. Mother, who didn't really know how, made them herself. My cousin, Shaheera, always wore immeasurably prettier clothes than I, since her mother had her dresses made by a professional seamstress.

Malaria, constant companion of my childhood, left me ailing and emaciated. My sallowness and skinniness were the source of constant teasing and hurtful jokes and name-calling: 'Come here, sallow-face; go away, green-skin.'

I heard exciting things about *Qadr* Night,[1] which Muslims believe to have qualities different from all other nights of the year. For instance, there was a tree in the heavens with as many green leaves on it as there were people on the earth. On the night of *Lailat al-Qadr* the leaves of those who would die that year would fall and new leaves would grow for those to be born. One of the privileges of *Lailat al-Qadr* was that the

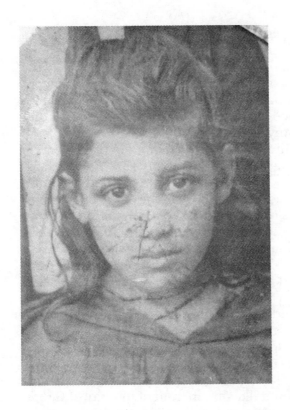

heavens were open to hear and grant prayers arising from troubled hearts. Therefore on *Lailat al-Qadr* I would seclude myself in a corner of the open courtyard of the house, or at the foot of a bitter orange tree, to raise my face to the heavens imploring them to make my cheeks a beautiful rosy colour so I would not be called yellow or green any longer, names that severely wounded my feelings.

My lack of appetite was one of the symptoms of my general weak condition. I was not at all a greedy child. This reminds me of a passing incident, which nevertheless had a painful effect upon me. Next to our house was one of the many shops that stand on both sides of the old market stretching from the east of the town to the west in a long straight line. This shop specialised in selling the sweets and *kunafa*[2] particular to Nablus. One afternoon I stood on the bottom step outside our door, which opened upon the market, watching a swarm of bees buzzing over a tray of *kunafa* displayed in front of the shop. The bees would hover, settle down, then fly off to return and hover over it once more. Completely oblivious of the *kunafa* itself, I was totally absorbed in the spectacle of the bees. All of a sudden my eldest brother pulled me by the hand towards the house, saying as we climbed the steps: 'It isn't proper for you to stand like that in front of the tray of *kunafa*. If you want some tell Mother and she'll get some for you.'

I looked at him in amazement without saying anything. I didn't try to set him right. Always unable to defend myself I somehow felt that whatever others supposed to be right, even if it was wrong, was what I had to accept. However, this particular incident humiliated me a great deal. Lowering my head, I gazed at the ground, grieved that my brother should consider me greedy while the truth was that food of any kind was the last thing I ever thought about. It was, anyway, abundant in a house where luncheon parties were the order of the day.

I yearned for things other than food: gold earrings, a gold bracelet, a beautiful and expensive dress, a factory-made doll. I yearned for my parents' love and for some special solicitude to be shown to me. I longed for them to grant some of my unfulfilled desires.

**18**

In our country, Palestine, people associate good or bad fortune with a new baby, a new mare, a new wife or a new house. This newness triggers optimism or pessimism, depending on whether it is accompanied by happy or unhappy events.

I wonder if Mother associated my arrival in the family with the misfortune that befell it. I mean the British deporting father to Egypt, exiling him from his family and country. I don't know. Perhaps she did it unconsciously. I don't want to misjudge my mother. At any rate, having neither the time nor the desire for me, she put me in the care of a girl named al-Samra, who worked for us. Mother's only duty was to breast-feed me.

When I was being weaned, al-Samra used to take me to her house, adjacent to ours, to sleep with her. She told me later she would merely have to pat my shoulder and back while whispering in my ear: 'I am al-Samra. You are with me', to soothe my cries, and make me feel secure in her arms. I still love her and her children, one of whom she named Fadwa, after me.

I often heard Mother tell little incidents or funny stories about my brothers' and sisters' childhoods, that would make us little ones laugh. I would wait for her to tell some story about my childhood, some joke, for example, or some cute thing I had done, like she told about them. But my long-awaited turn never came. In my childish simplicity I would forestall her: 'Mother, tell us something about me. What did I do? What did I use to say? Please tell us.' But she never quenched my thirst with one simple anecdote. Cringing with a feeling of nonentity I would tell myself: I am nothing. I have no place in her memory.

I used to feel a kind of discomfort which I was unable to explain. The bitter taste of the hurts we sustain in our childhood never leaves us, no matter how long we live.

The memories that left their mark on me for several years were those of my cousin, Shaheera. She was four years older than I and, when she died at the age of fourteen from

**19**

rheumatic fever, I was not upset. My feelings were quite neutral. Her haughtiness and superior attitude tormented me. She always looked at me with cruel enmity. We grew up in the same house and environment, so I could not understand why she hated me. She was the pampered darling of her parents, enjoying the affection and solicitude that I craved all my childhood. She had gold earrings that dangled against her white neck. I loved to see the earrings dancing whenever she moved her head, and I longed for some earrings like those glittering, dancing ones. But then no one was concerned with responding to my material, let alone psychological, needs. Our room faced that of my uncle's wife and her three daughters. The tradition in our house was that the parents did not sleep in the same room. The father always had his own bedroom, whereas the mother slept with her children in another room. Nothing separated our room from that of my aunt and her daughters but a small roofed-over courtyard, in the middle of which was a fountain set in a basin. Every morning before we left for school, my aunt would seat Shaheera in front of her to comb her long hair. At the same time I would be sitting before Mother so she could comb mine. Sitting there in my place I would see my aunt caressing Shaheera's hair, combing it slowly, whispering the endearments that a mother spontaneously and instinctively says, to satisfy her daughter's need for affection. This all went on before my eyes while I took the blows on my back from Mother's fists, as my fidgeting got on her nerves. She combed my hair in nervous haste, hurting me. She did not treat my long knotted locks with gentle patience.

More than once Mother treated me unfairly on account of Shaheera, who sometimes used the ploy of telling lies against me. Mother even punished me one day by rubbing red pepper seeds on my lips. Screaming at the injustice, I swore I was innocent, but the trouble was there was no possible way of disproving the lies. Having endured such situations with my mother for many long years, I began having dreams in which I would see myself face to face with Mother – even after her death. She would be silent while I, filled with feelings of suppressed defeat and a bitter sense of anger at the injustice, would try to scream out her unfairness at her, but my voice would stick in my throat. This dream was one of the many nightmares that continually troubled my sleep.

Filial love is often clothed in hate. Despite my extreme sensitivity to Mother's treatment, which to me seemed rough and cruel, I was at the same time closely attached to her emotionally. Fearing she would die and leave us alone, I would entreat God on *Lailat al-Qadr* that the leaf of her life would stay green, and remain hanging on the tree in the heavens.

## 5

Among the stories my older sister used to tell me at bedtime was one about a mother who died and left her children behind. The father married again: an evil woman who tormented her husband's children by fabricating lies about them to humiliate them and make them suffer. Such stories made me cling closer to Mother. As a child, my relationship with her was based upon a mixture of contradictory feelings. I was afraid of her while at the same time I feared lest she should die. How I wished, during my childhood, that she would give me the chance to love her more.

I would secretly feel very happy when, from time to time, I had an attack of malaria, as these were the only occasions when Mother manifested her motherly feelings, making me sense the true warmth of her affection for me.

The bond between me and my maternal aunt was immeasurably deeper than that between Mother and me: it was she who satisfied my longings for affection and compassion. I visited her frequently, spending the night with her every few days, enjoying the freedom she allowed me. Not having any children, Auntie had taken to raising plants to fill the vacuum in her married life. Her house was a rainbow-coloured garden. She was famous in the town for acquiring and growing different species of rare flowers.

Her husband was neither a fanatic nor a slave to tradition,

so she was able to enjoy the company of women friends, exchanging visits and frequenting places of amusement. Through Auntie and my childhood companion, Alya, I became acquainted with many seasonal celebrations and social festivities – the *Nairuz*,[3] for instance, when families would set out very early in the morning, before sunrise, for the meadows at the foothills to enjoy the fresh spring morning. They would bring along containers of coffee and tea, different kinds of pastry, cheese and eggs.

The celebration of these seasonal holidays was forbidden to the members of our household. I used to wish I were the daughter of Auntie and her husband. I hated belonging to the family to which bad luck had assigned me. I wished I could belong to a family with less money but more freedom.

I even stopped playing with the dolls Auntie and my friend Alya made for me from sticks and pieces of cloth, when Mother scolded me one day, saying: 'My God, haven't you played with dolls long enough? You're a big girl now.' At that time I was eight years old and since that day I have not cradled a doll in my arms. My attachment to dolls was stronger than my attachment to anything else. In my arms the doll became a living being, a little child whom I petted, joked with, got angry at, punished and sang to sleep. Mother rebuked me with the words, 'You're a big girl now', so often that I never made any move without first considering whether she would think me too old for it. I was lost in the perpetual quest for an answer to this perplexing question.

Mother wasn't cruel by nature. She was extremely sensitive, as quickly moved to tears and sorrow as she was to fun, singing and laughter. She had a cheerful temperament, open to human contact, and couldn't enjoy life without being with people. I always had a strange immunity to the infection of her cheerful, extroverted temperament.

However, I sensed a hidden thread of unhappiness running through her. After I had grown up, I realised that the source of that hidden unhappiness was the social restraint and subjugation imposed on the women in our household. It became quite clear to me later on that it was her isolation

22

from society that developed in her the inclination for sarcasm and wisecracks in order to relieve her feelings. Along with her beautiful Turkish features, inherited from her mother, she was surpassingly lighthearted, and possessed an extraordinary quickness of mind when it came to making stinging remarks. All her children have inherited her wonderful talent for mimicry.

She told me often how she would lose her appetite when Father or his brother allowed the women of the family to attend a wedding or other festive occasion in the house of one of the Nablus families. As she would say: 'My delight at getting out of the house and encountering the world outside knew no bounds.' This occurred only once or twice a year.

One of the delights she was allowed was to go to the public bath which, in those days, was the congenial social centre for the women in the town. Bath day was a happy occasion for me too. The unique atmosphere of the building fascinated me: doors and subterranean vaults. One door opened on to another; one wall led to another. A large pool of water stood in the centre of a courtyard under a huge glazed cupola which shed light on the hall and the stone benches that lined its walls. After that there was another passageway, another hall and another pool, where the air became hotter and hotter, until one ended this labyrinthine journey in a wide hall encircled by the bathing rooms.

I had to bend my head back to enjoy the sight of the high roof studded with small round glass skylights, that were like moons shining through the foggy air of the bath. The vapour rising everywhere, the peculiar strange smell conveyed to the senses by the warm intimate atmosphere, the lively women's voices mingled with children's cries and shouts, water dripping on to naked bodies from long flowing hair – all this mystical shadowy atmosphere would overpower my eyes, my soul, and my senses.

The poorer women thought nothing of moving around the bath rooms with naked breasts and buttocks. I was delighted with the spontaneity of these women, who lived in a much freer and more down-to-earth atmosphere than that of the bourgeoisie, which was characterised by falsehood and hypocrisy.

The manager of the bath – customarily the leaseholder's wife, sister or female relative – welcomed the ladies of affluence with deference.[4] She would bring the lady her wooden clogs, help her undress and wind the colourful striped *wizra*[5] about her waist. Then she would lead her to the bathing room, holding her arm lest she slip on the smooth wet bath floor. In the bathing room the women squatted before the *daya*, the woman who washed the hair, scrubbed the body with soap and a *lifa*,[6] then massaged it.

I noticed that, undressed, Mother appeared more beautiful and attractive than ever. In my eyes she looked like a fairy-tale houri. I also noticed how the ladies gathered round her, how much they liked her and how happy they were to chat with her. Her naturally gregarious disposition, along with her wit and beauty, seems to have attracted others to her.

If I have spoken somewhat bitterly of my relationship with my mother during my childhood, she is entitled to have some of her positive virtues pointed out, in particular her exceeding generosity and her great compassion for the poor. She also had a tremendous capacity for love and tolerance. She loathed hatred, peevishness, gossip, and anything of the like that was liable to stir up trouble, so much that her tolerant, generous nature became a weak point in her personality, hindering her from defending her family against the domination of my paternal aunt, and my paternal uncle's family, who stuck their noses into our private and public affairs.

Mother's love for life was boundless. I can only imagine the extent of the inner torment caused to her by the restrictions laid upon the female members of the family. I was ever astounded by the way she preserved her vitality and her capacity for fun and laughter while under this merciless weight of social suppression and subjugation.

She reached old age without the fire of her love for life dying down. Two years after Palestine's catastrophe of 1948 with the exodus of thousands of Palestinians from their homes to neighbouring Arab states, social changes of the kind that

24

often occur after wars began to transform our society. This was the turning point at which social life in Nablus gradually began to change. The most significant indications were the removal of the veil from women's faces, mixed attendance at cinema shows, and mixed family visiting. With the removal of the veil the formidable barrier separating the sexes in the city was removed. I say 'city' now, for the small town had gradually begun to expand.

Mother was the first woman of her generation in Nablus to remove the veil, and from that moment she began to breathe the air of freedom, as the chapter of generations of fanaticism was brought to a close. Seeing her vitality increase, due to her release from the confining chains in that detestable ancient prison, filled me with joy. Attending the cinema shows, along with exchanging visits, was a source of great delight to her. She loved singing, music and dancing. Books, newspapers and magazines were daily necessities. When her eye-sight failed in her old age, she resorted to the use of magnifying glasses. Reading was one of her greatest pleasures.

She kept her love of life up to the last moment of her life.


## 6

If I clung to my maternal aunt more than I did to Mother, my attachment to my paternal uncle, al-Haj Hafiz, was stronger and deeper than my attachment to my father. The way Uncle played and laughed with me revealed the warmth of his heart and made me feel he really loved me.

My memories of that play and teasing remain quite clear, while other recollections of him are muddled and disjointed.

To me he appeard an outstanding figure, a leader, a prince among men. But Father, in my view, was an ordinary man just like any other. The great vitality displayed at my uncle's gatherings in the family *diwan*[7] attracted me. The leading men of the town always deferred to him, and there was a perpetual procession of meetings and gatherings through his home. I would often run to him when he was sitting among his guests and he would take me in his arms and seat me beside him, something that Father never did.

Every spring the Nablus men celebrated the festival of the Prophet Moses. This idea had originated with Salah al-Din al-Ayyubi,[8] who made it an occasion for Muslims to gather in Jerusalem at Easter, as a precaution against sudden attack by the Christian crusaders thronging there to celebrate. Huge numbers of Muslim young men would flock from cities and towns all over Palestine to meet at the Prophet Moses' shrine between Jerusalem and Jericho. It became customary for the men and youths of Nablus to bring out the Prophet Moses' banner kept by the Nablus municipality. The procession was accompanied by beating drums, clanging cymbals and folk songs. After traversing the whole city, the parade would set out for Jerusalem to meet up with the Hebron banner-bearing procession and the Jerusalem one. The festivities would continue throughout the Easter celebrations.

In the Prophet Moses' procession, as in wedding processions, circumcisions and ritual recitations of the entire Quran, the parade would stop in front of our house, where it would turn into a patriotic celebration with hurrahs and salutations in honour of my uncle. One young man would climb on to another's shoulders to sing rousing songs, and wave a sword. The crowd would echo his words, 'We are men of the mountain of fire',[9] and the like. Meanwhile Uncle would look down on the parade from the balcony of the *diwan* and sprinkle orange-blossom water on the young men in the parade from a pitcher, or rather a small silver long-necked bottle.

This made me extremely proud of Uncle. After some time I came to understand why he was held in such esteem by the masses. In 1925 the National Party was formed in Nablus, in support of al-Haj Amin al-Husayni in the elections that took place that year for the High Islamic Council. Likewise a party in opposition to the National Party was formed. This was the People's Democratic Party. Uncle was a member of the National Party, which, soon after its victory in the elections, split into two factions: the populist and the council. The latter supported al-Haj Amin al-Husayni and the former

26

Raghib al-Nashashibi, the major of Jerusalem. To its detriment the country was divided between them.[10]

Father was not detached from the political scene; in fact, he was a member of various political societies and was imprisoned several times by the British Mandatory Government. However, Uncle was always the more prominent figure.

Uncle's death from a heart attack in 1927, when he was approaching the age of fifty-two, was the first time death knocked at the door of my life.

His death stunned me, leaving me in a stupor, turning in a whirlpool of bitter grief. His loss was the first bereavement I experienced. A person's life is a chain whose links are continually being severed, beginning with removal from the mother's breast and ending with loss of life itself.

I stood there gazing at him lying motionless on his bed. I was bewildered by his pallid face registering nothing but complete indifference to the weeping family and friends around him. It saddened me to see him so remote, after he had been the closest of all my family to me. For many years after, I kept the small pair of scissors with which he had pared his nails for the last time, hidden under my pillow. I would kiss them and cry over them before I went to sleep.

My simple mind, at that time remote from any complex philosophical contemplation, was occupied a great deal by this strange, terrifying thing called death. What puzzled me most was that the faces of the dead all had the same look: a look of indifference and absolute detachment. Alya, whom I regarded as another part of myself that I could not get along without, died before my eyes at the age of seventeen without my being able to share what she felt at the moment of death: she did her dying alone. Others of my dear ones died in the same way without my being able to share the strange moment of death with them. These thoughts certainly did not occur to me in this fashion; my perception of them was dim. Despite the fact that I was told that death took our loved ones to paradise, Uncle's death, followed by that of my beloved young woman teacher, Zahwa al-'Amd, and that of my

27

childhood companion and neighbour, Alya, remained, in my mind, completely unjustified. The question hung upon my childish lips: Why did they die and go away from me? – posed in all the simplicity and clarity of childhood.

## 7

From the day I opened my eyes upon the world, I was aware of al-Shaykha, my paternal aunt, only as a person of awe and authority, and the secret agent who worked on behalf of the heads of the family, giving them reports of everything that went on in the house, reports with a great deal of venom in them.

Just as tyrannical surveillance, repression and sugjugation in society give rise to the dual traits of submission and rebelliousness, the same is true of individuals. Anyone who grows up in an environment of secret police surveillance and oppressive family authority will emerge with a dual psyche. There are always acquired characteristics, arising as a result of social and, in particular, family subjugation. Al-Shaykha was one of those who worked at creating this dual personality in me: submission, on the one hand, and rebellion, on the other.

At the age of sixteen, al-Shaykha had returned to her father's house, divorced after a failed marriage that had lasted only a few months.

In her youth she had taken up the teachings of Shaykh Abd al-Qadir al-Kilani, escaping to a refuge in religion from the frustrations of her failed marriage. He was a blind Egyptian shaykh, a follower of the al-Kilaniya mystical order, who had descended upon our town and gathered around him, among others, some of the divorced women and widows. Meetings were held in the house of the administrative treasurer who, at the time, had given him shelter in the hope of receiving his blessing and had, along with his wife, joined the order.

The shaykh had brainwashed these women. His blessing spread over the place – or so they fancied – a musk-scented fragrance that so sharpened their senses that they could see

28

the invisible, and hear things that did not exist.

Talk about the shaykh's blessing induced my Turkish grandmother (Imm Azeeza) one day to attend one of those sessions. She couldn't believe what she saw. She launched an extended devastating campaign against the shaykh. From that day on a profound enmity grew up between my grandmother and al-Shaykha that ended only with both their deaths. Death alone puts an end to everything. However, al-Shaykha carried a deep grudge against Mother and us – with the exception of my brother, Ahmad.

As far as I could estimate, she was in her sixties the first time I saw her. She was given to much praying, fasting and glorification of God. She fasted the three months: Rajab, Shaaban and Ramadan; she would get up to say the night prayers and the special Ramadan night prayers as well as the daily forenoon prayer. I would see a huge string of prayer beads, called *al-alfiyya* (the thousander), piled on her cushion on the floor. This rosary was made up of one thousand beads, and on each bead God's name would be invoked in prayer. Al-Shaykha would put a thread mark between the bead where she had stopped her praises and the next, as if in that way she were presenting her account to God.

In my childhood I was obsessed with a desire to watch the dramatic movements of praying people, and I would stand at the door of the Bek mosque facing our house in the old market, staring at them, noting their different facial expressions and the contrasting ways they offered their prayers. There were those in a rush who appeared to be paying no heed to what they were doing. Then there were the patient humble ones, absorbed wholeheartedly in their prayers.

I would watch the movements of the hands as they were raised up behind the ears, then immediately came to rest on the breast with the right hand placed over the left. The lips recited the prayers in a whisper, then the uniform bodily movements would begin: bending the torso forward, standing erect raising the head high, bending again, kneeling and prostrating, kneeling once more with the palms of the hands resting on the thighs. Following this came the creed

**29**

accompanied by the raising of both index fingers, then the salutations with the head turning right and left and so on. Watching these movements fascinated me. I always wished I could learn why people used them to express their faith and piety. I did not realise until much later that all rites and rituals of worship, from primitive paganism to the appearance of the divine monotheistic religions, take on theatrical characteristics in expressing religious feelings. Our predilection for the mysterious may be innate.

However, al-Shaykha's performance at her prayers was exaggerated and affected. There was always a certain artificiality and insincerity about her extreme fanaticism when she was staging her prayers. Sometimes she would get into a dervish-like state. She would begin to shake and move her head violently from right to left, while rapidly reiterating 'God . . . God . . . God . . .', etc. without interruption; foam would gather at the corners of her mouth, as she assiduously repeated her movements.

This meant that God's spirit had descended upon her. The spirit would descend upon her even at a casual gathering with women visitors.

The rest of her time was dedicated to issuing orders and prohibitions to the women in the family, backbiting and criticising people bitterly, as is the wont of people who have had frustrating lives.

How suspicious al-Shaykha was! Often, she would attribute sexual connotations to people's actions. She would never allow any of the girls in the family to establish a friendship with a female relative, school friend or neighbour. In her opinion the devil was always lurking there between any two people. She would drive every school friend and neighbour out of the house.

Whenever I rendered her a service or bought what she needed from the market, it was done with a yearning to gain her love and approval. But she never so much as bestowed a smile or a look of tenderness or affection on me. She stood like a wall covered with ice where no green plant grew. In my heart I compared her with my maternal grandmother – what a difference! – here was warmth, gentleness and tenderness, whereas al-Shaykha was a treeless desert with no springs of water. She was like a cruel goddess who had set herself upon an invisible throne.

She felt haughtily superior, and was dominated by a mindless blind class arrogance. She was the pious one, to whom the simple-minded women took themselves with their sick children, carrying water jugs in their hands. Al-Shaykha would recite Quranic verses over the children's head and breathe her 'pure' breath into the jugs, allowing her healing blessing to permeate the water. This was al-Shaykha: an ascetic for God and in God. She had a strange view of the oppressed classes, a hateful obsolete view that filled her with haughty disdain. 'We are at the top of the ladder . . . you are at the bottom . . . This is God's will.'

In those days this was a commonly held view. Class was ordained by God and His irreversible will. I continually heard this sort of abhorrent talk: 'Master, mistress, at your service, master; at your service, mistress; at your service, my master's son.' Traditional assumptions will remain powerful as long as people are receptive to them and do not rebel against them. Today we reject Aristotle's words: 'The slave is like an animal', but in his time his words were not rejected: he was simply expressing the prevailing ideas of his era – the ideas of the slave-owning Athenian society.

I recall a lady once saying to al-Shaykha at a festive occasion in our house: 'Please come and honour us with a visit. We always visit you but you never visit us.' Giving her an icy look, al-Shaykha replied with her customary arrogance: 'Listen, you've always visited us and we've never visited you. Why violate this rule now? What's happened to the world? Has everything been turned topsy-turvy?'

The woman was abashed and my heart sank in pity at her embarrassment. Rushing to Mother I told her how al-Shaykha had embarrassed the poor woman. I was too young to understand the meaning of one human being cruelly and mercilessly crushing another, but I had a spontaneous, instinctive loathing for these attitudes, for I was very sensitive. I was probably unconsciously influenced by Mother who disapproved of any class superiority. She criticised al-Shaykha's arrogance to us, lest we be afflicted by her disease. She would say to us in all simplicity: 'We were all created by the same God and we are all coming to the same end. Al-Shaykha is hard-hearted. One mustn't treat others with contempt, no matter what their social standing. Offending the poor is one of the cruelties that will be punished by God.'

Mother used to talk to us quite sweetly and freely about the democracy of death that put everyone on an equal footing. She also taught us, indirectly, the true meaning of the words 'human being' and its universality.

I, in turn, was astounded at how a person such as the religious al-Shaykha could be so cruel. Afterwards, I came to understand how al-Shaykha's religious hypocrisy prevented her religiosity from modifying her human sentiments. She did not comprehend the true meaning of religion as love, mercy and treating others well. She was as illiterate in mind and feelings as she was of the alphabet.

She had an odd and confounding standard for what was lawful and what was forbidden, what was proper and improper. If she caught me wearing a short dress, she would shout at me: 'Why don't you show more of your thighs . . .? You and your mother who sewed this scandalous garment are both going to hell!'

This used to confuse my simple childish serenity of mind. Was God going to send Mother and me to hell just on account of a short dress? I pictured God as a fearful, harsh, merciless master.

Whenever I was alone I would burst into singing: 'How often we have sent our greetings on the breeze to the beautiful loved one where . . .' Al-Shaykha would burst in like a whirlwind: 'Silence, shut up! The next thing you know you'll be a *jinkiya* in Hind and Sareena's band.' My voice would suddenly break off, leaving the song hanging incomplete in the air.

Hind and Sareena were professional singers in Nablus, and the word *jinkiya* was the name given to a professional singer. It derives from the word *jink*, the Persian name for a stringed instrument resembling a dulcimer.

If al-Shaykha could have probed the depths of my heart at that time she would have discovered a lurking desire – my aspirations to one day become a *jinkiya* or a dancer. As far as I was concerned, the words *jinkiya* and dancer were tied to the thing dearest to me: freedom. A professional such as these women possessed a freedom unknown in the world in which I lived. There was on one to wield authority over the singer or constrain her. To me singing and dancing were the most beautiful things in the world. When Mother crooned in her tender moving voice I would run to sit beside her, listening very attentively . . . 'Where are you going, my consoler?' . . . 'Assemble the tribe and gather the dear ones' . . . 'Oh, Mash'al' . . . 'Visit me once a year' . . . and other songs I still love. I picked up tunes and lyrics very quickly. Singing was my joy and delight and learning to play the lute was an ambition that preoccupied me until I mastered it through hard work and much effort, for the lute was a forbidden instrument in our house and I could practise only when the heads of the household were out. Making music and singing were an outlet for expressing my repressed emotional needs during my girlhood and youth. I found in music and singing, whether in listening or practising, a relaxation from the tension I suffered. This art, like poetry, remains a means of self-fulfilment, releasing the abilities locked up inside me.

One of my most forbidding memories of al-Shaykha is of her one day entering our room, the girls' room as it was called, or the south room. Every room had its own name to distinguish it from the other rooms of the large dwelling. When she came in al-Shaykha was taken aback by the presence of my older brother, Ahmad, who was clarifying some of the basic rules of prosody for me. In his hand he held one of my poems, or rather one of my first attempts at poetry. Standing silently above us, she finally burst out in a tone of bitter reprimand: 'Even you?', addressing Ahmad, then added: 'A girl must be subdued every time she raises her head.' Ahmad joked with her flippantly then turned back to me and my poem.

'Even you?' – an expression of shock and distress at discovering Ahmad's indulgence of mind, for he was the only one in our household she bestowed any love upon, and regarded him as sensible and judicious. She had no love at all for Ibrahim. In her eyes, he had violated the family traditions by freeing himself from its harsh bonds.

From that day on, trying to build any bridges between us was useless. I gave up this hopeless task. To the world of my childhood and adolescence, al-Shaykha remains a nightmare that left its mark on my life for a long time.

She was one of those who played their role in my life, then quickly disappeared in the folds of time.

## 8

When the Turkish tourist, Awliya Chelebi, visited Nablus, he recorded his comments on its gardens and springs, mentioning its many children. He also said: 'If you asked any of the inhabitants about his lineage he would tell you he was a descendant of one of the apostles or prophets.'

My faith in the veracity of the history of genealogy is somewhat shaky, nor do I see much advantage in going back to the pages of history to search for the roots of 'the family tree', especially when these roots reach as far back as early nomadic life.

At any rate, it is quite certain that the origins of the family I descended from do not go back at any apostle or prophet.

However, the knowledge handed down for five centuries indicates that our ancestors pitched their tents in the desert between Hims and Hama, where the hill known as Tel Tuqan still stands and where tribal branches of nomadic Bedouin still live to this day. I recall that some Bedouin from the Tuqans of that area arrived in Nablus some forty years ago, looking for their relatives. They were guests in our house for a few days – a very impressive event that was a source of great delight to us of the younger generation.

It is well known, in fact confirmed, that some of the descendants of our ancestors who emigrated and settled in

Nablus after the Ottoman conquest became professional soldiers in the army, known as the Janissary, later renowned for its high-handedness in political affairs. The great-grandfather of the branch that Father's family came from was an army man. It was he, Ibrahim Agha al-Shorbaji, who built the house that has passed down from generation to generation to the present day.

The house is one of the most ancient of the old Nablus houses, reminding one of the palaces of the harem, adapted architecturally to the needs of the feudal system. In it could be seen arches, vaults, wide courtyards, gardens, water fountains, upper chambers and spiral staircases. A visitor had difficulty finding the way or knowing where to go without a guide. In such houses one never knew if one was heading for the reception room, the chicken coop, or the kitchen.

In this house, within its high walls that shut off the harem society from the outside world, where it was buried alive, my oppressed childhood, girlhood and a great part of my youth were spent.

The man dominated family life, as in all homes of our society. The woman had to forget that the word 'no' existed in the language, except when she repeated, 'There is no God but God', in her ablutions and prayers. 'Yes' was the parroted word instilled in her from infancy, to become embedded in her consciousness for the rest of her life.

The right to express her feelings or views was prohibited. Laughing and singing were also taboo and could be indulged in only secretly, after the men, the lords and masters, left for work. Personal independence was a concept foreign to a woman all her life.

If we leave those women to live their empty lives in that house, that prison , and turn our attention to the family in general, we see many contradictions: religious bigotry existing side by side with tolerance, and national and patriotic sentiments abiding in harmony with an educational tradition, which Father and Uncle strove to inculcate firmly in the family, of sending the boys to foreign schools to acquire the knowledge and enrichment of a western education. For others, al-Azhar[11] had been the place towards which seekers of knowledge in our city had always turned their faces.

One of the forms this inconsistency took in our extended family was the wide gulf between the dispositions of the members of the two families: Uncle's family and Father's. Uncle was natural and cheerful. He talked to the women in the family, making us laugh and sharing in our childish games; whereas Father was without humour. He would not give my sisters or myself a chance to get close to him. From my childhood, his presence upset me. I used to wonder at the friendly smiles he showered upon Uncle's daughters and witheld from us, his own.

Nevertheless, the members of Uncle's family remained aloof. They raised barriers of emotional coldness and layers of silence between themselves and us. Their gloominess and the pervading atmosphere of secretiveness were a constant source of amazement to me. My brothers and sisters were a lively bunch, filling the house with high spirits, laughter and song. Everything about them was open and frank, while Uncle's family shut themselves away from us with a tight taciturnity and secrecy.

It is worth mentioning the absence of dissension in the family atmosphere. Father and Uncle absolutely forbade the stirring up of gossip and family bickering, making the rhythm of life in the house appear sweetly harmonious from the outside. But in fact there was something like a silent aversion between the members of the two families or, at least, I would say, the incongruity between the dispositions of both was profound.

Quarrelling between adults was something very rare in the family. The neighbours reviling, shouting and fighting, with the women's voices mixed with the men's, was anathema to our ears. Shouting arguments always gave us the impression that the quarrellers were riff-raff.

One thing that had no place in our house was faith in superstitions, and the belief in the existence of *jinn* and *afareet*, or making use of amulets and incantations as a means of protection to ward off evil and harm. These things evoked our laughter and sarcastic comments. So I grew up sheltered from superstition.

Yet I have a hidden propensity for the supernatural, although my mind rejects it. I am both pessimistic and optimistic by nature. I fear envy, and a bad dream can spread a mantle of gloomy apprehensiveness over me the whole day.

Humanity is still influenced by a legacy from the infancy of its prehistoric mind: the legacy of paganism and idolatry, confirmed by the fact that, even amongst the educated, there are those who believe in superstitions and dreams despite all that the scientific age offers them. Nablus was famous for the presence of the Samaritan Jewish sect. In this sect the family of the Samaritan priest inherits the profession of magic and sorcery, the preparation of incantations, as well as the task of palm-reading. Many people from the city and countryside still resort to him, not only for magic and amulets, but for advice in matters of marriage and other areas of life. This the Samaritan priest gives from a knowledge of astrology which he is expected to learn.

## 9

One of the pleasantest things I have ever read by the great travellers who visited Nablus in the past is the comment of al-Shaykh Mustafa al-Luqaimi al-Husayni in his account of his travels entitled: *The Congenial Benefits of My Journey to the Valley of Jerusalem*, in 1143 hegira. After describing its natural beauty, its resources and abundance of springs, he says: 'Its mild climate, because of its gentleness, is well-suited to the tender feelings of people in love.'

Whenever I walk through the streets which skirt Mount 'Aibal and Mount Jirzim or run along their heights, I am taken back to the world of my childhood: a world of discovery and wonder. The faces of the past pass before my eyes, filling me with nostalgia for the old town and its gentleness. What a penalty a small ancient town pays to become a large city keeping up with the modern age! A high price that has taken away its virginal beauty, its ancient architectural features, and much of the beauty of nature around it!

Where are the paved covered markets, the old bridges, the narrow alleyways steeped in the odour of history? Most of this has vanished, leaving little behind. Where are the orchards that covered the area around Ra's al-Ain on Mount Jirzim, and which extended along the green valley between the two mountains?

I look around searching for its innate, gentle charm and its lush greenness, but catch only a few glimpses of either. The almond, walnut, peach, apricot and lemon trees have given way to stores, modern multi-storey apartment buildings, and to more paved streets for more cars, buses and lorries.

When I traverse the streets of Ra's al-Ain, my eyes search for the bed of the flood stream in the mountain, and for the waterfalls, shining in the spring sunshine, as they gush madly from the inner recesses of the mountain, cascading to its feet to be swallowed up once more in the earth's belly.

During February and March, the season when the springs burst forth, the town women would go out to these springs and waterfalls, wrapped in their black cloaks, carrying baskets of local pastries, mixed roasted nuts, and Nablus sweets. Today, when I enter the vast phantom world of memory, I see troupes of young children wading barefoot and bare-legged in the water rushing between the mountain rocks, washing lettuce and pelting one another with its green leaves, shouting and teasing one another. Their laughter floats over the surface of the falling water in company with the lettuce leaves, orange and sweet lemon peel, all finally blending in the roar of the water.

The water from the springs is now held in storage tanks; the fountainheads and waterfalls have disappeared along with many other things. The cordial, friendly faces are absent and only the memory of them remains alive in the soul.

Where is my childhood companion, Alya?

My childhood had few joys and most of these are associated with Alya, our neighbour Imm Hasan's daughter.

She was four years older than me, but, despite such a great difference in age at this stage of our lives, we enjoyed perfect harmony, mutual understanding and affection.

I used to beg Mother to let me go to Ra's al-Ain with Alya, where her mother's sister lived in an isolated house surrounded by gardens and hidden from view by trees with intertwining branches. Whenever Mother gave me permission to accompany Alya to her aunt's house, my eyes would light up and my heart fill with joy. As we went out of our house together, I would pray to God to grant me a safe getaway without meeting one of my uncle's sons, Father or my brother Ahmad, who would send me back where I came from, sadly disappointed.

We always went in the late afternoon. The uncultivated beauty and the overwhelming silence of the empty countryside filled my soul with ecstasy.

The fresh, cool winding paths, the ripple of invisible water, the densely tangled raspberry bushes whose fruit I loved . . . I can still sense their sharp sour taste whenever I recall that distant past.

On these narrow paths shaded by overhanging trees, paths too narrow for us to walk side by side, I would follow behind Alya, and to me it was another world.

Feelings of freedom, of breaking right away from the atmosphere of the ancient house choked with its prohibitions, endless commands and restraints, exhilarated me. Those dazzling moments overwhelmed me with a sensuous, insatiable desire to devour what was around me. I was overcome with a yearning to possess the world around me; I wished that those living shapes leavened with the yeast of unfolding life were something I could grasp with my hands or fold to my bosom, in order to take them and hide them under my pillow, along with the childish possessions secreted there.

I grew intimately attached to the trees of that area with its narrow paths and fresh, cool winding ways. I lived with them in profound harmony, feeling deep and true joy. Everything there aroused my wonder, everything was new to my eyes and my imagination, sending waves of fresh ecstasy through me. There, my childhood, in all its throbbing spontaneity, was set free to embrace a new world of virginal greenness that grew

40

freely, unbounded by any barriers. I loved the chaotic growth in the trees, if freedom can be called chaotic. I would gaze at nature around me much as a nursing baby gazes into the face of its mother, discovering it feature by feature, day after day.

Through Alya I became familiar with many aspects of our town and the rhythm of its life, which I would not have got to know so closely had it not been for this dear friend, bubbling over with such lively energy.

She introduced me to seasonal and community cele-brations: weddings, the prophet's birthday gatherings,[12] the *Haj* festivities, parties in celebration of a child's recital of the entire Quran, the birth of male children, and circumcisions. She often took me to the house of one of her relatives during the month of Shaaban. It was customary during that month for the head of the family in Nablus to entertain the women members of the family: maternal and paternal aunts, paternal cousins and other female relatives. This was a means of preserving kinship ties, as well as an occasion for the women to enjoy themselves at the Shaaban rendezvous. They would wear new clothes, henna their hands, and put bunches of jasmine, carnations, sweet basil or other aromatic flowers on the right side of their heads. The singing sessions they held, giving free rein to their beautiful voices, fascinated me most. I was amazed that the men of the household allowed them to have such a good time. This joyful atmosphere was unknown in our house and was not allowed. There the preservation of kinship ties took place in a silence devoid of colour, move-ment or any expression of joy.

During spring and summer, Thursday afternoons were special outings for the women, when they went to the green meadows at the foot of the mountain carrying with them various kinds of food, fruit and mixed nuts. I was introduced to these gay social gatherings forbidden to the women of our family, by Alya and my only maternal aunt, Imm Abdullah Asqalan.

I would also accompany Alya and her mother to shrines and tombs of saints and dervishes. The dervish shaykhs had the custom of holding *Dhikr*[13] sessions, accompanied by the beating of drums and cymbals and the raising of large green banners. At some saints' tombs I would often see lighted lamps at the sides of the tomb, which was draped with a green cloth embroidered with Quranic verses. From Alya's mother I learned that barren women resorted to the tombs to plead for children. They would light lamps there in order to gain the saint's favour, or to fulfil a vow. This would kindle my imagination, drawing me into a lovely state of mystery. However, when I returned home and told Mother what I had seen and heard, I would invariably be struck by her lack of response and by her calling all this stupid bosh. She used that exact word. This would kill my fantasies and dispossess me of that mystery world that always fascinated me.

Sometimes when I pass the Hanbali Mosque in the old market in the city centre, memories of evenings of the 27th of Ramadan suddenly rush to the surface of my mind. I see myself entering the mosque with Alya, just before the evening prayer or immediately after it, I don't remember precisely. It would be crowded with the women who had rushed there to get a blessing from the Prophet's hairs kept in a vault to the right of the *mihrab*.[14] These hairs had been brought from Istanbul by order of Sultan Muhammad Rashad. On the mosque pulpit, one can see the following inscription: 'The mosque was renovated and honoured by Prophet Muhammad's hairs, by order of Sultan Muhammad Rashad Khan V, may God grant him victory.' How often did I try to make my way with Alya through the crowd to get near the vault to see Muhammad's hairs! Feeling I was about to be crushed by the pressure of the women's bodies, I would hang very tightly on to Alya's skirt for fear of being separated from her and lost in the crowd.

The greatest thrill of the festivals was going with her to the fairs. I didn't like swinging because, whenever the swing flung me forward, a feeling of numbness at the end of my spinal cord would upset me. I would avoid this, preferring the ferris wheel, where I would sit with Alya in one of the boxes fixed to a huge wooden wheel resting on iron posts set in the ground. The owner would start it up and the ferris wheel would revolve, lifting the boxes then lowering them. It would keep turning, bringing us to the highest point then the lowest with every revolution, building up the excitement. The ascent gave me a sense of fear of a sudden crash, whereas the descent gave me a pleasurable feeling of tumbling down which I felt under the seat belt, as if it were tickling me gently. Sometimes we would forget ourselves in this fun, moving from one place to another, playing and buying fresh green almonds, lupines and beans soaked in salt water. Why shouldn't we enjoy ourselves to the full when our pockets were stuffed with the feast money always given to us on the feast morning, and heavy with piastres?

I remember one feast day when, suddenly overtaken by sunset, we began to quicken our pace, sometimes running through the now almost empty market. The ground in the market and all its nooks and crannies were littered with remnants and traces of children's daytime activities: silver chocolate wrappers, empty candy and nut bags, peanut and pistachio shells, and shreds of coloured ride tickets. All this, added to the creeping dusk and lingering silence, intensified my forlorn fear of the inescapable punishment awaiting me. The nightmare I was in made me forget the day's pleasures. To this day, when I walk through that market, I feel the fingers of the fear of those moments knocking at memory's door.

The early morning hours of the first day of the feast bring back the most pleasant memories. I would hurry to the market to stand at the door of the Bek mosque, opposite our house, watching the men and boys arriving for prayer, dressed in their best. The feast *takbeer*,[15] arising humbly and fervently as a collective recitation, stirred the emotions, filling me with tenderness, honing my senses to the point of transcendence. I still love listening to it every feast morning, broadcast over the Arabic stations. In my early poetical stage I composed a song for the feast for Palestine Radio, expressing my spontaneous childish sentiments. Watching the congregation stand in prayer on that morning, my attention would be drawn to Father and others of the town elite standing side by side with the poor and simple folk at the feast prayers. Although most of the song has gone from my memory, I still remember these bits of it:

Welcome feast, joy of the heart . . .

What a wonderful sight, at dawn
When people go to the mosque with poignant feelings . . .

They stand to glorify, row behind row
Rich beside poor, shoulder to shoulder . . .

By God, how the feast *takbeer* captivates the heart!
It satisfies my spirit's hunger more than the songs of birds.

When the feast prayer ended, Alya and I would follow the group of worshippers to the cemetery, where the palm branches set up over the graves made it look like a green forest. With the men's entry, the veiled women, concluding their visits to their loved ones resting there, hastened to leave.

I loved the sight of the men in their new clothes, especially the shiny *qunbaz*[16] with its narrow light-coloured stripes. As they walked, the two edges of the *qunbaz* rubbing on each other made a slight rustling sound, like the rustling of leaves on a tree.

The young men put silk handkerchiefs in the breast pockets of their elegant jackets. As they walked along, the edges of the handkerchief hanging over the pocket looked like birds flapping their wings. Some young men put carnations or rosebuds in place of the handkerchiefs.

For us little ones, the greatest moment was when we heard the cannon shot, announcing the good news that the feast was to begin.[17] The town would resound from end to end with the shouts of children, for this moment was the culmination of childish joy at the happy feast.


## 10

Memories of my childhood before I reached school age remain so confused, faded and disjointed that I cannot

44

straighten out the muddle and set them in order. However, the pictures I remember clearly from this important stage of life, during which a child begins to be conscious of its social self, are those of Father's and Uncle's friends and their interest in me; likewise friends of my brothers, Ahmad and Ibrahim, along with the neighbouring shop-owners. Any time I encountered one of them visiting the family or in the market, they would laugh and joke with me. With them I felt more appreciated than within my family. I felt the same after I started school. The headmistress' and teachers' attitude helped me think better of myself.

I remember nothing of my first day at school, nor of the time when I learned to read and write. What I do distinctly remember is having always enjoyed trying to read anything written that my eye fell upon.

There were only two girls' schools in Nablus: the western Fatimiyyeh School and the eastern Ayishiyyeh School. The highest grade was the fifth primary.[18]

I spent the first three years in the Fatimiyyeh School, then moved with the whole class to the Ayishiyyeh.

In school I was able to discover some parts of my lost self. There I established myself as a person, something I had not been able to do at home. My teachers liked me and I liked them. Some of them paid special attention to me. I recall how my heart would beat faster whenever my favourite teacher (Sitt Zahwa al-Ahmad) spoke to me. I loved her more than I loved anyone in my family those days. She had a beautiful face and figure, and was elegant and very attractive.

I would gaze lovingly at her as she explained the meaning of a selection of reading or gave us a bit of dictation. After writing the paragraph dictated, I would raise my head in anticipation of the next paragraph, happy to look at her face. When she stood before my desk in the front row, set aside for the younger, smaller pupils, and laid her white fingers on the edge of my desk, I wanted to kiss them. And whenever she bent over me to look at my exercise book, the fragrance of the delicate perfume she always wore penetrated my senses, making me wish she would stay beside me for ever.

Suddenly she stopped coming to school. My beloved teacher was sick. She was absent for a long time. I knew loneliness then, tasting the bitterness of the absence of a dear one and the burden of waiting.

She lived with her family in an isolated house, far away in the Balaibus area on the west side of Mount 'Aibal. Her elder sister was the teacher of the elementary class in the school. I went to her, along with some classmates, to ask permission to visit Sitt Zahwa.

We entered the silent house trembling and apprehensive, holding our breath in anticipation. In her room we sat cross-legged on cushions on the floor before her bed. Her listless eyes swept over our faces, one by one, and when they lighted upon my face she smiled. I felt as if my heart was melting with sorrow. Ever since we had entered, I had been choking back the tears. But now I was unable to restrain myself any longer. I hid my face behind a classmate and wept silently.

When Zahwa, my young teacher, died it was the second blow death had dealt me.

Throughout the few years I spent at school, I cannot remember any of my teachers wounding my feelings or treating me badly. School fulfilled many of the psychological needs that remained unsatisfied at home. I had a high profile amongst my teachers and classmates. One cause of happiness was that my Arabic language teacher sometimes saddled me with the job of coaching the weaker students in the class.

I preferred school to home. It suited me better. At school I discovered the taste of friendship and loved it. The girl who sat next to me, a student of the same age named 'Inaya al-Nabulsi, was my nearest and dearest friend. Our friendship reached such a point that we devised a bizarre way to consolidate it. One day we pricked our thumbs. She licked a drop of blood from my finger and I licked a drop of blood from hers, thus sealing us as inseparable blood sisters.

I haven't met 'Inaya since our school days. She left Nablus after her early marriage. But 'Inaya, the little girl, remains in a warm corner of my heart, a place she has never left.

At puberty I outgrew the bouts of malaria fever and began to enjoy good health.

I began to notice my developing body. I was afraid, embarrassed, and confused by the now noticeable growth of my breasts. I tried to hide this development, and watched it all with great chagrin, as if I were committing some shocking sin worthy of punishment.

I had arrived at this stage of my life knowing nothing at all about love. This was a subject no one in the family discussed in the hearing of us younger ones.

With the arrival of spring, I experienced this thing called love that has continued endlessly to spin its cocoon around my being.

Here was the answer to the question Mother had denied me. It came borne on a jasmine flower redolent with scent that fastened itself to the walls of my heart. Even now I can feel an invisible hand pushing me into that past every time the scent of jasmine drifts towards me.

There are dozens of years behind me now as I recall that event, but the excitement it aroused in me and the wonder born of that excitement are things I will never forget. I had discovered something new in me and in the world, something very strange that made me stand breathless at the wonder of first love.

The depths of my soul were filled with the wonderful, mysterious scent of the jasmine flower. Something defying description was stirring within me; I now felt my heart was melting under the influence of songs steeped in warm eastern emotions. Since that time Muhammad Abd al-Wahhab's songs have taken root in my heart and he remains the prince of singers for me – 'Let's submerge ourselves in love,' 'A heart left in our valley, at the point of death', 'May the Prophet be with you. Don't deprive my heart of you' – it was these songs that gave shape to my vague, formless emotions. This was, perhaps, the first time I felt the throbbing beats of my heart. The meaning of the songs was beyond my comprehension, but my senses lapped up the emotions in the songs and the singer's voice, quenching my thirst and increasing the intensity of its flame.

I lost my appetite. For the first time I experienced blissful sleeplessness full of fantasies and delightful imaginings; and for the first time I knew how one person's face can obliterate all other faces, and invade the whole of existence.

He was a sixteen-year-old boy and the affair did not go beyond his following me daily as I came and went. How could one like me swerve to the right or left? Obedience was my outstanding characteristic and I was continually haunted by fear of my family. The only contact between me and the boy was the jasmine flower, which a little boy came running and handed to me one day in al-Aqaba Alley, when I was on my way to visit my aunt.

Then came the curse that puts an end to all lovely things!

Someone, who had been watching us, denounced me to my brother, Yusuf, who came at me like a whirlwind: 'Tell me the truth . . .' I told him the truth to escape the language he usually used with others, and the harsh blows from his iron fists – he was blessed with a huge muscular body, caused by excessive practice at weightlifting.

He issued his magisterial sentence: compulsory confinement to the house till the day of my death. Threatening to kill me if I crossed the threshold, he left the house to punish the boy.

I stayed within the geographical bounds Yusuf had set me, dazed, frustrated, not able to believe what had happened.

What great harm is done to the basic natural disposition of the young and adolescent through faulty upbringing and misunderstanding.

As I mentioned earlier, Uncle's family was closed in upon itself: when they conversed they whispered or shut the door. We knew nothing of what went on among them.

But our family reflected the influence of Mother's personality. Our affairs were open and frank, the public property of our uncle's family and my paternal aunt. There, there was concealment, secretiveness and silence; here, openness, overtness, spontaneity and noise.

Had what happened to me happened to my cousin, Shaheera, no one would have heard about the affair. It would have been handled with secrecy and perfect restraint. However, since it happened to me, there was no getting around the drum-beating and bells ringing for everyone in the household to hear and see, even the women who helpd with the housework.

My aunt and the members of Uncle's family magnified the innocent childish episode, inflating it beyond the bounds of reality. They began fixing me with their accusing looks, forming unfair opinions about me, and treating me accordingly.

The seeds of low self-esteem were planted in my tender young soul. I developed the habit of walking with my head bowed, not daring to raise my eyes to the faces that met me morning and evening with scowling aversion. They debased me in my own eyes.

My maternal aunt, noticing the unnatural way I walked and sat, continually begged me, with her customary solicitude, to lift up my head and straighten up when I walked.

One morning Father came back to the house on some business. When he found me helping Mother make the beds he asked her: 'Why hasn't the girl gone to school?' She replied: 'There are many stories going around about girls these days and since she's reached this age it's better for her to stay at home.'

'Eh . . . good', remarked Father, and left!

Often when he wanted to tell me something he would use the third person, even if I were there where he could see me. He would say to Mother: 'Tell the girl to do such and such . . . Tell the girl that she drinks too much coffee. I always see her sipping coffee day and night.' And so on!

It was the most difficult thing I had to endure – being deprived of going to school and continuing my studies. When I used to see my sister, Adeeba, sit down every evening to prepare her lessons for the next day, open her satchel, spread her copybooks around and begin studying and doing her assignments, I would fly to my bed to hide my tears under the covers, a crushing feeling of injustice deepening within me.

Sometimes I would go to the kitchen to stand before the kerosene tin with a box of matches in my hand. However, afraid I wouldn't be able to bear the physical pain, I would leave, trying to think of a way out that was less drastic than being consumed by fire.

I often thought of taking poison, but who would get it for me? Moreover, it causes severe pain before death. That was enough to make me change my mind.

Suicide was the only way I could take back the personal freedom that had been taken from me. I wanted to express my rebellion against them by committing suicide. Suicide was the only way, my one chance of revenge on the family's tyranny.

Neither Yusuf nor any other family member could sentence me to life. I would leave them disturbed, tormented, remorseful. Here I paused a while. What about Mother?

I felt pity for Mother. She always took my part when any of them treated me unfairly; however, her individuality had been so debilitated by subjugation, she was unable to save me from the men's decision.

Throughout these difficult months, the same dream kept haunting me over and over again: I would see myself running in a dark alleyway, fleeing from an old man who was pursuing me and whose features bore an aggressive, hostile look. But a solid wall would prevent me escaping. I would turn into another alley only to find the same dead end. The old man kept running after me like an enraged wild beast while I panted with fear, breathless from this perpetual chase. Then I would awake bathed in perspiration and gasping for breath. Fear of this suffocating dream made me hate to go to sleep.

I became accustomed to withdrawing into myself and becoming oblivious of my surroundings. Detachment fortified me. I was with the family when, in reality, I was as far removed from them as possible. I lived in a private world they could not invade, a world closed to them that I never allowed any of them to discover.

My ability to separate myself from the real world and bury myself in daydream increased significantly. By means of these dreams, I burst out of my prison bars to roam the streets alone, to travel to unknown countries where I met strangers who loved me and whom I loved.

I would always exclude all members of my family from my imaginary journeys, for the family was the prison from whose locked doors I wished to escape.

The ability to detach myself from the real world was nothing new. From childhood I used to sit under a tree in the yard and fix my eyes on my left thumb without blinking, doing this with such concentration that my thumb, and eventually my whole hand, seemed extraneous to me, lacking any sense or meaning, something that had absolutely no connection with my body. Then I myself would become a stranger to myself. In my silent contemplation, I would repeat: Who am I? Who am I? I would repeat my name over and over in my thoughts but my name would seem foreign and meaningless to me.

At that point any connection I had to my name, myself, or my surroundings would be cut, leaving me submerged in a very curious state of non-presence and nothingness.

When I raised my eyes from my thumb to look around me, I would come back to myself and the outside world, rejoicing at the power I possessed to get out of myself in this inscrutable manner and then come back. It was an amusing pastime.

When I told Mother about it, she warned me not to do it again, lest it end in madness. Scared by Mother's remarks, I completely stopped staring at my left thumb, and abandoned my strange journeys of absence.

## 11

In July 1929 my brother, Ibrahim, returned from Beirut with a degree from the American University of Beirut and settled down in Nablus to take up teaching in the National *Najah* School. With Ibrahim's return good fortune shone upon me.

My fondness for him had grown out of several exciting childish pleasures he had given me. The first present I ever received was from him. The first trip I took was in his company. He was the only one to fill the vacancy Uncle's death left in my life. The child searching for another father to clasp her close in his arms, found the lost father in the first present and the first kiss accompanying it.

This gift, which he had brought from Jerusalem when he was a student in the Mutran School, was the first reason for my attachment to Ibrahim, an attachment that later deepened greatly. His treatment made me think that he cared about my happiness, especially when he let me accompany him on his trips to the west side of the foot of Mount 'Aibal.

Seating himself on one of the limestone rocks of the mountain, he would let me run off, while he gave himself up to meditation. I would go to the nearby mountain path, leaping like a goat from rock to rock, looking around, searching for sweet-smelling fennel greens, whose long, round, juicy stalks I loved to chew. I would also gather a bunch of cyclamen, red anemones and camomile flowers. Every once in a while Ibrahim would turn around, warning me not to stray far from him.

My delight in these simple adventures was marked by the absence of fear of family punishment. Fear had always spoiled my simple joys, but with Ibrahim I was free of any nagging anxiety.

A new chapter began in my life with Ibrahim's settling in Nablus. Serving him became my goal in life and a revival of my lost happiness. I tidied his room, dusted his bookshelves and table, and every morning prepared hot water for him to shave, and brought it to him.

In those days there was no system of pipes bringing water to the upper floor, so every evening I would carry water to fill the washbowl on the washstand in the corner of the room near the door. It was also my job to set the table for him at all his meals. I imposed all these duties and others upon myself, delighted that he had chosen me instead of any of my other sisters to serve him and prepare things for him. I clung to Ibrahim with the tenacity of a drowning person to a lifeboat.

In contrast to the other men of the family, Ibrahim would sit with his mother and sisters, chatting, telling us what had happened, what was going on in his own life and about public affairs in general. Or he would relate outstanding literary or historical passages he had read in *The Book of Songs* by Abu al-Faraj al-Asfahani, *The Unique Necklace* by Abd Rabbihi or *The Book of Animals* by al-Jahiz.[19]

As far as we were concerned, he was a well-spring of love and kindness, showering his gifts upon us, granting us his time and assistance when help was needed.

I was concerned that he should not receive an injury or become sick, and was forever preoccupied with keeping the floor clean and free from the orange skins and pips the children dropped on it, lest Ibrahim tread on them, slip and have an accident.

He alone became the air I breathed, the air of health and personal happiness. His love and special concern for me gave me a feeling of contentment as a human being.

The optimists say that the psyche, like light, cannot be corrupted, but I believe that, if a person is deeply humiliated and made into a nobody, she will change into a twisted creature, unless she finds someone to love her and shower her with tenderness. Affection is the basic ingredient of the atmosphere in which growth takes place, in either the home or the school. Good mental health cannot be achieved without affection. Ibrahim was the psychological healer that saved me from inner collapse.

Nature always abhors a vacuum; it refuses it and cannot live with it. The soul must be filled with something: love and goodness, or hate and evil; with constructive inclinations or with destructive tendencies that culminate in self-destruction, if they find nothing outside the self to destroy.

The various Scriptures say that the well into which

Joseph's brothers cast him had no water. Does this mean it was absolutely empty? Couldn't there have been poisonous reptiles lurking in the corners or slithering along the sides here and there?

At this very difficult period of adolescence, Ibrahim's hand was the lifeline let down to pull me up out of the desolate, enveloping darkness of my personal well.

## 12

My natural bent for poetry showed itself from my early years. I received great pleasure from repeating the poems I learned at school. I would stand breathless in wonder at the poems or short excerpts of verse I chanced upon in school-books or in the newspapers Father and my brothers brought home, despite my inability to understand their content.

There was a book entitled *al-Kashkoul* (*The Scrapbook*), containing a collection of outstanding poems, together with literary and historical information. It was in this book I first encountered the poem, 'Ayyuha al-Saqi ilaika al-mushtaka' ('Oh cup-bearer we complain to you').

This poem, or rather this *muwashshah*,[20] introduced me to a mysterious and enchanting world, probably produced by the external music arising from the nature of its metrics, characterised by a diversity of rhyme, while adhering to the rhyming of the last two lines of every stanza. This imparts to the *muwashshah* the rhythm that pleases the ear and calms the soul. However, most of the words carried exciting associations for me that the poet never intended.

In those days water-carriers supplied the houses of the town with water, except for a few houses of the ancient feudal estates who privately owned some of the many springs. Water reached these houses through underground earthenware pipes and poured into pools in the middle of their spacious courtyards. Whenever I began reciting the opening verse: 'Oh cup-bearer we complain to you, we have called you but you didn't hear', the word, 'cup-bearer' assumed, in my mind, a particular emotional connotation. It was associated with the image of the old water-carrier who supplied the houses in al-Aqaba Alley with water he carried from Ain al-Kas, east of the town.

The water-carrier's arrival at my maternal aunt's house in al-Aqaba Alley had a very pleasant effect on me. As soon as he set foot on the first step of the outer stairs leading to the house, he would call out the familiar words: 'Your protection, Oh God'. That was to alert the women to hide behind the doors.

I would run to meet the water-carrier and stand beside him at the large porous, clay water jar, watching him lift the waterskin from his back with his strong hands. Then, supporting it on his stomach, he would put its tied opening on the water jar's wide mouth, untie the thong, and the fresh sparkling water would pour into the jar that swallowed up four full waterskins or more.

In my imagination, the cup-bearer the poet was addressing always took the form of the old water-carrier of al-Aqaba Alley. The *nadeem* or drinking companion of shining countenance in the poem about whom the poet was ecstatic ('And you were ecstatic about a drinking companion of shining countenance') I imagined to be the son of our neighbour, the *taheeneh*[21] seller. He was a young, tall, slender, brown-skinned fellow bearing the name, Nadeem. In this way my fancy gave the words images and meanings relevant to me. I would avail myself of my father's and male cousins' absence in the afternoon to climb the uncovered outside stairway leading to one of the upper floors of the house. There I would stand facing the trees in the main courtyard, reciting the *muwashshah* in a ringing confident tone, imitating Ibrahim's recitation of the poem, imagining myself a poet reading her poem to an audience just like Ibrahim did. I would become so absorbed in this imaginary scene that, to my senses, it would become a reality. When I came to the end of the poem, I would recite it again, then a third and fourth time in a Sufi-like trance.

Twenty-six years later, on a June afternoon in 1955, I stood in the West Hall of the University of Beirut facing, for the first time in my life, the audience the Arabic Department of the University had invited to listen to selections of my poetry.

During the moments Professor Jubrail Jabbour took to introduce me, a short filmstrip passed rapidly before my eyes as I looked over the faces in front of me. I saw myself facing the trees in the courtyard, reciting the beloved poem to them: 'Oh cup-bearer we complain to you, we called you but you did not respond', and I smiled.

My smile might have appeared to be a greeting to the audience, but in truth it was a greeting to the image of that girl, captivated by her *muwashshah* poem and reciting it to the trees in the mystical Sufi state she would get into.

I progressed from merely reciting poetry to attempting to write it. At times I would be possessed by unfathomable feelings and a vague excitement, especially when listening to music or singing. Feeling the urge to give expression to something I sensed but did not understand, I would run to get a pencil and paper that in no time would be covered with a jumble of unconnected words. I would take the paper filled with this riddle to Ibrahim, hesitatingly requesting him to read the poem I had written. Ibrahim never disappointed me. He would read the words, smile at me, pat me on the shoulder and I would leave without hearing a word either of encouragement or of discouragement.

Music still gives me a feeling of tranquillity, inducing that dreamy mood in which I want to write a poem.

In the Old Testament I have come across prophets who made use of music for the Lord's revelation. Descending from the high place, preceded by the *rabab*,[22] tambourine and lute, they would prophesy as the spirit of the Lord descended upon them. Elisha said: 'Now bring me a lute.' And when he played upon the lute the hand of the Lord was upon him.

Indeed, music stirs up the emotions, excites the imagination and makes us dream of unseen worlds abounding with the vitality and movement of life.

What role does chance play in our lives? A trivial event, run-of-the-mill news, or a mere encounter can change the course of one's life. The path one is following can take a decisive turn, changing one's whole world. Had not that boy crossed my path and had not my brother, Yusuf, confined me within the old walls, my life would have followed the usual course. I would have continued my studies at the Ayishiyyeh School until the fifth year and Ibrahim would never have thought of making me his pupil.

He had learned from Mother the reason for my staying at home. However, being a man of broad vision, sympathetic, and knowledgeable about the human soul, his view of the affair was fifty years ahead of his time. He didn't interfere, nor did he impose his will on Yusuf, who was a severe man. He just showered me with loving kindness. Small matters kept piling up and eventually formed a bridge over which I could pass from one stage to another. All that was left to wait for was the opportune time: the sound of the bell from the invisible world announcing the approaching moment. Coincidence!

Ibrahim had just arrived to take his dinner. While washing his hands he was enjoying telling Mother about two of his pupils who, that morning, had brought him some verses free of errors of metre or rhyme. He was bursting with joy and pride as he talked about it. Involuntarily I said in my faint weak voice, 'Lucky them!'

Ibrahim looked at me in silence. Then all of a sudden he said, 'I'll teach you to write poetry. Come with me.'

Mother had dished out his food, but he quickly left the room. I caught up with him and together we went up the stairs leading to the second floor where his room and study were. Standing before the bookshelves, he moved his eyes over them, searching for a certain book. My heart was leaping into my mouth, making me gasp for breath. Two minutes passed. Then he came to me holding *al-Hamasa*, the famous anthology of Abu Tammam. After looking in the index, he opened it at the right page. 'This poem,' he said, 'I shall read it to you, explain it verse by verse, then you copy it into a special copybook so you can memorise it. I'll hear you recite it from memory this evening.'

He began reading:

## A Woman Laments Her Brother

He roamed about seeking freedom from death and perished.
My word, oh Dalla, what killed you?
What other beautiful things could you possibly have
possessed?
Anything can be a killer when you meet your appointed
time.
The Fates stand awaiting the youth on the path he follows.

When he explained the meaning of the lines I felt a shiver of
melancholy running through me. 'I chose this poem for you,'
he said, 'so you could see how Arab women write beautiful
poems.'

We went down to the dining-room, my heart beating with
the breathless anticipation of a new world. That evening I
recited the poem to him from memory without faltering or
making a single mistake.

When I went to my bed that night, I held in my arms a pale
green exercise book and a blue pencil; in my heart there was a
host of emotions. I was returning to exercise books, pencils,
studies and memorising; I was returning to my lost paradise.
The words I had written in my bad handwriting on the cover
of the exercise book for material to memorise caught my eye.
It was the handwriting of the thirteen-year-old pupil:

Name – Fadwa Tuqan
Class – (I crossed out this word, writing in its place:
Teacher – Ibrahim Tuqan)
Subject – Learning Poetry
School – The House

These were not just words to me; they were suns and moons.
Before them, my life had come to a standstill, not moving
with time. I had not known what to do with it. Now, here was
a life in motion, its pace quickening, giving me the feeling of
restored self-confidence.

How marvellous is the first step, how beautiful, how entrancing. I felt as light as a bird. No longer was my heart weighed down with grief and boredom. In one moment the mountain of ignominy had disappeared. The spaces of the future stretched in its place, bright with sunshine, vast and green like wheat-fields in spring.

How truly terrifying is the first step! The forces of evil, whether overt or hidden, never let up. They crouch in the corners, lying in wait for us. With the first step begins the clash between the will to live and the forces of destruction, be they random or preordained.

My sister, Fataya, thinking she was revealing exciting news, said to Father: 'Do you know that Ibrahim is teaching Fadwa to compose poetry?'

With a flick of his wrist, he resumed drinking his black coffee. This wave of the hand conveyed his complete contempt, making me cringe and recoil within myself. He doesn't believe I am good for anything, I said to myself. He has no feelings for me except indifference, as though I'm nothing, as though I'm a nonentity, a vacuum, as if there is absolutely no need for me to exist.

The rift between Father and me widened and deepened. Likewise, the scorn with which my paternal aunt and my uncle's family had looked upon the whole affair at the beginning now changed to real enmity. They tried to block my path on my new journey.

They were driven to use particularly clever tactics, for trying to persuade Ibrahim to relinquish what he had begun with me was not an easy matter. He was an independent in his thoughts, candid, courageous, and unable to submit to something he didn't believe in.

My journey with Ibrahim and poetry continued for six uninterrupted days, then Ibrahim suddenly broke it off. Three days passed without him summoning me to recite the last poem he had asked me to memorise, or to choose another for me to learn. This sudden silence brought back the old heaviness of heart, the slumped shoulders and bent back of my former wretched days.

Being naturally timid, I was not bold enough to impose myself upon others, even Ibrahim. I waited anxiously for him to say something.

By the fourth morning, taking courage from my confidence in his love and kindness, I decided to confront him with the question. I took the morning pitcher of hot shaving water to him as usual, put the small vessel on the washstand, while he stood before its oval-shaped mirror preparing to shave. He lathered his face and chin with the brush, while I stood silently watching him in the mirror, doing my best to form the question. Finally God helped me to find my tongue. 'Have you changed your mind?' I asked trembling. 'Have you given up . . .?' My voice broke, breaking down, in spite of myself, into tears.

'Not at all. I haven't changed my mind,' he answered immediately, one half of his face still white with lather. 'I wanted to make sure you truly wanted to learn. We'll resume our lessons today.'

I went down the stairs standing tall. The world had opened its arms to me afresh. The future was awaiting me. No doubt about it. It was there! This was enough to make me feel I was living.

A full oval-shaped face, large deep-black eyes, a smooth black fringe on the forehead, the shadow of a smile on closed lips, a theatrical pose of the head and body – the picture is still clear in my mind's eye. The long years have not erased any of the lineaments from my memory. And under the picture, or over it, or beside it, I don't remember, the name printed in large black letters: The Iraqi poetess, Rabab al-Kazimi.

An ideal image of Rabab grew in my mind, and became the high ideal I strove to reach. The emotional impression, and the deep psychological effect her picture made on me, had much to do with directing my thoughts towards poetry, even before I was sentenced to forced confinement in the house.

When I began seriously attempting to compose poetry,

the first poem I wrote, without metrical or grammatical error, was addressed to Rabab al-Kazimi:

> Rabab, crown of all poetesses
> Rabab, you've exceeded all intelligent women
> By God you are worthy
> Of praise among young women!
> Your father bestowed upon you
> A rich treasure overflowing with delights
> Al-Kazimi, who is al-Kazimi?
> He is the composer of eloquent verse
> Oh poets
> Do not stand in the way of women poets![23]

When her father, the poet Abd al-Muhsin al-Kazimi, died, some years later, I wrote an elegy on him to express my sympathy for Rabab.

## 13

A warm spring morning. Faisal Street, as yet without large buildings, is flooded with sunshine. Boys and girls are hurrying on their way to school, the children of the rich carrying leather cases; their classmates, children of the poor, carrying small cloth book-bags. I dawdle along until the most beautiful teacher, the one dearest to my heart in the Ayishiyyeh School, appears on the street.

I intentionally timed my going to school in the morning with her regular routine. I would walk by her side, happy to converse with her along the way, proud to have the other pupils see me in her company, talking to her. She was the prettiest teacher and had the most outstanding personality, not only in the school, but in the whole town. She was Sitt Fakhriyyeh al-Hijjawi, teacher of Arabic and English. Since she was also Ibrahim's foster sister,[24] she always asked about him and about his latest poem.

That spring morning I was telling her about the new poem he had read to us the previous evening when she interrupted with: 'Why don't you learn to write poetry from him? You have the talent, there's no question about that. The way you recite poetry makes me certain you have a love for it.'

Despite my immediate reaction, protesting the absurdity of the idea, my mind secretly registered the passing remark, storing it deep down. Indeed, the idea kept turning over and working on the subconscious, like the perpetual motion of a dynamo. I went to sleep and awakened with this dream. In my working hours I began seeing, in my mind's eye, the poems I had not yet written published in the papers, just like Ibrahim's and Rabab al-Kazimi's.

This passing conversation with Sitt Fakhriyyeh took place shortly before I was sentenced to confinement in the house.

Thus, in the end, our thoughts and aspirations become part of us. Strangely, what triggers these psychological developments and sets them in motion within us is usually a passing remark or otherwise insignificant event.

Putting all my misery and defeat behind me, I began living the future in the present that Ibrahim had turned into green meadows and promising fields of ripe grain. I could see the coming harvest in my daydreams. I could now anticipate time on the wings of a dream. To me the future was everything. These potentialities I possessed would turn into realities only in the future. The past with all its misfortunes was gone. Had I realised some months previously what the near future held in store for me, I should not have been so depressed at the state I was in. I should not have thought of suicide. If I had carried out that idea of sucide, this happy present would have become nothing but a future I had let slip through my hands during those wretched months.

I mapped out a daily programme for myself: I would wake up with or before the dawn call to prayer, make my coffee, sit down with my exercise book before me and set to work. Before going to sleep at night, I looked forward to this period of study, and awoke with the dawn full of enthusiasm at the thought of spending all morning studying. These hours were marked with a mental alertness and vigour which were disturbed only when the family wakened one after the other.

Ours was a large family, numbering more than twenty people, not counting the women who helped with the housework. When all these people woke up, the hubbub began: voices mingling with children's cries, kerosene stoves hissing – numerous Primus stoves all starting up at the same time.

The hours dedicated to study in the early morning filled my whole day with pleasure and energy. Poetry became the sole preoccupation, awake or asleep, of my spirit and mind. It became the love that remained throughout my life a mystical love, not in the religious sense of the word, but in the intensity of the love and dazzling ecstasy with which it overwhelmed me.

Sitting over my studies was my salvation. I do not recall who it was who said that, if we looked at happy people, we would see them either building a house, or composing a tune, or bringing up a child, or planting a field. This is to say, our quest for happiness lies outside ourselves.

My absorption in my new world taught me the taste of happiness. I was immersed in the act of creating myself, building myself up anew, in an eager search for the potentialities and abilities that constituted my life's capital.

The practice of giving the best we have, knowing that our days are not being spent in vain, gives us a sense of self-possession, peace and tranquillity.

Despite still being under sentence of confinement, studying and memorising thousands of lines of ancient Arabic poetry cleansed my soul from the torment of mulling over my feelings of self-pity and injustice.

The pre-Islamic, the Umayyad and the Abbasid poets lived with me. They ate, drank, did household chores and bathed with me. They talked to me and I talked to them.

I wasn't fond of them all at the same time. I would fall in love with one poet at a time, until I had exhausted his works, then, satisfied, I would feel the need for another poet and the discovery of another world. And so on.

My last love amongst the ancient poets was Abu Firas al-Hamadani.[25] For a long time, perhaps the longest of my former loves, I bore his longings and his suffering during his imprisonment and imitated his poetry in writing mine.

I was obliged to help Mother with the housework. Al-Samra and Khadija, the two servant girls, had married but, even though there was always a servant woman in the house, the family members were numerous, the house very large, and guests from the country flooded in upon us every day, some of whom would spend several days with us. Uncle and Father had friends and acquaintances from the country with whom they had done business ever since the tithe system of the Turkish era. The Ottoman Empire once had extensive holdings in Palestine, known as *al-Jiftlik* or the Sultan's holdings. The state allotted the land, in fief, to the inhabitants to plant grain, in exchange for a guarantee of payment in kind, of one tenth. The state gave notice in advance and the merchants offered their guarantees; whoever offered the best price got the job of collecting the tithe. At harvest time the guarantor of the tenth went to the threshing floor to set the days for the grain measurer. In the presence of a receipt committee and appraisers, the state's share was set aside to be taken in kind or in money, whatever the agreement had been. The British Mandate abolished this system.

Most of the burden of the considerable housework fell upon Mother's shoulders. My eldest sister had married her cousin and joined Uncle's family in the same house. Fataya and Adeeba had enrolled in an institute to learn dressmaking. When Father wanted me to enrol too, I refused, lest I lose my golden opportunity to learn poetry. For me, poetry took precedence over the chance to escape from the prison whose geographical bounds my brother Yusuf had set.

I performed my household tasks with a poem in my pocket. I memorised poetry while I ironed my brothers' shirts and trousers, while I made the beds, and while I washed the naphtha glass tops and filled the lamps with fuel. Lighting by electricity was not available in Nablus at the time, in contrast to other Palestinian cities. Our town council had boycotted the Jewish Rotenburgh project, when the British Mandatory

Government had, in the twenties, granted the contract for generating electricity to this company. The inhabitants of Nablus lit their houses with naphtha lamps until the beginning of the forties. That was before two or three families purchased generating systems and connected the power, in some parts of the city, to houses who wanted to share it. Electric lighting did not take over until the town council undertook the establishment of the large electrical plant to light the whole city, in the middle of 1957.

## 14

The professor of Arabic literature at the American University of Beirut, Anis al-Maqdasi, sent a proposal to Ibrahim, offering him a teaching position in the American University. Ibrahim was happy to return to Beirut, a city he loved.

I watched him descend the stairs then disappear from my sight through the outer door, like a delicate ghost. I went back to his room, wandering aimlessly around it. I stood looking at the empty desk – no papers or pens. I saw the torn-up papers in the wastebasket. I opened his wardrobe now containing only a few jackets. I touched the neckties he had left behind. I sniffed the shirt he had worn the day before. Everything I saw around me in the room spoke of his absence.

In deep desolation I threw myself on his bed and wept.

During the following days I often sat beside the pool in the open courtyard where the family usually gathered, except in winter. There I sat looking up at the closed windows of his room overlooking the main courtyard of the house. Through those windows his deep, full, melodious voice had spread through the house, as he recited poetry or verses of the Quran. My heart would swell with the reverberations of his voice mixed with the fragrance of bitter orange blossoms. My joy at hearing his resonant voice coming through the windows had been absolute.

Throughout the two academic years he spent at the university in Beirut, I lived on his unfailing letters, in which he guided and encouraged me in composing poetry, writing prose and pursuing my studies.

He had chosen a collection of books for my self-education and I arranged my time within a schedule I had laid down for myself. The early morning hours were devoted to grammar and syntax. I completed all the sections of *The Plain Grammar*, written by Ali al-Jarim and Mustafa Amin. I covered it all, section by section, from the primary stage to the end of the secondary level, including *Plain Rhetoric* by the same authors. The forenoon hours were set aside for memorising poetry while I did the housework, and the afternoons for concentrated reading.

From 1931 to 1940 I read *al-Bayan wa al-Tabyin* (*A Book on Eloquence and Exposition*) by al-Jahiz,[26] *al-Kamil* (*The Perfect*) by al-Mubarrad,[27] *al-Amali* by al-Qali,[28] and *al-'Iqd al-Fareed*.[29] I was often immersed in *al-Aghani* (*The Book of Songs*) by Abu al-Faraj al-Asfahani.[30] I also read al-Aqqad's books, *al-Fusul* (*The Seasons*), *Sa'at bayn al-Kutub* (*Hours with Books,*) and *Mutala'at fi'l-Kutub wa 'l-Hayat* (*Expositions on Books and Life*). I read Taha Husayn, Ahmad Amin,[31] in particular, *Fajr al-Islam* (*The Dawn of Islam*) and the volumes following it. For quite a long time, my interest lay in the works of Mustafa Sadiq al-Rafi'i,[32] on the one hand, and May Ziyada,[33] on the other. That was after I had followed Muhammad Said al-Aryan's series of articles in the Egyptian magazine, *al-Risala*, on the life of al-Rafi'i and the story of his love for May Ziyada.

I had great admiration for Muhammad Hasan al-Zayyat's writings and was influenced by his style for some time.[34] His translation of *The Sorrows of Werther* drew me to his style. I memorised all of 'Ossian's Song' from this touching romance. (I had the faculty of memorising both poetry and prose.) I remember memorising several rhymed literary selections by Ahmad Shawqi[35] from his book, *Aswaq al-Dhahab* (*The Gold Markets*), and al-Nashashibi's speeches and a great part of *Nuql al-Adib*, which he selected from our literary legacy and published in serial form in the weekly magazine, *al-Risala*.[36] This literary review, along with the review, *al-Thaqafa*, became my indispensable weekly spiritual food.

Whenever I felt the need for relaxation, I would take advantage of the absence of the heads of the household to indulge in playing the lute and singing. I had learned to play from one of my mother's relatives when I used to visit my aunt, Imm Abdallah Asqalan. Singing or keeping a lute in the house was forbidden, but having a phonograph was permissible. Father spent a great deal of his leisure time listening to the songs of Fathiyya Ahmad, Umm Kalthum and al-Shaykh Salama Hijazi, his favourite singers. I used to wonder: since he liked music, why did he forbid us to play and sing?

I would clasp the lute, sitting in front of the window which faced the main door, so I wouldn't suddenly be surprised by the arrival of Father or one of my cousins. I would play and sing in a low voice, and as soon as I saw one of their heads, in its red fez, come into view, I would jump up quickly and hide the lute in our large wardrobe.

Ibrahim, delighted with my playing and singing, would sometimes reward me with some money or with a gift that would make me very happy; he was deeply concerned about my psychological rebirth and the development of my natural inclination to realise my latent abilities. All his life his penetrating eyes saw into the far reaches of my heart, sensing its misery at its emptiness, and feeling its ambitions, which he tried to help me to fulfil. He was the only one who really saw me, and noticed my existence.

## 15

From the letters Ibrahim sent me from Beirut during 1931 and 1932, it is clear that I was progressing at a rate that I can now scarcely believe. His letters reveal that, during those two years, I learnt to write letters and poems free of errors of syntax, grammar and prosody. This was indeed a short time, considering that I had started from scratch and that there was no one in the house to help me or give me directions. I recall that during a visit my brother Ahmad paid us one day, quite by chance his hand fell upon a poem I was working on at the time. Praising its high standard – relative of course – he drew my attention to a few mistakes in its rhyme and metre. Although he had specialised in physics, he had some knowledge of the principles of poetry, which he loved and appreciated. It was long time before Ahmad believed in me and took my career as a poet seriously. Actually he went on believing, as did the others, that Ibrahim had a hand in my poems.

I only mention this to confirm the truth of the idea that, if a natural bent meets up with a driving urge for self-realisation, one becomes a hostage to ambition and aspiration. One's whole life becomes dedicated to realising these goals, revolving on this pivot alone in defiance of all obstacles and hindrances, and consequently producing incredible results.

In my uneven handwriting at the time, I copied down Confucius' wise saying: 'Even small birds can fly if they want to. Nothing in the world is impossible to the unvanquishable will.' I stuck the paper to the inside door of my small cupboard. These words were a source of confidence and hope during the first years.

Before a would-be poet progresses to being a poet she must, inevitably, pass through a stage of imitating other poets. Influenced by them, she endeavours to clothe herself in their styles until she takes on her own authenticity.

Ibn al-Rumi was my first love among the poets.[37] Ever since Ibrahim had chosen Ibn al-Rumi's elegy on his middle son for me to memorise, the poet's grief, tender feelings and extreme emotionalism had bound me to him. The first poem I ever had published in the newspaper was patterned on this lament in metre, rhyme and sentiment. My poem was entitled 'Longings for Ibrahim', or something of the sort. Just as Ibn al-Rumi had said in the opening verses of his poem:

Your weeping heals even though it is useless.
So weep on, my two eyes,
For one who equalled both of you, has died.

In my yearning for Ibrahim, I wrote:

In my heart my longings from afar have increased.
Does Ibrahim have the same feelings as I?
I tell the eye longing for sleep, 'First hold back
Your tears. Then you will be relieved of insomnia.'
How I wish you would return home
To drive away my heart's distress.

These are all the lines I can remember from that poem which
my brother, Yusuf, carried in his pocket one day to the poet
Abd al-Kareem al-Karmi (Abu Salma), to let him have a
look at it. Yusuf had by now become less oppressive.

I was astonished one morning to find the poem in the *Mir'at
al-Sharq* (*Mirror of the East*) paper, published in Jerusalem by
the Palestinian journalist, Boulus Shihada. I wasn't made
happy by this, but rather was struck with sudden fear and
great anxiety. What was this? My name in the newspaper?
How was Father going to take this grave matter? He would
definitely forbid me to write any more poetry.

I endured this nightmare until the afternoon. When Father
entered the house, I ran and hid in our room – the girls' room,
crouching there breathlessly, waiting for the roof to fall on my
head. But, to my astonishment, the roof didn't fall. Father
didn't even allude to it and I heaved a sign of relief.

My peace of mind now gave me the chance to think about
the boy who once loved me and whom I loved. What would
his feelings be when he read my name in the newspaper? Days
passed, followed by year after year, without my ever learning
the answer to that question. The boy disappeared and I never
heard of him again.

In the summer of 1932 Ibrahim resigned from his work at the
American University to teach in Jerusalem, where he took
me to live with him in the house of my brother Ahmad, who
had recently married. I looked after Ibrahim's needs, along
with applying myself eagerly to my studies and continued
attempts at writing poetry. However, before long I became

prey to anxiety and distress. Ibrahim's health began to fail rapidly and, at the beginning of January 1933, he was admitted to the German hospital in Jerusalem for stomach surgery. The outcome of this operation was very uncertain.

I returned to Nablus heavy-hearted, to write a very sad lament of which I can recall only the last lines:

> What is poetry but a complaint of the soul when it despairs
> And an echo of melodies when it sings?

It was in the metre of Ibn al-Rumi's poem: 'The branches and the hillocks yielded you grief'. When Ibrahim read it, after his recovery, his response was not encouraging. He had noticed previously that, in all my attempts at verse, I was absorbed in expressing feelings of suffering and pain. He had, at times, drawn my attention to it, warning me against continuing thus. He told me once: 'Sister, people aren't interested in our personal feelings. Don't forget this fact.' It would appear that my melancholy, introverted nature, which always made me withdraw completely within myself, was stronger than Ibrahim's excellent advice. There seems to be a certain immutability in our natural dispositions. Whenever I try to take a stand that goes against my natural disposition, I fail and return disappointed. My attempts at poetry have revolved mainly around my personal feelings and sufferings.

After his recovery, Ibrahim did not go back to teaching; he left it with no intention of returning. He remained in Nablus working as an administrative officer in the municipal office.

Travel books describe Nablus as the scene of dissent and revolt against the Ottoman government, its inhabitants characterised by their insubordination, disobedience, uprisings and great courage. This city has retained to the present its tradition of struggle and dissent and has been a great source of trouble to the authorities, ever since the true face of the British Mandate came to light and the secrets of the Zionist movement and of western imperialism were uncovered.

Nothing is born from a vacuum. What about our national-istic poets? Ibrahim grew up in a land whose depths were seething with events, and among a society in which the seeds of revolt were always present. Since writing his poem 'al-Thulatha' al-Hamra' ' ('Red Tuesday') about the heroic martyrs who were hanged in Acre prison in 1929, Ibrahim has been the voice of the Palestinian people; his nationalistic and social conscience was vigilantly aware of a reality which he rejected. His poetry, laden with the fervour of this reality, is a profound exploration of this Palestinian consciousness. In no time two other voices, no less effective, joined his – Abd al-Kareem al-Karmi (Abu Salma) and Abd al-Raheem Mahmud, Ibrahim's pupil and friend who later fell as a martyr defending his usurped country in the 1948 war at the battle of the 'Tree'. These voices created the triad that set the stage for later Palestinian poets, whose glowing poetic output lit bright torches on the long night journey.

Directly after the British occupation, men from Nablus founded the National Najah School, now the National Najah University. Before long, a club was established in connection with this school which, in a short time, became the site of national festivities on various occasions. The Arab Club began inviting thinkers, men of letters, and Palestinian and Arab poets to read, which gave the city a cultural incan-descence, in addition to its patriotic political fame. The club also founded a Boy Scout group which had a great influence on the young boys of the city up to the 1936 revolt. The Arab Club became the centre of patriotic fervour that generated demonstrations by angry crowds. Echoes of Ibrahim's nationalistic poems reverberated under the ceiling of this club, kindling in the masses the desire for freedom and independence.

During the period between 1933 and the beginning of 1937, I occasionally tried to clothe myself in Ibrahim's poetical robes and to imitate him by writing patriotic verse. I wrote a few nationalistic poems, one of which I remember was about the Palestinian leaders banished to the Seychelles Islands by the Mandatory Government. It was published in

Beirut by Ibrahim's close friend, Dr Omar Farroukh in his magazine, *al-Amali*. These poems did not spring from a true political consciousness or sentiment; they merely revealed my cleverness in versifying and in copying al-Buhturi and Abu Tammam[38] and other classical poets, along with my relative competence in the language and capacity to express myself. Ibrahim was overjoyed to see his seedling producing its first fruits.

## 16

From the beginning, Ibrahim had cautioned me against memorising modern poetry, with the exception of some poems by Shawqi, Hafiz Ibrahim, Ismail Sabry and Khalil Mutran, which he chose for me and advised me to learn. Since, during this period, young Arab poets were mostly inclined towards romanticism, their works, published in newspaper and literary magazines, were not to Ibrahim's artistic taste. Ibrahim felt strongly that the Arab poetic heritage was sacred. He belonged to a generation that had grown up aware of a widespread movement to revive this heritage through resurrecting its artistic values; its terseness of phraseology, its clarity of expression and its beauty of style, beginning with al-Barudi at the dawn of the revivalist movement, on through Shawqi and his contemporary Egyptian, Iraqi, Lebanese and Syrian poets. The poetry of the young men of the 'Apollo' school at the time, which resembled the poetry of the Arab poets in north America (the Mahjar group) was, in Ibrahim's view, colourless and weak in style, not comparable to the eloquent poetic expression which distinguished the ancient poetic heritage. He continually pointed out to me that the strength of phraseology and the ability to master the language would never be attained by the poet who does not return to the original fountains of Arab poetry: its classical heritage.

I stuck to this poetic heritage for many years, during which it remained the pattern I followed in my attempts at poetry. Throughout the whole period between 1933 and 1940 my interest lay in what was termed a grandiose style and expression.

How proud and pleased I was to see Dr Omar Farroukh introducing one of my poems, which he published in *al-Amali*, with these words: 'These are the verses of a rising young poetess. At a time when we see many men composing soft feminine poetry, we find this young woman, in the first stage of her life, reawakening in our minds memories of Abu Tammam and al-Mutanabbi[39] and reviving Shawqi's style.'

My interest in traditional poetic expression grew to the point where my thoughts and feelings were deflected from genuine experience to a concern for phrasing and selecting words with a ring and reverberation to them. I wrote much love poetry in this style, signing my poems 'Dananeer'. Sometimes I used to send them to *al-Amali* and, at other times, to *al-Risala* review in Cairo. In my mind, the word 'love' was associated with disgrace and shame – an association imprinted upon me from my infancy. The first time I thought of publishing two of my amorous pieces in *al-Amali*, I quoted, in all simplicity and innocence, the words of Abu al-Faraj about the poetess Dananeer, Yahya al-Barmaki's slave girl,[40] in his *Book of Songs*: 'Dananeer was honourable and chaste.' I used this sentence as an introduction to the two verse pieces to shield me from the shame of love and to convince the reader that love poetry did not remove the qualities of 'chastity' and 'honour' from the female writer of poetry.

At that time I was living with Ibrahim and his wife in Jerusalem. Ibrahim would sometimes bring his friend, Abu Salma, an employee, like himself, in the Palestine Broadcasting Agency, home for lunch. One day at table, I was surprised by Abu Salma asking Ibrahim a question I had not anticipated. 'Ibrahim,' he said, 'in your reading in *Kitab al-Aghani*, have you come across these two selections of Dananeer's published in the latest edition of *al-Amali*?' 'No indeed,' replied Ibrahim, 'I don't recall having read them before.' Abu Salma said nothing more and I didn't speak up. Hiding my embarrassment and confusion behind my silence, I pretended to be occupied with cutting the piece of meat on my plate, lest my sudden blushing disclose the secret that eleven centuries separated the Barmaki poetess, Dananeer, and the author of the poetry published in the magazine, who belonged, like the others present, to the twentieth century, but wrote poetry completely lacking any flavour of her times.

I did not hide the truth from Ibrahim for long, but owned up after a few months, secure in the knowledge of his love for me, and his tolerance and openmindedness towards women. Delighted at learning the truth, he proudly revealed it to Abu Salma, proud that his pupil was able to write such forceful poetry with a strong linguistic construction.

However, I began to feel that this classical style, and this preoccupation with a choice of words that were resonant but contrived, was an obstacle to the flow and movement, the spontaneity and truth in the process of creativity. I could sense an artificiality creeping into my poetry, giving it a dryness and rigidity. I was unable to breathe real life into my poem and to furnish it with the vital sap that could flow through it and give it life. I was, in fact, hewing away at a rock; there was something stifling the emotional truth inside me, and checking the smooth easy flow of the current of feeling through my poem. I did not find my authentic poetic self until the day Dr Muhammad Mandour introduced me to the work of the Arab poets in North America.

Mandour was a critic and outstanding revolutionary thinker who now occupies a leading position in the history of modern Arabic literature and criticism. His writing first appeared at the beginning of 1940 in the Egyptian magazine *al-Thaqafa*, where he wrote a series of articles criticising the strident tone prevalent in Arabic literature, and commending the muted tone which characterised much of Arabic poetry and prose written in North America. I found the works of those North American poets closer to my psychological and mental make-up. During that period, I also chanced upon poets of the Apollo school, such as Ibrahim Naji, al-Shabbi, Ali Mahmud Taha and al-Tijani.[41] From that time, I turned my back on the Abbasid style, my main ambition being to write poetry deriving its beauty from simplicity, flexibility, truthfulness, and poetical expression free of affectation.

In the late forties, the avant-garde poetess, Nazik al-Mala'ika, published her first poems in free verse. Nazik is to be credited for her pioneering role in the evolution of form in contemporary Arabic poetry and for the extraordinary speed with which the poets of the fifties accepted this novel method. Nazik shone during the fifties, and her poetic and critical eminence, characterised by a special charm and wide influence, was dazzling. No innovative movement can succeed and spread rapidly unless the voice raised on its behalf is distinctive, and can arouse a strong response in others. Nazik, truly, had such a voice.

I was convinced of the viability of free verse. I abandoned the traditional two-hemistich verse with its long lines and monotonous rhythm, and began applying myself to the writing of the new poetry. It wasn't an easy task at first. I was faced with a difficulty I had not experienced when composing a poem whose single verse of two hemistichs had the same balanced number of feet in each hemistich. Ever since I had been taught prosody, I do not recall having fallen into any error in metre. The music of the regular monotonous measure had led me, automatically, along a fixed, straight, narrow path, quite different from that of the free verse poem with its irregular use of feet. I found myself stumbling at the beginning, for it is no simple matter for an ear accustomed to the music of monotonous poetic measures to familiarise itself with irregular melodies, as they lack the basic unity that distinguishes the single verse in the traditional poem. In the free verse poem, characterised by organic unity, the poet pouring out feelings through lines of differing lengths does not usually stop until the end of the idea, to start over again with a fresh idea, and so on to the end of the poem.

My position on freedom from the bonds of ancient prosody is still one of support. This does not mean that I go along with those who advocate the abandonment of metre and rhyme altogether. Poetry continues to be distinct from prose and there is nothing more charming than musical durations as they echo within lines of differing length, and nothing more beautiful than rhymes alternating in a free verse poem, some*imes appearing distinctly, and sometimes disappearing. Despite the opposition to the modern poetry movement encountered from the traditionalists and their unequivocal rejection of it, it has held its ground and established itself by attracting the gifted poets of the fifties, who shine today in the history of contemporary Arabic poetry.

The story of the struggle between the old and the new is eternal, but the struggle is inevitable for renewal. Rigidity and permanence are impossible. Since everything moves towards change and mutability, refusing to remain as it is, and since the tendency to change is a law of life, the poet will definitely be subject to this law. Rigidity is impossible, and when we demand that the modern Arab poet preserve a fixed structure and form in poetry, it is as if we are asking him or her to go against the law of movement and development.

It would seem that even this modern poetic movement, already over three decades old, also faces the risk of repeating itself, and will, doubtless, have to face in the end the trend towards renewal and the desire for new experiments.

## 17

Between 1932 and 1933 I developed a close friendship with the daughter of a government employee in Nablus, a girl of Kurdish origin. This young girl, recently arrived from Damascus after a visit to her maternal uncles, lived in an atmosphere altogether different from that of our house. Her parents and brothers lived in the midst of artistic surroundings and every family member was a skilled lute player and singer. One of the sons later became a star in the Egyptian cinema world.

This slightly dark, very attractive girl, Wujdan, often visited her grandmother who lived next door to us. Her friendship was a breath of fresh air to me. She would come to me, whispering in her pleasant Syrian accent: 'Write me a letter to Fouad . . .' Fouad lived in Damascus. He was her cousin and fiancé and had fallen in love with her during her visit. From this adolescent friend, Wujdan, I learned to dance the Charleston. Ibrahim had bought a phonograph that delighted us all. There was all sorts of music recorded on the 'Odeon' records and 'His Master's Voice' and others. Among them was tango, foxtrot and Charleston dance music. The rhythm and boisterous beat of the Charleston helped release the frustration I endured from social pressure. I got so I could perform the Charleston with as great versatility and sublime ecstasy as the eastern Arab dervishes, or the poor American Blacks when they resort to dancing to a loud rhythmic drumbeat to get relief from external pressures.

It was the same with my paternal aunt, al-Shaykha, whose absorption in dervish exercises, whenever the spirit of God descended upon her, helped her to get rid of her tensions.

Sheltering under Ibrahim's wings afforded me a sort of protection from al-Shaykha who could no longer pursue me with her scolding and her reprimands. But she continued to nurse a profound anger at me and at Ibrahim's interest in me, and she tittle-tattled to the heads of the household, setting them against me.

I had a feeling of being continually under observation. My cousin tore a dress I was wearing one evening. The dress didn't lack modesty in any way; its one fault was that it made me look pretty.

This world I lived in continued to have such a deadly effect on me that I was weighed down by feelings of repression and servitude, especially after Ibrahim moved to his work in Radio Palestine in Jerusalem. I used to feel that the hired help in the house was freer and happier than me, and I was prevented by my inadequacy and weakness from having any control over what was going on around me. I was conscious of the humiliation of this situation and my inability to break out of the mould I was forced into. Thus a perpetual conflict arose between two parts of myself, a self defeated by repression, and the grim reality of life, giving me a split personality: one appearing submissively obedient, while the other was in such a thunderous state underneath the surface that it was almost destroying itself. I went on suffering the drama of the wild current running under the surface of calm waters, like one of Chekhov's characters.

My adolescence continued to be exposed to the sword of the 'executioner' I mentioned later on in my poem, 'He and She', and in many of the poems of my first collection, *Alone with the Days*. This scourge fell upon my teenage years under the guise of traditions and tyrannical moral standards. I realised that the pressures ere not so much linked to traditions, as they were an outlet for anger and rancour at the poetic path on which I had begun, with strange mystical fervour, to make such phenomenal speed.

I was looking for an opportunity to study English, but Nablus lacked the appropriate facilities. Unlike other Palestinian cities such as Nazareth, Haifa and Jaffa, it had no private foreign schools. There was only the convent school, St Joseph, which I had always wanted to join. It was quite distinguished for Nablus. It taught its pupils – and how few they were! – French, piano and oil painting. After my eldest cousin died, when I was twenty-five years old, my aspiration was realised. I studied there for two years, for I had continued to be haunted by the dream of the school life I had been deprived of in my youth.

In 1939 I got the chance to study English, when Father permitted me and my sister, Fataya, to take private lessons from a young Christian girl who had recently graduated from the Friends' School in Ramallah.

We had the first lesson, then the order to stop was issued. Some of the heads of the family had raised objections to this freakish behaviour when they learned about it from al-Shaykha. Father was eager to please them.

The men dressed in European style; they spoke Turkish, French and English; they ate with knives and forks; they fell in love. Then they lay jealously in wait whenever one of us girls aspired to better things or tried to assert herself in quite natural ways. They represented, in the most flagrant manner possible, the rigidity of the Arab male and his absolute inability to maintain a personality that was healthy and whole. They represented, now as ever, the dual personality of the Arab: one half going along with development, con-forming to the spirit of the times and adjusting to the rhythm of contemporary life; the other half paralysed, informed by an age-old egoism rooted in the Arab man's soul, with all the eastern haughtiness that has dictated how the male should treat his female relatives. Everything around me oppressed me. I even felt that the thick ancient walls of the old house were closing in on me. How I wished I could sleep under the open sky: no roof above me, no walls around me and no relatives near me.

I always took a passive stand, giving in to things that annoyed or even angered me. Never once did I have the courage to raise my voice in protest. However, my sister, Fataya, had an entirely different temperament; she didn't bow her head and didn't care whom she pleased or dis-pleased.

Fataya stood up to Father, protesting against his change of position over our learning English. 'I know the reason,' she said angrily. 'It's they . . . they . . . they are the ones who advised it! What have they to do with us since you have given your permission?'

Father appeased her by saying: 'Your brother Nimr will take on the job of teaching you and your sister.'

Nimr obediently took on the task with no less enthusiasm than we did. Although very young at the time, he was upset by the women's position in the house. It was he who later convinced Father to send my youngest sister, Hanan, to Schmidt Girls' College in Jerusalem, to obtain the secondary matriculation certificate.

Yes, I lacked the courage to rail against their hostile attitudes. But the feelings of hate and aversion – in compensation – were assuming huge proportions in the depths of my soul, like a satanic tree. No matter how easy-going one may be, there is no way to escape the savage claws of hatred created and fomented in us by those who rob us of our freedom, and mistreat and mistrust us.

In their eyes, I was the discordant note in the house, the

sheep going astray from the fold. From the outset they dealt with me accordingly, in order to stifle my strivings for self-realisation. They tried in various ways to sow the seeds of self-doubt and misgivings about my abilities. The peril of this method lies in the fact that, by nature, we see ourselves as others see us, and it is other people's ideas about us that we absorb, especially in the formative period of childhood and adolescence.

I know a lady whose empty mind has nothing more to occupy it than her continual problems with her servants, and her conversation is limited to this subject. In her view, the servant is always marked by baseness and lack of self-respect: 'If the servant did not possess these characteristics, he would not accept such menial work.' These could only be the views and judgments of one whose children have never known the pangs of hunger. For I remember Imm Hasan who worked for Uncle's family, Imm Afeef who worked for us, al-Haj Nafi' who worked in Father's and Uncle's soap factory, and Sulaiman who cleaned the reception hall and lit the lamps in the corridors every evening, as well as shopping for our daily provisons such as fresh vegetables, meat and so on. I knew all of them, and others like them, and have the fondest memories of them all. They spoiled me; they loved me and I loved them. I had a strong attachment to al-Haj Nafi', in particular.

However, when I was little, I used to believe everything that lady said. Children always believe what older people say, but, at the same time, I would get confused between the truth as I knew it and sensed it through my direct association with this downtrodden section of humanity which contra-dicted that judgment, and what that lady used to say. I did not understand, at that time, that the superior conduct of the master towards his servant and his opinion of him were the main factors in creating lack of self-respect in the servant, if what the lady said was correct. We definitely come to be as others see us, since their opinion dominates us and motivates our behaviour.

As far as my actual situation at home was concerned, I now stood between two forces: Ibrahim's faith in me, which charged me with self-confidence and self-respect, and with expectations of some day making something of myself, and the continual attempts of others to shake this confidence. I fluctuated between these two forces according to the measure of negative and positive feelings in my nature, and consequently had to wrestle between my aspirations and the reality of my existence in a backward community amongst relatives whose thinking was not the slightest bit liberated.

A small seed within me refused to be satisfied with what was, and yearned for innovation and change. It wanted to become something different, refusing to lie dormant. I could feel this seed stirring within me with a perpetual dynamism, while feeling at the same time the steely mould I was crouching in working to choke off this seed. Eventually, my inner aspirations were to erupt like a volcano at any moment.

My world of books, papers and pens gave me strength; it helped me to hold on and plant my feet firmly on the ground that was quaking under them. My constant dream was to break off all association with whatever represented authority in the family: Father, male cousins, paternal aunt. I avoided them all and thus learned to loathe whatever represented despotic domination and unjust authority in all social institutions. However, my aversion remained passive, rather than becoming a positive force to change society for the better.

Later, I felt grateful to those who wanted to stifle me with cruelty and harsh treatment. Had it not been for their boorishness, my capacity to hang on tenaciously to the literary goals I aspired to would never have developed. Had they used gentleness and affection in their attempts to kill my aspirations, they would have extinguished the latent spark in me; had they given me the silk-glove treatment in their attempts to smother my ambitions, instead of the iron fist, they would have succeeded. The soft, smooth, silken cord is usually more proficient in strangling.

Whenever I fell prey to their heavy-handedness, I would sometimes feel I was actually going to pieces. I would be drowning in a sea of despair. However, this breakdown would bring me to the point where something else would result. When one falls into the abyss of despair, the spark of life creeps in, driving one to take action to get out of the abyss. Thus, my struggle with those forces that opposed me would intensify anew and would convince me, later, of the soundness of the dialectical view of life.

All along this leg of my journey, the harshest stage of my life, Ibrahim's support remained the driving force in transforming my repressed feelings into productive energy. I would again become totally absorbed in my studies, my readings, and my attempts at writing poetry and prose.

I recall having seen some years ago on a London stage a play about the life of a woman schoolteacher with high aspirations, discernment, warmth and compassion who, through her strength of personality, was able to leave her mark on her young pupils' lives and later became the major influence in directing those lives. As the curtain was falling her voice could be heard from a distance saying: 'Give me a young girl in her formative years and I'll make her my disciple for the rest of her life.'

## 18

Autumn 1935 . . . The winds were blowing through the Ya'bud forest, a village in the Jinin district, a region pregnant with revolutionary energy and forever anticipating events. Shaykh 'Izz al-Din al-Qassam was raising his faithful Arab fist to strike the first blow for the rebellion. No sooner had he done so than eternity opened its doors for him to join, along with others of his group, the ranks of the immortal martyrs.

The fire kindled by the martyrs flared up again in April 1936, showering its sparks amongst the masses. The *fellahin* and labourers were inflamed . . . Jaffa declared a strike that included the port workers.

The populist uprising intensified, and compelled the traditional leadership to change its strategy, bringing it into confrontation with the heat of the rebellion.

On 20 April there was a large patriotic rally in Nablus and the 'National Committee' was formed. The committee issued a declaration, expressing 'The Arabs' displeasure at the policy of a government whose goal is the extermination of Arab rights in their own Arab country'.[42]

The leaders of the national parties were swept along in the swift current of events that ended in a general strike throughout Palestine. Political and armed strife involving all sections of the Palestinian people broke out. One of the most intense chapters of the Palestinian struggle was written then along the mountain paths and in its villages. From there the immortal voice of the people rang out: 'We're the ones defending the homeland and we kiss its wounds.'

Nimr Sirhan, Palestine's famous folk singer, would echo, saying:

Sell your mother and buy a rifle
The rifle's better      than your mother
When its action      dispels your grief

Turning back in memory to those Palestinian days, I find that I was in Amman, detained, on account of the general strike in Palestine, in the house of my brother Ahmad, who had recently been commissioned by the Mandatory Government to take up the post of director of education in the Emirate of Trans-Jordan.

My brother's wife complains and reproaches him for leaving her alone, some evenings, to call on his various men friends:

'But you are not alone. I brought my sister here to keep you company.'

'Your sister only stays with me for a short time. After eight she shuts herself up in her room.'

My brother's wife was justified in her complaint for I never was any use at entertaining people. I still lack this talent for amusing others. A talent for being satisfied with my own company on the one hand, and with the companionship of my books and exercise books on the other, was what governed my conduct.

At times, a sort of imbalance or disturbance would occur in my relationship with others. That would happen when I clashed with the unexpected, or when my ideal was shattered. At that point, I would become unable to integrate, and would experience a sense of alienation and resort to my safe refuge: my own self, my books and my solitude, the pivots of my existence, affording me the opportunity to read and meditate, and giving me a sense of security.

The reasons for secluding myself were not necessarily always the result of clashes with other people. For even during the periods when I was at peace and harmony with the world, with people and things in general, I still enjoyed my own company and could only find it by isolating myself. This was my tendency most of the time. This natural introverted withdrawal later became the cause of the inner struggle I endured in my poetic career, especially when I emerged into life and could feel it with all my being.

Fawzi al-Qawuqji's[43] popularity rose to fever pitch. Echoes of the rebellion and its achievements reached me from a distance, as I sat back in my brother Ahmad's house in Amman. My imagination and senses having been stirred by Fawzi al-Qawuqji's heroism, I set myself to composing a poem expressing the fascination of the romantic young woman with the personality of the legendary revolutionary leader:

> Hero of heroes, flower of all young men
> Come and tell us about your wondrous exploits.

Time passed and, with the setting of Fawzi al-Qawuqji's popularity and the waning of the public's adoration of him, this poem went the way of all the other failed attempts.

At the end of autumn 1936, the Supreme Command of the rebellion requested, in a communiqué signed in the name of al-Qawuqji, a halt to the operations of the rebellion . . . After a few days the Command announced a withdrawal from the battlefield. The kings and princes then decided to support the negotiations, relying upon the 'good intentions' of the English towards the Arabs!

The strikes in Palestine having ended, the siege around me in Amman relaxed, making it possible for me to go home. The year of detention in Amman remains a blank period in my life. The experience of travel and the absence from home did not afford me anything of value. Amman, the Emirate's capital, was a poverty-stricken town, small, insignificant, lacking any outward appeal or anything worth investigating. The severe social restrictions and customs did not differ from the norm in those Arab countries which were still under-developed socially. As for my brother Ahmad, he always raised that barrier the oldest brother puts between himself and his brothers and sisters. He dominated us like a father, so my relationship to him was marked mostly by unease, reserve and formality, along with silence. And silence is the language of strangers, even strangers united by blood.

I returned to my own corner in our large room in Nablus, the girls' room. I returned to my cupboard, my table, my chair and my coffee pot and cup. All my life I have had a strong attachment to my personal intimate things. The fact of their being mine has always had a very strong appeal for me.

Being in Amman I had missed the experience of living through the Palestinian rebellion of 1936. But here I was, after some months, enduring it at first hand, when it flared up again over the partition plan and the murder of the English Governor of Nazareth, Andrews, along with his British guard, at the end of September 1937.

The assassination incensed the authorities, giving rise to acts of suppression, torture and mass arrests. The Arab High Command and the national committees lost their legitimacy after the authorities proclaimed them illegal organisations. Then al-Haj Amin al-Husayni disappeared in strange circumstances, and some leaders fled, while others were banished to the Seychelles. However, the rebellion grew stronger and, along with it, the acts of repression.

We would constantly be taken unawares, for example, by the sudden announcement, at any time during the day, of a curfew preventing people from leaving the places where they were, to return home.

One day I remember standing with Mother in the market, stammering before the British armed forces. The way to our house was closed off: we did not know where to go. When some soldiers pointed towards the east, we understood we were to go eastward. We walked to al-Manara Square to knock at the door of some friends, where we waited until the curfew was lifted, allowing us to return home. Police raids to search houses became a common affair, night or day. The imposition of martial law on the country indicated the violence of the clashes between the masses and the British authorities.

One of those days stands out in my memory in all its minute detail. My sisters and I awakened to the sound of soldiers' heavy footfalls. There was a troop of them standing in the room in the darkness of the last hours of the night. We sprang up from our beds, and they told us to leave immediately, without giving us a chance to change our clothes. However, quickly snatching our coats from the wardrobe and hap-hazardly putting on our headgear, we went out into the market with the rest of the women, men and children of our quarter – the Yasmineh Quarter. In response to the orders of the soldiers in the search party, the men went one way and the women and children another. Amongst the women was a neighbour of ours who had given birth ten days previously. I saw her raising her veiled face high, revealing her white neck and some wisps of red hair, as she said while they groped around the baby's wraps: 'May the Lord defeat you and widow your women.' She said it in the pure Nablus dialect. Al-Shaykha, my paternal aunt, was suffering from such a bad attack of bronchitis she could not walk. So our neighbour, al-Dahdouh, the fruit and vegetable merchant, carried her on his back in the women's file.

We ended up in the Ra's al-Ain district at the foot of Mount Jirzim, where we spread out under the open sky at daybreak. Suddenly, from the other side, a long double line of men from the besieged quarters came in sight. Amongst them I saw Father wrapped in his cloak. A feeling of sadness and compassion crept over me. The sight of older men and those advanced in years in such a situation arouses feelings more bitter and sad than would be occasioned by the sight of young people. I saw men known to be strong, impetuous and haughty being forced to move quickly along the double line; this brought home the irony in this humiliating sight.

We returned to our homes before sunset to see the results of the worst plundering raid ever. My olive-coloured pen was one of the things taken. I missed it grievously for a long time: it had been the first fountain pen I owned. The main reason for my disturbance at its loss was that it had been a present from Ibrahim. He had given it to me, a few years previously, as a reward for an elegy I had written on the late King Faisal.

The rebellion had deepened the antagonism of the Palestinian people towards the British. From the beginning, the Balfour Declaration had been a devilish British intrigue. The Qassam rebellion had originally been a revolt against the British. They were the root of the evil, the agents who fulfilled the ambitious and momentous designs of the Zionists. When Abu Salma said in 1936: 'Had my God been English, I would have preached blasphemy', he touched a most sensitive spot in the hearts of the Palestinian people. He was speaking for them, expressing their angry, inflamed feelings.

The cloak has arrived! . . . The cloak has arrived! . . .

This was the watchword in the Nablus streets and alleyways. Whenever the city faced trouble or danger from outside, a common bond would unite the Nablusites. This is a natural tendency with groups at all times and in all places. The fear and dangers people sense from the enemy without, brings out in them a shared community spirit towards the common foe.

'The cloak has arrived . . . The cloak has arrived!' The watchword would echo through the markets and alleys, warning people of the approach of a military raiding force. Those who needed to hide hid; and those who had to take precautions could do so.

Afterwards, the colloquial phrase, 'The cloak has arrived', became one of the legacies of the popular rebellion in Nablus.

Nablus, like Hebron, was a stronghold of fierce resistance and the day arrived when the British authorities were forced to relinquish control of the administration of these two cities. The resistance reached such a degree of violence that the courts in Nablus were abolished and their dossiers removed to the military barracks outside the city.[44]

Stories of heroism, news of violence, death, arrests, banishment and treason . . . these all penetrated the walls of the house, reaching my ears by various means: my brothers, the newspapers, visiting women, the butcher's boy, the grocer, the milkman, and others like them. When we heard the voices of the demonstrators first at a distance, then slowly drawing nearer, I would go downstairs, my head wrapped in a large covering concealing my face and most of my body. Running to the stone ledge in the reception hall, I would look down upon the market through one of the windows. The ledge would be crammed with women from the neighbouring household. When I saw the great mass of angry people in the demonstration, my eyes would fill with tears and sometimes the tears would roll down my cheeks. Ever since, I cry and am deeply moved at the sight of a dense crowd. My tears on such occasions were probably a result of my inability to participate in the struggle effectively. I did not experience the flavour of this participation, or come to know its intensity and sweetness, until after the war of June 1967. The Israeli occupation brought back to me my sense of being a social entity. It was only under the shadow of the occupation, when I began meeting large audiences through my peotry readings, that I realised the value and true meaning of a poetry that ferments and ages in the earthen wine jugs of the people.

The pounding of the rifle butts of British soldiers on our door awakened us at midnight. When Father got up to answer them, our hearts were in such a state of panic that we felt they were hanging on a rope. What now?

Deep inside we knew what was coming. When knocks came on the door at such an hour of the night, one knew there would be an arrest.

Father did not return.

In the morning he was on his way in handcuffs to Acre prison, along with Dr Mustafa Bshnaq and Fa'ik al-Anabtawi, there to meet up with hundreds of victims of collective repression.

My emotional relationship with my father see-sawed between neutrality in times of peace, when he was in good health, and overflowing compassion when he was in prison or sick.

Days, weeks and months passed with the fury of events unabated. News of Father's illness in prison reached us. By nature he was slender of build. I awakened in the silence of night, in my warm bed, while the winter cold was so bitter outside it would 'cut through a nail', as the saying goes in Nablus and the surrounding countryside. In my imagination, I saw Father lying sick and sleepless within the icy prison walls and a wave of deep compassion swept over me. My old feelings of suppression and tension caused by his presence in the house completely vanished, giving way to a sense of desolation, compassion and sorrow.

Outside, water was dripping from the leaves of the trees as regularly as the ticking of a clock. That complete silence gave birth to an unusual mental experience. In my mind's eye, I saw a poem I had not yet written, published on a page of the magazine, *al-Risala*. I also saw in my imagination the title in black letters, 'To My Father'.

The moment vanished.

But the imagined picture did not; it lived on in my mind for days to come, until it became a reality on the poetry page of *al-Risala*, a magazine I had often dreamt of reaching, but had found no way to do so.

The poetic experience in my poem, 'To My Father', was the result of all the emotions I had experienced, which had accumulated inside me since the 1936 rebellion. I could not usually write poems under the immediate influence of events and commotions, when I would be in a seething emotional state. For example, I was struck completely dumb for two months after the June War and my ability to write poetry was paralysed for months after the September massacre.[45] When the storm calms down, my ability to compose returns and the poem begins to form in my mind in the jelly-like state of the foetus in the womb. At this stage I do not know exactly what I want to say. Then, gradually, thoughts find a way to crystallise and, in a very vague way, I find myself writing the first line, then the second. After that comes the personal conscious effort.

The owner–editor of *al-Risala*, Ahmad Hasan al-Zayyat, God rest his soul, opened up the magazine to outstanding Arab writers and poets, along with Egyptian writers. *Al-Risala* was the most widely read Arabic review published in the Arab world. Al-Zayyat showed proper concern for Palestinian revolutionary literature. At this stage Egypt, in the words of the historian Sati' al-Husari, 'discovered her Arab identity and was zealously active in the Arab revolutionary movement'. The furious Palestinian reaction to the scheme to partition Palestine between Arabs and Jews resulted in the 1938 Cairo convention under the sponsorship of the Wafd government, distinguished at that time by the fervour of its popular appeal. Representatives and members from the parliaments of the Arab countries as well as deputies from the nationalist movement in Morocco attended the conference. Egypt also played host to the historic Cairo women's conference, in which representatives from women's organisations in Syria, Lebanon, Iraq, East Jordan and Egypt participated. The resolutions passed in both conferences included the confirmation and support of the Palestinian demand for the formation of an independent national government, an end to immigration and a ban on the sale of land.[46]

I copied out the poem that had occupied the night hours of two winter weeks. In fear and trembling, I hesitated in the face of my desire to surprise Ibrahim by finding it published in *al-Risala*, the magazine I had become infatuated with. I felt that my ambition to be published in it exceeded the bounds of my narrow literary scope. Al-Zayyat had only heard of me once before when he had, some months previously, published a piece of prose I had written, commenting on an article I had read in his magazine with the title 'Does the animal have an instinct for the unseen?' I used the article as a forum to express my Palestinian sentiments of the time: in my comment, I spoke very emotionally about the silence of the lonely night surrounding 'the mountain of fire' before the return of the 1937 rebellion, and of how the jackal's eerie howls would come across the mountain as if they were warnings of the tragedies to come and of the future victims who would fall as a result of aggression and torture. Then I spoke of how that animal's instincts had correctly anticipated the heroic but tragic martyrdom that occurred later.

When my comment appeared in *al-Risala* I could scarcely believe my eyes. For many days, I would go back and read it in the magazine, reliving the sensations of delight and joy at the realisation of 'great literary' achievement! This beginning was the starting point for my ambitions. I dreamt of seeing my poems published in *al-Risala*, the magazine of highest literary repute in the whole Arab world at the time.

Now my hesitation did not last long. Overcoming my trepidation, I decided to try my luck. Without showing the poem to Ibrahim, I sent it to *al-Risala*, then began counting the hours in an effort to speed up the days and nights.

The first time of anything always has a special taste and aroma that does not return with repetition. My name shone out when I saw it amongst the names of illustrious authors in the table of contents of *al-Risala* at the beginning of 1939. The poem took Ibrahim who, at the time, was director of the Arabic section of Radio Palestine in Jerusalem, completely by surprise. He sent me a short letter, addressing me as Umm Tammam,[47] and congratulating me on the excellent poem, saying that Is'af al-Nashashibi,[48] Khalil al-Sakakini[49] and others had all given it the highest praise! I wept with joy.

Father's condition worsened and he was moved to a hospital in Acre. My brother, Ahmad, who had returned from Amman to his post in the Department of Education in Jerusalem, began proceedings to have Father released. He was told that his release depended upon payment of a given sum of money to one of the British officials responsible at the time.

When Ahmad went to hand over the bribe, he found that the official he was bribing had been a colleague of his when he was a student at Oxford University in England. However, this surprise discovery made no difference. The English officer took the designated sum, the two exchanged the familiar English words of thanks . . . the matter was closed.

After some days, Father left the prison hospital, banished for the second time to Egypt without permission to visit us in Nablus before his departure.

Throughout the thirties, a number of new faces appeared amongst the Palestinian poets, young men contributing committed verse reflecting a national consciousness and a sense of patriotic responsibility. Poetry, whether formal (written in classical Arabic) or folk (written in colloquial Palestinian), was an activity which, together with journalism and various other literary genres, contributed to the awakening of the people's patriotic and political conscious-ness in cities and villages alike. All this led to the outbreak of the 1936 Palestinian rebellion. The Balfour Declaration, Jewish immigration, the glorification of all kinds of sacrifice for the sake of retaining the land, were all equally the focus of poems of the thirties, regardless of the disparity in artistic level and poetic authenticity. There was always a strong tie between the Palestinian poet and the movement of the struggle. The Palestinian poet was the direct product of the current struggle in Palestine and at the same time an effective force influencing that struggle.

## 19

It was my misfortune to have been born or raised to worry about others' opinions of me. I was therefore always careful, when I was in a crowd, to express myself without being assertive or presumptuous. I became so sensitive to this that I would don a mask to hide what was going on inside me. This mask was device to ward off the hurt of other people's deep probing curiosity.

The Nablusites have their own social rules and to gain approval one must conform to these rules. The most important rule was to be careful when amongst people not to show that you are more knowledgeable than they are, otherwise you are regarded as conceited, pretentious and detestable. Biting sarcastic criticism is common amongst Nablusites, and I was therefore unwilling to impose myself on others by speaking on subjects far from their concerns. I lost the desire to discuss and argue back and forth. In most situations, my communicaton with people was merely polite and devoid of any real interest.

Between the 1930s and the 1940s, I was not allowed to leave the house unless accompanied by a family member: Mother or my paternal aunt or my sisters or female cousins. Visiting, which was the only relief, did not hold any attraction for me. However, I felt I had to accompany them sometimes, just to get away from the confinement of the high walls, if only for a couple of hours. At any rate, Mother and the other women of the household were only allowed to leave the house once every month or two.

At that time women in general were illiterate. Most of those who knew how to read and write had not gone beyond the elementary stages of education. There were a few who had completed their studies in the government teachers' training college in Jerusalem, where the highest level during this time was second-year secondary.[50] The women teachers in Nablus and other Palestinian cities consitituted a socially acceptable group which was respected by the townspeople; the teacher, therefore, always felt self-confident and proud of her achievement. In Nablus the teachers formed a particular social group, and it was the aspiration of every ambitious girl to belong to this group. The young woman teacher knew, for the first time, the value of economic independence, and shared with her father or her brothers in the support of the family. It was enough for her that she was no longer a burden on her family, not to mention the fact that she had become a valuable economic factor in the household.

However, that did not mean she was emancipated from the prevailing backward social concepts. She still had to submit to restrictions, traditions and subordination to men. Her level of learning was so very limited that it was not enough to make her personally independent, an individual confident in her capabilities and potentialities. She remained under the man's protection, relying upon him, not even having the right to choose her mate. She was also at the mercy of her brother, even if he was unemployed and no use to himself, his family or society.

Nevertheless, a teacher's situation was much preferable to that of others. It made her feel superior within the female society around her, influencing her social conduct, and lending her a certain snobbishness, conceit and pomposity.

In that era teachers were not familiar with books outside the school's sphere, neither were they concerned with educating themselves through serious reading. Their interests were centred upon fashionable clothes and making themselves look pretty, since economically they were able to satisfy their material needs. There were of course some exceptions, but they did not significantly change the general reality.

This group of little-read teachers did not welcome me in a spirit of friendship, but sometimes in one of hostility, with the exception of one who did not fit into the general picture. She was one of those who individually sought knowledge and the further cultivation of their minds, Sitt Fakhriyyeh al-Hijjawi, my former teacher in the Ayishiyyeh School, who had always

94

given me special attention and care at school and outside.

Sitt Fakhriyyeh was delighted with my pieces in the papers, in particular *al-Risala*. Her encouragement and praise of the progress I was making in my poetry elated me. When I met her I would not shy away from talking to her about a book I had read or a poem I had composed. In her I found a sensitive response that sent a soft glow of deep joy through me.

With the exception of Sitt Fakhriyyeh, that privileged female community of teachers was bent on hurting me and facing me with negative feelings which were reflected in the hostile arrogance with which they treated me. Their sharp tongues would repeat: 'Her brother Ibrahim writes the poetry for her and puts her name at the end of it.'

These negative feelings towards me prevailed even after Ibrahim's death. I suffered a great deal from this enmity for at the time I did not realise that one must pay the price for the success one achieves, even amongst one's family and closest relatives.

'The flute player has no merit in his home town.' This is a psychological truth I learned later and accepted.

This is the picture of the female community that surrounded me in my town during the 1930s and 1940s, an unlettered bourgeois society, in which I appeared a peculiar antisocial creature.

The breach between me and the female community widened. It had nothing to offer me and was incapable of taking anything from me. It was a society of sharp tongues, and unceasing gossip and backbiting. Prattle is a sign of backwardness in societies that do not read. I should have realised that the world was functioning as usual before I discovered a fertile world of books. But I did not realise that at the time. Had I done so, the breach between me and that wretched female community would not have been so wide.

## 20

Despite the fact that the Palestine rebellion, which lasted

from 1936 to 1939, was aimed at resisting the British and at making the Mandatory forces its target, Zionist forces did not stop their villainous attacks on Arabs in all parts of Palestine. This villainy reached its peak in July 1938 when bombs exploded in the Arab markets in Jerusalem, Jaffa and Haifa, killing dozens of Arab citizens. In May 1939 the White Paper was issued, containing an explanation of the meaning of a 'national home for the Jews': 'Britain does not understand the expression "establishment of a national home for the Jews" mentioned in the Balfour Declaration, and in the Mandatory Statute, to mean changing Palestine into a Jewish state.'[51]

From that point on Zionist terrorist actions were aimed at both the British and the Arabs.

The Palestine Broadcasting Station had recently moved to its new building in the Musrara quarter in Jerusalem, a large two-storeyed building with its interior adapted to the requirements of a modern broadcasting station.

The date, 3 August 1939; the time, Wednesday afternoon.

Ibrahim and the two radio announcers, Tawfiq Abu Sharif and Muhammad Bushnaq, are moving back and forth from the control room to the studio checking the sound in a complicated programme in which twenty-one Arab children and their instructor are participating in a musical. They are all rehearsing for the programme with the help of the engineer Adib Mansour. None of them is aware that they are walking on a floor concealing the most dangerous kind of explosive device.

Ibrahim goes down to his office on the first floor to clear up some unfinished work. Muhammad Bushnaq is with the children in the studio on the second floor where the rehearsals are going on. The clock strikes five and with its strokes the evening broadcast begins in three languages: English, Arabic and Hebrew.

Ibrahim is in his room, with the announcer Tawfiq Abu Sharif. At 5.14 they hear the sound of a powerful explosion. It does not occur to them that it is in the building, as it happened in one of the small well-soundproofed broadcasting rooms. Upon hearing a commotion in the hall, they immediately come out to confront a pale-faced Muhammad Bushnaq surrounded by terrified children. 'Fire,' says Muhammad, 'fire caused by a short circuit.' A few moments . . . Engineer Adib Mansour and his assistant arrive from the second floor carrying the wounded British announcer, Mrs Weizenberg. The engineer and his assistant return to the second floor. The wounded woman is moved to the dirctor's room where Ibrahim and one of his assistants stay with her. When she asks about her legs, Ibrahim and the other man make light of the matter, while brushing the dust off her face. The wounded woman is on the point of fainting. Ibrahim rushes out of the room to ask for water while holding on to the door to prevent anyone entering. As Ibrahim takes the glass of water from the servant, another explosion shakes the building. The ceiling above Ibrahim's head splits open. A few steps from him a large piece of the roof falls on the telephone switchboard, smashing it. Looking around, Ibrahim notices children in imminent danger of falling. He and Muhammad Bushnaq shove them out of the building. One of the British guards tries to prevent them leaving the open-air courtyard for the street. Ibrahim and Muhammad overcome him and force the door open. The guard is still hovering round them trying to stop them when another explosion is heard . . . followed by another. By now the guard, realising the gravity of the situation, becomes preoccupied with his own safety . . . Another explosion accompanied by a high-pitched scream from Adib Mansour. His legs are crushed from the hips down. The ambulances arrive quickly, providing first aid. No one knows if the disaster is over or if there is more to come. Ibrahim thinks of his two sons, Ja'far and Uraib . . . and discovers how precious and sweet life is . . . He eventually hurries home dazed and burning with anger.

'What about the Jews working in the Arabic section?'

'It emerged afterwards that the building was empty of all Jewish employees at the time of the explosion!'

I quaked inside as Ibrahim told us the story of those terrible moments. As for Mother, she was cutting the meat to be distributed to the poor of the Yasmiyyeh Quarter, an offering of thanks for Ibrahim's safety, her perplexed face wet with tears.

1939 was bidding farewell to autumn, winter was returning with its generous gifts, and Ibrahim was spending a short holiday with us.

'How are you progressing with your new teacher?'

'The progress stopped before it started.'

'Why?'

'You know . . . orders!'

'Get yourself ready to leave with me tomorrow.'

I went to pack my suitcase, breathless with glad anticipation. I had never dreamed of this.

My life took a new turn, unprecedented since I had set out on my journey in poetry. It was a starting point from which my personality began, for the first time, to blossom outwards. In addition to enrolling in evening classes at the Jerusalem YMCA to study English, I participated in the presentation of some broadcast interviews, and in dramas and songs with the radio vocal troupe. I also composed a number of songs that were set to music and broadcast in some of the programmes. One day the aritist, Muhammad Kareem, player of the *buzk* (long-stemmed lute), spoke to me about a tune he had composed, named 'The Withered Violet', asking me to write the lyrics for a song of this title. This made me deeply happy and in a few days I presented him with the words of the song. It became the most popular of his songs broadcast over Radio Palestine:

My youth has faded; my stem has withered
Though I'm still in the spring of my life
Oh this life of mine that was young and fresh,
Now consumed by the fire of passion
Heart's desire, come close to me,
You will restore my bloom of youth,

You will restore the life to my soul,
I live again by the touch of your hand.
Suffering has bowed down my head
Since I lost the fragrance of my early days.

I was delighted with my new world, happy to be far away from the stern rule of my family, and from faces that did not love me and that I did not love. Ibrahim's protective wings filled my days with a feeling of warmth.

Aside from all those things, there were the well-stocked libraries, the cinemas, and the public concerts that the broadcasting agency held, by which the Arabs in Jerusalem flocked in great numbers. Moreover, private literary and artistic evenings were held in Ibrahim's house or in that of Yahya al-Lababidi, director of the music section of the broadcasting service, whenever Radio Palestine was hosting a famous writer or musician from one of the Arab countries.

I was living in the midst of a free society where the modern woman's personality was not undermined by men's severity and crudeness. This was apparent in her dress, her conversation, and her natural behaviour in a society where the veil separating the two sexes had been lifted, a society in which the young woman had the opportunity of a better and broader education.

In this expansive atmosphere of cloudless healthy unrestraint, I breathed, for the first time, the sweet breath of life; I experienced peace of soul and mind, and savoured a life free from gloomy faces and hostile looks. Ibrahim's gentle, even-tempered wife helped to produce the harmony and accord in my new life. Imm Ja'far was neither a jealous nor a bossy woman. She was beautiful and self-confident, and could therefore understand my attachment to Ibrahim. She accepted his love for me and for us all: his mother, sisters and brothers. I never felt that she was upset by his interest in me and the special attention he paid me. Thus, during my stay in Jerusalem, I was provided with an atmosphere free of attempts to dominate or efface me. That healthy climate ensured for me an independent personal existence that I could not have enjoyed had Imm Ja'far not been a person of such a gentle and lovely disposition.

In the last quarter of 1940, October to be exact, Ibrahim was dismissed from his work in the Palestine Broadcasting Station. There were a number of factors behind this dismissal. Ever since he had taken over the management of the Arabic section, the Jews had been lying in wait for him. The Zionist faction was not at all happy with someone like Ibrahim in such a crucial position, one with such influence on Arab public opinion in Palestine. To the Zionists, he was a troublemaker, using his high position in broadcasting to act against Zionist interests. There were numerous attacks on him by the Hebrew press. The finger of accusation was pointed at Ibrahim for the speeches he wrote and broadcast and the interviews he arranged for the Arabic programme, with Palestinian writers who presented various literary, social and religious topics

A political interpretation was always put upon what was broadcast. The Jewish faction would create an imaginary nation, a state, governments and mandates, out of the simplest story, just as it saw incitement under the guise of religion when discussing moral questions. In their opinion, political propaganda was also disseminated through historical subjects. Moreover, talks on the Prophet and well-known religious parables were the most dangerous, as these reminded mothers to raise healthy strong children. The source of danger, according to this claim, was that behind the purpose of bringing Palestinian children up to be strong lay the hope that they would be able to resist and fight in the future! The majority of interviews in the Arab section were evaluated in this manner. Ibrahim was criticised and held responsible.[52] This was going on at the same time as Chaim Weizmann was corresponding with the British Colonial Secretary, telling him about the 40,000 Jewish fighters in the Hagana who had finished their training.[53]

The historical subjects Ibrahim presented, came close, in the view of the Hebrew press, to anti-Semitic propaganda. On this, one of the Jewish papers wrote: 'Freedom of speech in Palestine has reached the state where Palestine Radio yesterday broadcast an anti-Semitic speech. The speaker was himself a Semite and the hatred towards the Jews was broadcast in a Semitic language. This Semite is not an ordinary man. He is a high-ranking employee called Ibrahim Tuqan, the Arab assistant to the programme director in Palestine Radio.' Then the paper touched in the subject of this 'anti-Semitic' talk, which was based on the story of Sumaw'al and the pre-Islamic poet, Imru'u al-Qays,[54] on the one hand, and al-A'sha's[55] poem in praise of Shuraih Ibn Sumaw'al, on the other.

The next day another paper, commenting on the same subject, said:

The deliberate misrepresentation in the Arabic story, because a Jewish poet was eulogized in it, is significant. It is frightening in its situation and in its application, and is of more consequence than killing a few people with a bomb. This is not merely a perversion of historical fact, it is propaganda for this bomb. But this is not a unique incident of this nature. Ibrahim Tuqan, director of the Arab section in Palestine Radio, has several times previously – without it occurring to anyone to follow his work regularly in the broadcasting agency – been caught red-handed in waging propaganda against the Jews, clothing it in a flimsy gown of well-known stories. And we must say that strict surveillance can bring to light further treachery in the broadcasting agency which has such a great power to disseminate information; this agency for which the Palestinian government is completely responsible. Instead of being a government radio standing for peace in its highest form and for facilitating discussions that can defuse the situation, it has become quite clear that it disseminates hate and provocation in the Arabic language. So will the Arabic director be called to account, or will he be left to continue his work in peace?

When Ibrahim was called to account to the government circles responsible, his rebuttal was as follows:

Sumaw'al is one of a number of characters in Arabic literature that were and still are subjects of debate in literary circles. There are those who categorically disavow

**101**

this period of literary history, considering it legendary and without any foundation. The reason for this is that the literary history of the earliest period, and with which we are concerned at present, has been taken from the mouths of the storytellers, who added to or subtracted from it. It has therefore fallen under the influence of several factors: the varying ability to memorise, tribal solidarity, the popularity of storytelling and the desire for financial compensation on the part of the story-teller. All this necessitated an uninterrupted succession of material and a refurbishing of it. This encouraged the storytellers to plagiarise and invent in the stories, the poetry and the chronicles. When the period of recording came around, a mass of this legacy was accumulated in our books. Due to their discrepancies and diversity of origin, we have a strong incentive for thorough scientific investigation, demanding skill in distinguishing the genuine from the forged, in verifying the texts and in commenting on them.

Sumaw'al's relationship to the history of Arabic literature and to the greatest poet of the pre-Islamic period accords to every specialist in our culture and its history, the right to talk about him just as he talks about any poet or author, regardless of his race or religion. My choice of Sumaw'al, as a literary and historical research subject, was scientific and no different from a number of previous studies I began at the time I was student at the American University in Beirut. My plan was to deal with the life of a poet and the various stories connected with it, and to examine his works. In this way, I would produce an organised biography, built upon pure scientific criticism, complying with modern research methods. Amongst those poets, I have studied al-'Abbas ibn al-Ahnaf,[56] Deek al-Jinn al-Himsi, Muhammad ibn Munadhir, Sibt ibn al-Ta'aweedhi and al-Sarriyy al-Rafa'. I broadcast some accounts of their lives and samples of their poetry. Sumaw'al was one of them and the method of examining his life does not go beyond that of examining the above-mentioned poets.

Reliable critics have taken an interest in al-Sumaw'al,

critics such as Père Louis Cheiko, the Jesuit, and Rauhi al-Khalidi, who died in 1914. The discussions appeared in reputable magazines, such as *al-Mashriq* (*The Orient*) and *al-Munadi* (*The Herald*) and in well-known books, among them *The Poets of Christianity*.

The research revolved around the Jewishness of al-Sumaw'al: al-Khalidi supported it, while Père Louis Cheiko refuted it. Likewise, research weakened the validity of the transmitted story about the connection of Imru'u al-Qays with al-Sumaw'al, casting doubt upon it.

The Hebrew press was not fair in referring simply to the outcome of the research without the proofs that led to this conclusion. If they were free of bias, they would see that I dealt with Imru'u al-Qays, our greatest poet and the most devoted Arab of them all, with severe and merciless criticism. I revealed the points of weakness in his character, stating that I was of the opinion that he had conspired against his people in resorting to the Byzantine Emperor for aid. I accused him of high treason for falling back upon the foreigner for help against his Arab kinsfolk. However, the trustworthy source I relied upon in my comments on al-Sumaw'al was Abu Faraj al-Asfahani, author of *Kitab al-Aghani*, of whom mention was made in the radio talk.

Then came the Second World War, and the Mandatory Government imposed censorship. Some of the censors, Arab rivals of Ibrahim, were the initiators of inflammatory propaganda against him to the British authorities. There were dirty campaigns against him in which he was accused of lacing his programmes with propaganda against the Allies.

He was dismissed from the Palestine Broadcasting Agency, so his rival could take his place. Ibrahim left the country with his family to teach in Iraq. I returned to Nablus, sad at the turn of events, very disturbed over Ibrahim. Would his ailing health withstand the harsh Iraqi climate? A few months passed; he became ill; he returned to Nablus and died.

Something inside me broke. The agony of orphanhood overwhelmed me.

Fear has been my constant companion since childhood, a mindless blind force striking on all sides, with no one to deliver me from it. The roof might suddenly fall in; a sudden tremor might swallow this mountain up into the plain; a hammer blow, carried on a wailing voice announcing the death of a loved one, might strike the head.

> My heart quakes with fear
> Forever quakes with fear
> Forever terrified
> a bridge might collapse
> The earth under me trembles,
> spinning wildly without axis!
> Who will deliver me from this fear?

My love for Ibrahim remained a constant source of inward distress throughout my attachment to him during his short life. My joy at the presence of this loving brother in my life sometimes made me tremble with fear, from my exaggerated dread of his dying young. The terrible earthquake in Nablus in 1927 had sown the seeds of constant fear of Ibrahim's death in my childish heart that clung so closely to him. On that unforgettable day, the ceiling of the room in which he was taking his midday nap collapsed. However, by sheer luck, his bed wasn't under the part that fell in. He escaped from death to live for another fourteen years.

I still have to this day some small things that belonged to Ibrahim and my late brother, Nimr, to whom I transferred my devotion and love after Ibrahim's death: a small leather wallet, a pocket notebook, a necktie, a small comb, a ledger containing addresses, telephone numbers and appointments.

I still have these things and others like them that I handle with sorrow and love, as if I were trying to negate the death and decay of these loved ones by keeping their small possessions alive in my cupboard.

It was Thornton Wilder who said: 'There is a world of the living and a world of the dead, and there is no connection between them except love.'

104

## 21

The prisoner complex still lay latent within me. Our childhood complexes influence us all our lives. Those who generated them in us pass on; the days and years roll by with these problems still crouching there, curbing and directing our steps.

The heads of the household were incapable of accepting the obvious fact that a woman is a person who feels and longs for life and happiness, just the same as any other human being. There is no power that can defeat or halt the workings of nature. Their opposition only increased a thousandfold the promptings of this nature within me, pushing it to bursting point. But it would run up against immovable barriers, at which point something resembling a volcanic eruption would occur.

I bid farewell to the broad horizons of Jerusalem to return to Nablus, to meet an estranged family. Ibrahim's departure and untimely death intensified that estrangement. I went back even deeper into my profound inner exile, into journeying inside my self. The most important thing is what happens inside us, not to us. From that time on, grief became the chief element in my life.

At that time, the wide emotional gulf which separated me from Father remained. Silence was our common language; the gulf increased, especially after the burst of anger he let loose on me when he entered the room one day, to catch me red-handed smoking a cigarette.

Now when I recall Father's coldness towards me personally, I can find only one explanation for his maintaining the curtain of formality between us. Perhaps my prominence in the family as a novel personality, differing from the norm, led him to fear this would end up in a headstrong revolt against the established rules. He used his aloofness and inflexibility towards me as a bridle to curb my aspirations for change and transcendence, and to prevent me from overstepping the boundaries set for a young woman belonging to an extremely conservative family. The mark of the house was the mould into which the girl's personality was poured: the same mould all the females of the family were forced into.

In that environment, in the midst of those circumstances, it was difficult for me to develop a spirit of open rebelliousness, since neither rebelliousness nor defiance were natural to me. I sometimes considered running away in search of freedom from the anguish and the pain. However, I felt great pity for Father's old age, in spite of everything. I was never so hardhearted that I became indifferent to others' suffering for the sake of achieving my great ambitions. I had no recourse except complete detachment from the complex human relationships around me; to escape from my miserable state to a fictional one at times, or to daydreaming and reading poetry at others.

The reality of life in that bottled-up harem was humiliating submission. Here the female lived out her dark, pinched existence. Looking around me, I saw nothing but faceless victims with no independent life. They would sit back at home, where the man would cause his sisters and female cousins to age prematurely, a decline accelerated by subjugation and coercion. I never knew these victims as other than old women. Each had been an old woman since the age of twenty-five. I never saw them, except in their chaste, ascetic garb: a white kerchief covering their hair as they sat within the constraining walls. They had no friends; they had no private life. Young girls with grey hair and faces prematurely wrinkled by repression. Marriage of a girl to a stranger would go against family traditions, so it was either a paternal cousin or virginity to the grave.

My mental isolation within this reality was as difficult as was living amongst the clamour of voices and an unbearable uproar that never subsided. Ever since childhood, noise has tormented me. I had no private life during those days and a long time passed before I had a room of my own. Even that did not save me from being in the midst of the clamour in the communal reception room, the open courtyard, the large kitchen, and by the brazier fire around which the family gathered on winter nights. My constant hunger for peace, quiet and solitude was never satisfied. Whenever I had the opportunity to slip away to the olive groves by way of Rafeedya, a small green village, I would sit in the shade of a large olive tree, drinking in the peace and quiet and dreaming of having a small wooden hut in one of these groves, where I could live my life independently.

One of my most enduring dreams was to take a trip around the world. They say that the majority of those who have a passion for travel have endured a life like that of animals confined in cages behind iron bars. I actually lived that sort of life. How often did I follow, with my eyes, the sparrows taking off from their nests in the courtyard trees for the world outside the walls, unrestrained in wide space, free from fear and prohibitions. I would watch them sadly, wishing and dreaming I had wings to set me free. But the blows of reality would strike me, robbing me of my dreams and frustrating my desires.

## 22

I was not in a position to participate actively in the kind of life necessary to a poet. My only world, in that dreadful reality, empty of any meaningful emotion, was the world of books. I lived with the ideas to be found in books, isolated from the world of people, my femininity whimpering like a wounded animal in a cage, finding no means of expression.

While I was in this state of alienation and psychological siege, Father often came and asked me to write political poetry. He wanted me to fill the empty place Ibrahim had left behind. Whenever a national or political occasion arose, he would come asking me to write something on the subject. A voice from within would rise up in silent protest: *How and with what right or logic does Father ask me to compose political poetry, when I am shut up inside these walls? I don't sit with the men, I don't listen to their heated discussions, nor do I participate in the turmoil of life on the outside. I'm still not even acquainted with the face of my own country, since I am not allowed to travel.* With the exception of Jerusalem, which I came to know, thanks to Ibrahim taking me in when

he worked in Radio Palestine, I was not familiar with any other city beside Nablus.

One of the immutable laws of nature is that plants and animals cannot live and thrive without particular environmental conditions. As for me, the home environment in which I grew up did not nourish a concern for the outside world and its struggle.

Father was demanding that I write on a subject totally removed from my interests, and which had no connection with the psychological struggle going on inside me. Feelings of inadequacy so overwhelmed me that when I went to bed I would give myself over to weeping.

When we come to a point where things beyond our natural capabilities are demanded of us, the resulting shock and the difficulties we encounter often cause us psychological harm. Father thought I was capable of composing on any subject. Despite the fact that I had already planted my feet firmly in poetry, my mind was moving in a direction completely different to that in which Father wanted me to move. A poet must be familiar with the life of the world around, before dealing with it in poetry. Where was I to obtain the suitable raw material required? Where was I to find the intellectual and psychological environment conducive to writing such poetry? Would I derive it from the newspaper Father brought every day at noon when he came home for lunch? Reading the papers, however important, was not enough to light the flame of political poetry within me. I was completely isolated from life on the outside. This isolation had been imposed upon me; I hadn't chosen it of my own free will. The outside world was taboo, forbidden to the women of the family, who were deprived of any community activities or political concerns. Mother was a member of a women's charitable committee, but that made little difference. She seldom attended their meetings, nor was she permitted to travel to the women's conventions, as other members were. Above all, she was absolutely forbidden to participate in the women's demonstrations. Family tradition would never allow that.

A women's committee had been founded in Nablus in

1921, under the leadership of the late Mariam Hashim (who died in 1947). This society was, at first, of a charitable nature. Then in 1929 it united with the general Arab Women's Federation, founded in Egypt by the late Huda Shaarawi. At this time, the Palestine Women's Federation undertook the organisation of Palestinian women's participation in the political struggle in most of the cities and sometimes in the villages. The city women's activities were confined to demonstrations, to sending telegrams of protest and convening meetings, through the women's organisations which the bourgeoisie of that era had created. Being unveiled, the country women had greater and more effective freedom of movement. They were the ones who carried arms and food to the rebels hiding in the mountains.

With this total isolation imposed upon the women of our household, it was not surprising that the atmosphere in the female quarters lacked any political or community awareness. The house was like a large coop filled with domesticated birds, content to peck the feed thrown to them, without argument. That was their be-all and end-all. The vocation of those tame birds was limited to hatching the chicks and wasting the days of their lives moving between the large brass cooking pots and the firewood burning constantly in the stoves, winter and summer.

As happens in backward societies where a woman's life revolves around trivialities, the female environment in our house did not deviate from this pattern, one which prevailed in all families and all homes. So the family environment offered me nothing; rather, it increased my burden.

I developed a deep hatred for politics. During this period I suffered severe psychological and intellectual conflict. I was trying to comply with Father's wishes, in order to please him and win his favour, while everything in me was protesting, refusing and rebelling. Since I was not socially emancipated, how could I wage war with my pen for political, ideological or national freedom? I still lacked political maturity, just as I had no social dimension. I possessed nothing but a literary dimension that itself was still incomplete.

**110**

I knew myself; I was aware that the self could not become complete, except in a community of people. But between me and the community out there, beyond the walls that confined me, lay the distance of many centuries of the world of the harem . . .

Feelings of inadequacy continued to overwhelm me. The ability to write poetry failed me. I even stopped composing personal poems. Poetical barrenness overshadowed this whole difficult period of my life.

My keen awareness of the repression and tension I was under affected both my spiritual and physical self, making me lose more weight. I was scarcely ever without a headache; mental weariness weighed down every part of my body; at night I was bathed in sweat.

Life no longer held any meaning or relish for me. When I tried to unravel my private anxieties and personal feelings, it was as if something had been broken inside; misery inflated my consciousness of myself and my own existence. I was bleeding from the two-edged blade of that old proverb: 'If I am not for myself, who will be for me; if I am for myself, who am I?' My weak connection with reality and my need for contact with the outside world remained the source of a psychological conflict which I endured for a long time. Father was the one who had sowed the seeds of this conflict, which haunted me in other ways as well during the later stages of my poetical career.

I went on feeling completely alone, knowing that there was no one who felt my misery except myself. It was my being that was being stretched taut, torn apart; the heart that was constricted and crushed was my heart; and the ordeal that was reaching a crisis was my ordeal. There was no other being to share all this with me, no other person.

As the misery of repression and subjugation increased, my feelings of individuality and identity also increased. My existence inside the harem wing of the house made me shrink and recoil, so that I was bottled up inside myself. I got to the point where I could do nothing but stare into the reflection of that self, all repressed and bottled up. The poetry I published in the papers was the one social activity I could use as a bridge to link me with others, as I crouched within those ancient walls. Thus my feelings of alienation deepened, and my sense of being robbed of my dreams, my desires and aspirations began to take the form of a sickness.

It was during this period that I swallowed the whole contents of a bottle of aspirin. The family doctor, Nadeem Salah, saved me from the death that had become my only means of escape from the torment I was in.

I did not have any strong attachment to my father. My feelings towards him remained neutral: I did not hate him, neither did I love him. He never had any place in my heart, except when he was sick, imprisoned or in exile for political reasons. To me, he was the tent that sheltered us; if we lost him we would be exposed to the storms of life. I was continually in fear of him dying and leaving us to the mercy of others. Thus my emotions see-sawed between a sense of need for his presence and a sense of estrangement and lack of any emotional connection to him. He never showed any sort of concern or affection for me. Whenever I fell victim to malaria in my childhood, he never came near me or asked how I was. That neglect hurt me. Thus Ibrahim, with his overflowing compassion and love for me, replaced the father who never let me feel the warmth of fatherly feelings. When Ibrahim died and Father was still living, I truly felt like an orphan. At the time Father passed away I was going through a deep psychological crisis caused by the severe emotional repression that I had endured all those years. I tried to write an elegy for him, but failed. However, I missed him severely later on when the winds of family problems began to blow our way.

I never took sides in any dispute or quarrel; I always stood apart from the disputes, seeing, hearing and suffering. During this period, I wrote 'A Life', one of the few poems I composed in a few consecutive hours. In this poem, my true feelings at the loss of my father are revealed: feelings that went very deep.

## 23

Father died amid the tumult of the 1948 débâcle.

Thousands of refugees, moving eastward in their flight, arrived in Nablus. Houses, mosques, schools and the caves in Mounts 'Aibal and Jerzim were jam-packed with them.

Many long months passed after this first scandal on Arab soil, before I returned to writing poetry. Behind this silence, a process of preparation and storing up was going on all the time deep down in me and I no longer suffered feelings of emptiness and desolation.

Eventually my tongue was freed. I wrote the patriotic poetry to which Father had so often wished to see me dedicate myself in place of Ibrahim. I wrote that poetry quite voluntarily, without any outside coercion.

After Father's death my reaction to politics was no longer lacking. Although it was not strong, it still swayed me at different times, but lacked the quality of permanence. It would catch fire, on certain occasions, when things were inflamed, then die down when things were calm; it would flare up when there were general outbursts and cool off when there were lulls. With the status quo of the Palestinian situation, a numbness began creeping over my political sentiments. I entered into life, drinking it in large draughts, touching it and clinging to fleeting moments, not allowing them to escape me, enjoying it second by second and minute by minute.

In the first half of the fifties, I escaped from the prison of the harem. When the roof fell in on Palestine in 1948, the veil fell off the face of the Nablus woman. She had struggled for a long time to free herself from the traditional wrap and thick black veil.

Before the final lifting of the veil, Nablus women had succeeded in changing their outer covering, by stages, over a period of thirty years. In the twenties they got rid of the full black flowing skirt, substituting a black or brown coat or one of some other sombre colour. At the beginning of the forties they got rid of the tringular bolero-like cover that was worn on the head and came down over the shoulders to the waist, concealing the shape of the upper half of the body, and behind which the woman would fold her hands over her breast, so the men could not see her fingers. In the middle forties the transparent black kerchief became more transparent, revealing the face under it, and in the middle fifties the black veil was finally lifted, allowing the God-given beauty of their faces to speak modestly for itself.

The evolution of the veil in Nablus was slow compared to Jerusalem, Haifa and Jaffa. The path our development took was neither easy nor smooth. Nablus remained a bigoted city, clinging to the old traditions in which social change was not easily effected. The established moulds and patterns remained the prevailing order, despite the many well-educated young men and women. It is strange that this city, whose inhabitants are famous for their dynamism and great enterprise, remained adamantly against anything new touching their traditions. However, the inevitability of development eventually overcomes all resistance. It is life's march, impossible to check or halt.

My hunger for life was relentless. Someone who has squandered many years of her life in the desert of the Empty Quarter cannot turn her back on a green oasis when the doors are opened to her. The child of life emerged now into the life that had given her birth. Being wholly sincere, she faced life with a genuine and natural frankness which society, with its stern rules and customs, insists on counterfeiting and covering up with a false mask. This child of life was not selfish: she took and she gave. Giving was her way of life, an inseparable part of her nature. Previously, when she stole out to the wheat-fields, she would feel downcast and sad at seeing the gift the wheat had to offer, when she had nothing to offer. A heart filled with love suffocates if it finds no one to love.

The time arrived for this daughter of life to speak and, when a truthful woman speaks, it is life that is speaking.

Our eastern Arab society suppressed the sentiment of love,

just as it continually oppressed women. The magic hand of this beautiful human emotion touched even the hearts of prophets. It was because of this emotion that the noble Prophet Muhammad (God bless him and grant him salvation!) said: 'Praise be to God! Praise be to the director of hearts!' the moment he saw Zaynab Bint Jahsh suddenly appear to him. In Arab society, this beautiful human emotion is a casualty of the split nature of our society and still carries connotations of disgrace and shame.

As far as I'm concerned, love is a wider concept than the affirmation of a woman's femininity. To me it is the affirmation of my crushed humanity and its very salvation. All my life I have been drawn to love, driven by a poetic sentiment difficult to explain. Just as birds respond instinctively to the magnetic field in determining the path of their flight, so have I always responded to love. It remained to me the most attractive torch that beckoned me among life's various inducements.

I am not straying far from the truth when I say that, with me, love remained a concept; an absolute world. For me the 'other' was the embodiment of that idea, whose horizons I was never able to relinquish. It has become an instinct and a natural impulse, forever warm and throbbing in my heart, and I'd plunge into the warm sea of emotion to cleanse my soul of bitterness. This abstract concept had no shore or harbour where I could cast anchor. It was a vast sea where, sometimes, the waves were so high that they became a whirlpool within which I turned until I lost all sense of the world outside.

Before emerging from the harem, my adolescent emotions were on fire. I was a repressed soul who responded to the first word of love received on the page of a letter. Love by correspondence. I would fall into this sort of imaginary love and wallow in it, while the old walls of the harem lay between me and the actual experience. So that imagination and the exchange of letters were the length and breadth of my sphere of action. I hungered for something that did not exist; I was lost, alone, possessing nothing but this heightened imagination.

**115**

Liberation came at last. I found myself merging with the 'other', discovering myself through the compass of reality. My heart has ever been a fresh garden ripe for love. During moments of love we feel our humanity intensifying. We leave the far distant icy pole to travel to radiant sunshine. The 'other' becomes the bridge to a world whose scattered parts have been brought together to become one inseparable whole; a world which, by its sweetness and bitterness, its contradictions and ironies leads to mental and spiritual well-being; it is a beautiful, harsh, tender world, just like life itself. And after all is said and done, love is preordained like life and death, especially for those with poetic natures. For them there is no escape from it.

There is nothing sweeter than when love touches even trivial things, transforming them into things of beauty and worth: a restaurant bill, a theatre ticket, a dried flower, a ballpoint or fountain pen. All these and similar trivial things become rare and priceless when touched by love.

My vivid imagination created a magic halo around the beloved, projecting upon him what he did not have. I would see the faults but, in my view, the faults did not stand in the way of love. Which of us searches for a Christ to love? In my opinion, exemplary people make poor lovers. Their idealism makes them review the affair in a manner that strips love of all its great excitment. I have always believed that love is a treasure whose worth we can never assess until we have exhausted it or lost it in a gamble.

When time – that gigantic force of destruction – has played its role in things and relationships, I do not linger amongst the ruins. I do not remain faithful to the past, when it is over and done with. I do not allow the past permission to rob the future, for the past is a thief that takes away but does not give.

It is not strange for the heart to love more than once. It is unnatural that one's heart should be bound up in one person all one's life. It is normal for more than one relationship to form and for love to recur in the heart. And each time one falls in love, the emotions are just as strong, and just as sincere and sweet as the previous time. But there has never been a place in my heart for casual love, for frivolous and reckless relationships.

I often find that the past has gone not only in its physical sense, but in its psychological sense too. What is past has a value that differs entirely from my present view, so it loses its psychological significance. I feel that I am another person with no connection to my former self, no longer acquainted with it except in memory.

The world of my childhood is the only one that has not lost its psychological meaning for me. It is the only world to which I return with the old warmth of heart. With that exception, everything, it seems to me, submits to the laws of change.

## 24

My emergence from the harem coincided with a dramatic stage in the Arabs' struggle against new western imperialism. With the fall of Palestine in 1948, the traditional structure of Arab society was shaken, politically, socially and culturally. The reactionary regimes in Egypt and Syria fell, the popular movements grew stronger in Egypt and Iraq. The concepts of socialism and Marxism began to penetrate the minds of the Arab people, directing them towards the fight against imperialism, on the one hand and, on the other, against society's traditional concepts.

With the winds of change and revolt, poetry left its ivory tower to march along with the Arab masses, expressing their asprirations for freedom from repression and exploitation. The poet's cause became collective rather than individual. Then there was the dazzling rise of Jamal Abd al-Nasser, the Arab leader who became everyone's idol, his name on everyone's tongue. This devoted leader suddenly appeared to a nation that had been awaiting his arrival for many generations. He caused a fresh sense of confidence and power to gush forth in its life blood, making it beat anew, despite all the forces of evil opposing it.

I, along with millions of other Arabs, loved Jamal Abd al-Nasser. I lived through the nationalisation of the Suez canal and the tripartite aggression against Egypt with extreme emotion and excitement.

In Nablus during this period – between the years 1956 and 1957 – the mixed cultural club founded by Dr Waleed Qamhawi and some progressive young men, filled the cultural and social void which dominated the city. Despite the many reactionary and hostile voices raised in the mosques against the mixed club, and the offensive graffiti written on the walls of that rigidly conventional city, the club was able to realise some of its objectives with regard to intellectual, literary and social acitivities. I say it realised some of its objectives, for the governing regime of the day was not long in closing the club because of its secret political activity.[57]

I was a member of the club. This was the first time I joined and fitted into a group. When the tripartite aggression against Egypt broke out in 1956, the atmosphere in the club became electrifying. We felt we were suspended by a thread, swinging between hope and fear of a fresh defeat. The stand the Kremlin took delighted us and we were swept away by a torrent of love for Russia.

In the sphere of western politics, the Eisenhower–Dulles doctrine had appeared before that which advocated filling the vacuum Britain had left behind. Since it was quite obvious to America that Jordan was the best place to fill that vacuum, troubles began to beset the progressive government of Suliman al-Nabulsi.

On 10 April 1957 al-Nabulsi's government was dismissed, in the wake of the emergence of the nationalist officers' movement in the Jordanian army, the majority of whom belonged to the Baath party that supported the government.

The Palestinians dominated the progressive political parties that unanimously backed the fallen government of al-Nabulsi, foreseeing the suppression of freedom that would result from this resignation. Demonstrations were held on the West Bank, protesting against the king's demand that the government be dismissed. When the new government was formed under the leadership of Dr Husayn Fakhri al-Khalidi on 16 April, the progressive elements in the country refused to accept it. On 22 April a conference was held in Nablus, known as the National Islamic Conference, attended by more than 200 delegates, representing all the progressive political parties, in addition to various national leaders, and twenty-three parliamentarians. The total membership participating in the conference represented the majority of the Jordanian parliament.

The formation of the new government signalled a period of major transition, anticipating internal political restraint that would put an end to political freedom in the country and cut off any co-operation with the progressive regimes in Egypt and Syria. For this reason the resolutions passed by the National Conference called boldly and unequivocally for the resignation of al-Khalidi's government and the formation of another government composed of national socialist parties. They also demanded the rejection of the Eisenhower doctrine and the expulsion of the American ambassador and the American military attaché from the country. Likewise, the conference decided to hold a general strike on 24 April to back up these demands. Accordingly, on 24 April people awoke to a general strike in most cities in the kingdom. Violent demonstrations were held, especially in West Bank cities.[58]

On that day the government resigned to make way for a new government, formed on 25 April under the leadership of Ibrahim Hashim. Marital law was declared, all political parties were abolished, and a curfew was imposed on Amman, Irbid, Nablus, Jerusalem and Ramallah. There were sudden, widespread arrests, which prevented many of the ideologically committed members of the conference from returning to their cities. Some fell into the trap, to be led away to prison, while luckier ones hid in friends' or relatives' houses.

Around the middle of May, the weak rays of the afternoon sun were shining into the club's west room, from time to time stolen from the walls by passing clouds. Some of the members were discussing our usual topic: the gloomy political situation in the country. In the chair opposite sat a friend, the teacher (S). Her gleaming eyes were on my face. Something in those black eyes told me she was disturbed and not really with us. Suddenly I saw her jump from her chair and come quickly to sit beside me. Her head was close to mine and her lips touched a strand of hair over my ear. She whispered: 'Have you a safe place for a hunted comrade? We are in a critical situation; our district is under surveillance. He must leave his present hiding place tonight before they hunt him down.'

My mind worked fast. In those days there was freedom of action in the house. Those who remained of Uncle's family were cut off from us by a chronic quarrel. We didn't meet each other or speak to each other. The west room on our upper floor was remote and suitable. Mother and my young sister, Fataya, were always with me. My brother Rahmi would definitely welcome the guest. Rahmi had been with the comrades and for them ever since he was sixteen, even though he hadn't joined officially.

I whispered in her ear: 'Yes!' and we agreed on the time to carry it out. At half past eight in the evening we three were in a taxi, she beside the trustworthy driver and, on the back seat sitting beside me, a silent man I did not know, wearing a white *kaffiyyeh* and a black *igal*.

The weather was on our side!

Unexpected rains during a month which usually brings the breath of summer poured down in torrents. The taxi entered the old market. The shops were closed. The town was completely deserted except for a cat curled up in a dark alley. A passer-by, his head hunched into his shoulders and his hands thrust into his jacket pockets, was running to escape the sudden rain, trying to avoid the water spouts from the roofs on both sides of the alleys.

The taxi came to a stop in front of the door of our house. We got out to climb the many straight and spiral steps. The reception room on the third floor drew us in. The introductions were made.

Dr Abd al-Rahman Shuqair (I had often heard of him) was

**120**

the leader of the progressive party in Amman and the most weighty opponent of the reactionary regime. His attacks on the present system in Jordan were vehement. Should he be discovered, it would be a great coup for the forces of political repression.

My brother Rahmi came home and, to his surprise, found our distinguished guest, whom he received with open arms. The hunted political activist hid in the remote upper room with the curtains drawn over its narrow windows and glass door.

Early the next morning I went to Amman to reassure his patient wife and three small daughters. Having had no word of him, they were very anxious. Afterwards they left for Damascus.

During his stay with us, I took care that things in the house should appear normal, so as not to arouse the suspicions of Uncle's family. When Mother set up his meals on a small tray, I would watch for a time when the main courtyard was empty, then run with the tray of food to the upper room. Through that time I also deliberately kept on going to the club and the cinema, so as not to seem haunted with anxiety and fear.

Before leaving the house, I would lock the stair door leading to the upper floor. I was happy to perform the tasks I had taken upon myself, although my happiness was mixed with suppressed anxiety. If someone followed me in the street, I was filled with trepidation, fearing he might be an informer. I do not pretend to courage when I say that my secret fear was not for myself. My only concern was for the political activist's safety, on the one hand, and my brother Rahmi's, on the other, for the country was suffering a ruthless form of political repression and persecution.

Eleven days passed during which our guest remained hidden in the closed upper room with its curtains drawn, before arrangements were completed for him to slip from his hunters, to Damascus.

I was drinking my morning coffee in restless suspense.

The ringing of the telephone in my room drew me from my seat in one eager bound.

I lifted the receiver – Damascus.

'Talk to Damascus.'

The soft Damascene voice of Dr Shuqair's wife reached my ears: 'Hello ... good morning ... thanks for the present ... it arrived yesterday in good condition.'

'Thank God ... No need for thanks. It was my pleasure ... How are the children? My salaams to all.'

I put down the receiver.

I took a deep breath and relaxed!

## 25

At the beginning of the 1950s I became acquainted with Yasmeen Zahran – who later received a Ph.D. in history. The bonds of friendship between us were firmly cemented from the beginning. Our meetings and outings together in Jerusalem, Ramallah and Jericho took place over many years. Yasmeen was one of the most outstanding of the breed of educated women in the country. Through her I learned to love Proust and the Holy Bible. She was steeped in western thought, and espoused progressive ideas, leaning emotionally and ideologically towards the Baath party. Her house was the meeting place for her Baath friends in Ramallah and Jerusalem. She always claimed that mental and spiritual factors were among the most significant and basic elements deciding a people's destiny, more important than economic, social and political elements. History bears witness to this: for example the Arab conquests behind which lay neither economic nor social drive. It was nothing other than a spiritual outburst, and a creed for whose sake the Arabs fought and died. At the time, she had a weekly column in some of the local papers that she used as a sounding board for her progressive ideas, emphasising the necessity of the Arab individual's faith in the strength of the Arab people and their right to a dignified life. Unless this concept matures in the heart, and becomes a spiritual driving force, the individual

Arab will never be capable of change and self-determination.

Her house, in her home town of Ramallah, brought together the cream of the educated members of society of both sexes. The new young Palestinian women had now begun to enjoy the benefits of higher education. Even the daughters of some Muslim *shaykhs* in Nablus and other Palestinian cities were graduates of American and British universities.

The Nablus friends – Labeeba Salah (Ph.D. in Education); Yusra Salah (English language inspector); Saba Arafat,[59] and her sister Afaf, the creative artist – these, and others like them, open-minded and aware, of Yasmeen's generation in Ramallah and Jerusalem, were all beads in a necklace strung together in Yasmeen's lovely house.

At her place I became acquainted with my well-remembered friend, Jameel al-Budayri. He liked my poetry, but was continually urging me to get away from the subjective realm of the self. It was in Yasmeen's house, too, that I got to know the poet–martyr, Kamal Nasir.

At the time he was a Palestinian representative in the Jordanian parliament. We would spend fascinating evenings in Yasmeen's garden, when everyone would be his or her natural self. Kamal was always in a state of restless excitement, laughing, rebellious, and perplexed. Our conversations revolved around current circumstances, poetry, love, death, strife and suicide. We would read poetry, feel sad, be happy, be hopeful and fall into despair. Because of his dynamic, warm personality, Kamal was very close to his friends.

In 1957, during the dramatic period of our history with Jordan, I mean the period of martial law and the violent attack on the ideologists, the newspaper *Palestine*, published in Jerusalem, would every week offer its readers a new poem signed with the name of Abu Firas. The fervour, sincerity and genuineness of these poems caught my attention, making me wonder who this Abu Firas could be.

When I asked my friend, Raja al-Issa, chief editor of *Palestine*, about the unknown poet, he answered smiling: 'Who do you think he is?'

'There's the breath of Kamal in the poems', I replied.

'Shh . . . Don't let anyone hear you,' said Raja.

Then I realised that Kamal had gone into hiding and had not managed to slip through the blockade as I had thought. I was devastated.

On my way back to Nablus, images of the wonderful evenings, when friends met in Yasmeen Zahran's garden, began going round and round in my head and heart.

The following week I went to Raja al-Issa with a new poem dedicated to the imprisoned songbird.

During the week, a poem arrived from Kamal, in return. After that I started meeting Kamal in his safe hide-out.

One day I found him suffering from toothache. The risk of slipping out to a dentist was too dangerous. I suggested going to Jerusalem to bring back our relative, Dr Burhan Abd al-Hadi, to treat him. The following day I did just that.

During the days I spent with Dr Abd al-Rahman Shuqair and Kamal Nasir in their hide-outs, I discovered the difference between a person's feelings and thoughts when acting alone and those when working with a group. I tasted the joy of collective co-operation: getting outside myself and being part of a group delighted and overwhelmed me.

But the problem which remained for me was that the enthusiasm that waxed whenever things were at fever pitch waned when they were over.

I truly wished that politics could always arouse my enthusiasm; that I could join one of the progressive parties; that I could rid myself of being forever torn between my individualism and my national sentiments – those sentiments that were only aroused when situations were heated. I wished with all my heart that I could throw myself into the midst of the group, live its life, its concerns, and share its stand on national affairs. However, the realisation of this desire was beyond my capability. Dealing with people in the public world was not in my nature. So my complete inability to merge with a group gave rise to a sense of dissatisfaction. I wavered between these conflicting states, distressed by the clash between the force of my dominating fundamental

**124**

nature and my discontent, rather my loathing of this nature that created a guilt complex in me. In fact my incapacity was a tragic situation, corresponding to Engels' definition of tragedy: 'the collison of need with the impossibility of fulfilling this need.'

Not one of the poets of my generation failed to rally round a party or take a committed stand, which was the source of inspiration for their poetry. I was prey to an intricate clash between highly subjective sentiments which I could not transcend and my deep awareness of a deficiency in my poetry because of my inability to commit myself to any particular ideology.

I sometimes tried to philosophise about my lack of group spirit. Introspectively, I would ask myself: is it possible for a person with a poetical nature to strip herself of her personality to the extent demanded in this age? Why are poets all driven by one thing, politics alone? There are many sides to life; its facets are numerous, and a subjective tendency is one of these facets. So why eliminate it from poetry, since poetry is the reflection of life's various situations? A poet is, above everything else, a person before being political.

Thus, I would rationalise my situation: a poet is an individual like all others and represents all human beings in their intrinsic nature. The poet suffers at the death of a brother or a loved one, loves the opposite sex, and responds to the gifts of nature and life. So why ask the poet – as a poet – to lay aside these gifts, giving no expression to them in poetry?

Sometimes I would go so far as to persuade myself that party activities in our Arab countries were deficient. Politics still remained a personal loyalty to individuals, rather than to principles, and that took people's minds off the real task.

Undoubtedly in reverting to this immature way of thinking I was simply searching for a rationalisation. I was well aware that the poet could pursue national activities through poetry, without joining designated political organisations. It wasn't necessary to be tied to party activities to fulfil the role of a poet, in touch with Arab reality.

Thus my poetry writing remained bound to my unpredictable moods. I did not experience a lasting sense of reality, nor an abiding emotional attachment to the communal cause, until after the June War.

## 26

I read, so I exist. I continued to be a voracious reader and this voracity heightened my sense of deprivation from academic studies. Someone with high ambitions comes to harbour feelings of bitterness, arising from that vacuum left in the soul by being deprived when young of the chance to study. She becomes a bookworm.

My reading was not systematic. I would read any book I could lay my hands on: from literary, historical, social and philosophical subjects to books on simplified science. Salama Musa, al-Aqqad and al-Mazani were amongst the writers who opened my mind and taught me what I did not know. From the forties on, I stuck closely to psychology and to novels.

In novels I found the distillation of human experience; I found ideas, poetry, philosophy and psychoanalysis. They deal with life, that is with all that lives. Humankind is treated in the novel in all its turbulence, contradictions, vicissitudes, and all the contrasting elements that go to make it up. Thus the world of famous western novelists became my world, teeming with life and movement, while I was imprisoned within the walls. I read these novels in Arabic or English.

In novels, philosophical thought in particular continued to attract me: the problem of good and evil, matters of sickness and death, of divine justice and whether there actually is such a thing. Being pessimistic by nature, I was always drawn to the sceptical characters in novels, those who were dominated by anxiety and who asked many questions about the world and life. Was our destiny preordained in heaven or was it subject to our own actions? Did fatalism come from an outside power, or was it, as modern psychology teaches, a latent component of the self, inseparable from it? The existentialists say that we are free moral agents, with the ability to choose, and we alone weave the web of our existence. But what about the age we live in and the circumstances that surround us? What about the strength of hereditary forces? Aren't we the prisoners of our environment, circumstances, times, and psychological and physical make-up? Have religions saved an anguished humanity from its suffering? Are we born with a natural bent to sin or is it the influence of our environment? When I was small, I was disturbed by a story Mother often told us, as we sat around the brazier in winter. It was the story of the prophet Moses when he passed by a poor man, crouching in a pit that covered half his body, in order to hide his nakedness from passers-by. Distressed by the poor man's state, Moses ascended Mount Sinai to talk to his Lord, imploring Him to grant the man a means of living. God granted him His promise. When Moses returned joyfully to town, he was startled at the sight of the poor man's lifeless body hanging from the gallows.

Stunned, Moses immediately returned to the mountain to rebuke his Lord: 'Oh God, I asked you to give him his livelihood, not to hang him.'

The Great God replied: 'Be quiet Moses, I created him and I know him better.'

As we listened to her, perplexed and astonished, Mother would finish the tale and then explain what had happened: 'One of the owners of the house under whose walls the poor man sheltered was shaking out a tablecloth from which a gold dinar fell. Picking up the dinar, the poor man went to the tavern where he drank and caroused, then picked a quarrel with one of his drinking companions. He got up and, with what was left of the dinar, bought a knife and stabbed the man to death. At that they took him to the judge who ordered him to be hanged.'

This story troubled me: 'I created him and I know him better.' But why did He create him thus, then punish him?

The Old Testament was one of the books I returned to from time to time. In some of its books I discovered images of humanity, touched by the art of storytelling, emerging vital with life. Job's story is the story of a man under stress wrestling with the forces of evil that obstruct his path. Then there are the philosophical issues this book addresses: evil and misery. Who is responsible for them? Is there divine justice in the universe and where is it to be found, if it exists? Whenever my spirit was under siege from questions to which there is no satisfactory answer, or whenever I felt that the threads of my life were too scattered for me to bring back together, I would turn to the Book of Ecclesiastes: 'Vanity of vanities . . . What profit hath a man of all his labour which he taketh under the sun?'[60] It was as if that sage who put all his pessimism into that book was repeating what Gilgamesh had said earlier: 'This is the world: no house is lived in for ever; no contract is carried out to its conclusion; nothing is permanent.'[61]

However, the echo of Christ's cry in his affliction: 'My God, why has Thou forsaken me?' has taken root in my heart and there it stays.

In some of my old papers I came across two verses I had written down under the title, 'Torch of Faith':

Oh Lord! Rescue the embers of my dying fire
My doubts have almost swallowed the light of my faith.

If You are its kindler, please fan the flame
But if You are its extinguisher, forgive my denial.

In these two lines lay the seed that, many years later, gave birth to my poem, 'Before the Closed Door'.

When faith is shaken, the earth is shaken, spinning one around with it, as if it had no axis and, along with the unanswerable questions still in abeyance, life becomes an unbearable burden. In vain I endeavoured to adopt William Blake's motto: 'Do what you want. This world is only a fairy story built upon contradiction.' The person without spiritual insight is incomplete, as the Indians say.

In *Fear and Trembling*, Søren Kierkegaard expressed our need for religious faith: 'If mankind did not possess a consciousness of immortality, and if the basis of creation is a blind force beset by unconscious and inexplicable emotions from which springs everything sublime or base, then life can be nothing but despair.'

128

Islamic thought had drawn me, from an early age, to philosophical questions. The first to influence me in that direction was Zaky Mubarak in his book on al-Ghazzali.[62] Then I found intellectual satisfaction in reading the writings of the al-Mu'tazila and their debate about fatalism, freedom, justice, reward and punishment.[63]

My brother Rahmi, though my friend, was always at variance with me. He was ever a kind brother, with many of Ibrahim's characteristics, especially an affectionate nature and a love of being helpful. However, Rahmi did not show enthusiasm for my concerns, my reading, or my poetry. He was a Marxist by inclination and thinking. He went to sleep with Lenin and woke up with Stalin. He had been imprisoned at the age of seventeen, charged with being a communist. Ever since the late twenties, party members had suffered persecution from the British authorities and, after it, from feudal leaders and the Jewish bourgeoisie.

Rahmi pestered me about the necessity of commitment to the realities of the country, saying that we lived under conditions and in a time when no one should remain indifferent. Otherwise, there was no need for, or significance to, all the poetry I wrote. This disturbed me. In it I found a threat to the meaning of my life itself. Poetry was all my life.

I didn't concern myself with communism. I had no real understanding or clear picture of it. The (communist) League of National Freedom in Palestine had decided to accept the resolution of partition. After the creation of Israel, the party members, under the leadership of the late Fouad Nassar, Secretary General of the Central Committee, demanded the establishment of an independent National Palestinian State according to the resolution of the United Nations of 29 November 1947.

In those days, agreement to the partition resolution was considered treason to the country and its people. This was the reason for my spontaneous alienation from the communists and the flaring up of the dispute between Rahmi and me. With my weak political sensibility at the time how could I realise the astuteness and farsightedness of the position of the League of National Freedom? The Palestinian communists had anticipated us by thirty years in their stand on this issue; now we are claiming what they demanded three decades ago. We are demanding, like them, the exercise of our right to decide our future and establish the independent national state that the United Nations' resolution had stipulated in 1947, but to no avail.

## 27

When I emerged into life, I was defenceless, vulnerable, without experience or an understanding of people. So the confrontation was tedious, difficult and one-sided. Books alone are not sufficient for understanding life and the complications and clashes that arise in human relationships. We must experience life itself; our own personal experiences are the fountainhead of this knowledge.

Feelings and ideas remote from the world of people and reality . . . a social consciousness lacking real growth because of its chronically crippled state . . . Suddenly these came face to face with people and the hustle and bustle of life after the isolated world of the harem I found myself in a state of bewilderment and anxiety. Social life and what it had to offer were on one side, with me on the other. It was a situation that gave rise to astonishment, frustration and food for thought.

To know life and touch it means knowing people and touching them, and clashing with others, putting our fingers on their tender and their rough spots, their love and hate, their weakness and strength, their nobility and baseness, their sincerity and hypocrisy – this whole blend of contradictions. Along with this there was the inescapable high price one has to pay: good will and innocence.

I discovered that the world of human relationships is fraught with complications and strife. My nature was never a combative one, which might have helped me in a world that I found so alien to my make-up. I was in a turmoil between my love for people and my fear of them; between the depth of the

130

human relationship that bound me to friends and people, and my discovery that quite often words were not always truthful, but concealed a secret coldness behind a veil of pretence. I alternated between periods of accepting others and enjoying their friendship, and periods of weary apathy towards people, when I frequently took comfort in the lines of the beautiful old poem:

If you do not often drink impure water
You will be thirsty. What man is perfect?

In these lines I found a wonderful summary of the whole psychology of friendship, and human relationships in general. However, my ties to people continued to be subject to my moods.

Then my tendency to romanticism would pull me deep into myself again. The lack of anything compelling me to make contact with the outside world contributed. I had no job or position to occupy part of my thoughts and I never felt any inclination to do charitable social work. So my sympathies and emotions found no outside goal to reach for, nor any alternative to take me out of myself. I was convinced that my happiness lay only in isolation. However, individual happiness is in continual conflict with one's sense of duty to society. So what was the solution?

I came to realise my complete inability to break through this isolation, no longer forced upon me by others, while at the same time I was incapable of justifying this seclusion. This gave rise to a struggle of another kind with my life and myself. I began to search for a way out of this crisis.

England was one of the distant dreams that continually beckoned me. I told myself: I'll go on the train of life on a new journey to another station, where I'll cross new horizons. I'll stay there in the heart of civilisation for a year or two.

## 28

The last week of August 1961. A mild, clear evening in the public garden in Nablus. Visitors to the garden were enjoying the fine weather after a hot day – in particular those returning from the Gulf States, and the Kingdom of Saudi Arabia for a holiday in their own dear country between the arms of Jerzim and 'Aibal, always outstretched to welcome them.

In a corner shaded by the high branches of the trees in the garden, my cousin Farouq and I sat sipping coffee and chatting. Farouq was a close friend, closer even than my closest relative. Bonds of love had united us since his early infancy. I still remember how he fell asleep one evening sitting in my lap and, when his mother tried to move him to his bed, he suddenly woke up and started to cry, clinging to me, refusing to give in. I was very attached to the children in the family and, when they grew up, the bonds of love with most of them remained strong.

On that summer evening in the public garden, Farouq talked to me about his studies and experiences in England. At the time he was a student in New College, Oxford, and was to receive his university degree the following summer.

In turn I talked to Farouq about my remote dream and my aspirations to live in England for a year or two. Farouq endorsed the idea enthusiastically. He assured me he would make all the arrangements and preparations himself, immediately upon his return to England.[64]

Oxford, 8 October 1961

Dear Fadwa (God protect her),

I am writing to you from the oldest university city in the world. Today is Sunday. Every week on this day I hear the church bells ringing from morning until the early hours of the evening; I see the people of the city wending their way to the houses of worship, Bibles in hand, to meet with their Lord once a week, imploring Him to ward off the spectre of war, for they have tasted its misfortunes twice in this century. You don't find them seeking for wealth or livelihood – they have already attained that – they seek peace and security.

132

The hubbub of social life has begun in the university. Classes will begin on 13 October. Yesterday, Saturday 7 October, I was invited to a reception at the residence of Sir William Hayter, head of my college. Both he and his wife, Lady Hayter, welcomed me warmly. Lady Hayter, a Cambridge graduate, is a very gracious person. I spent almost a quarter of an hour chatting with both of them and they invited me to have dinner with them on the twenty-first of this month.

Enclosed you will find a clipping I took from the *Times* advertising section. I'm sending it to you so you can get an idea about such matters. I have marked some of the advertisements I would like you to read. For instance, there are two advertisements, each one pertaining to a lady who wishes to live with a family. However, you should know that these ads appear daily and an hour after they come out they are read by those interested and all snapped up. The best proof of this is that they aren't repeated the following day. So you can't depend upon reading them in Nablus, then writing to them. You will find you have missed the boat. Along with that, the English newspaper reach Jerusalem two days after publication.

What I'm suggesting is this: it would be advisable for you to come to England after December, where you will receive the warmest welcome from me. You will live with me in Oxford for as long as you choose. During your stay in Oxford, you can put an ad in the *Times* stating all your requirements, after you determine what they are. I assure you that, after December, I'll be in the new apartment. It has two bedrooms. I also assure you that you will not put me out in any way. On the contrary, it will be a source of joy to me. I welcome your coming from the bottom of my heart and your living with me for as long as you wish. I think it best for you to come to Oxford, so that the change won't be too sudden for you. I'll introduce you to my men and women friends in the college; I'll show you where to buy vegetables and meat. The bread and milk are delivered to the house every morning. I'm sure I'll be able to ward off all the difficulties you will run into at first, as every foreigner does when first coming to live in Britain. You will find life here much simpler than we imagine it to be in our country, that life here is good, and you will be free of everything that causes headaches and upsets.

Lastly, I beg you to give this idea some thought and to try to take courage about coming to England.

Warm regards and greetings to all family members. Sincerely,
Farouq Tuqan

Oxford, 15 October 1961

Dear Fadwa (God protect her),

I was delighted at your firm intention to come to England, especially to Oxford at first. I have begun thinking about drawing up a programme for you, so you can make the best of every moment you spend here. I pray God will help me in preparing all that you need. I want you to know that some of my friends are anxious to meet you and talk to you. I'm convinced you will find that the atmosphere at Oxford suits you very well.

As for the time of arrival, you are welcome at any time you choose. If you wish to spend the winter season in England, you had better start out now. But if you want to avoid England's cold, the first of March seems to me a suitable time, although there isn't much difference between the cold in February and March. At any rate, please get in touch with me as soon as you finish the necessary documents – visa and residence. Let me assure you that everything in England is well organised and the visitor finds no difficulty at all in obtaining anything. We are waiting for positive news from you.

Life in Oxford goes on as well as one could wish, this term. I am up to my ears in my weekly essay preparations, along with going to various parties, the most important of which was the party given by my friend who visited me in Nablus along with two others. You do remember, don't you, how excited they were over bathing in the public baths in the old city? Yesterday I was invited to dine at the professors' table in my college which we call the High Table.

I was the only student in my college to be invited to dine at that table this year, just as I was the student invited to dine at it the last academic year. This is a very great honour at Oxford. After dining we moved to the professors' magnificent hall, with the furniture many centuries old where, by candlelight, we drank sweet wine with walnuts, bananas and other fruit. This ritual takes place once a week, every Tuesday after supper.

I carried on a discussion on numerous subjects with the college professors, for two hours. Thanks be to God who helped me answer their questions well; some of these questions were quite cunning as they were directed to dicovering a person's mind and ideas. My answers were all supported by proofs and evidence.

The Christmas holidays begin Friday, 8 December, and last for six weeks. I am going to Austria to ski and from there to Germany for a few days, then to Paris. I haven't told anyone about this trip yet, but I'm going to write to my father to get his permission to travel, as usual. I shall also tell Uncle Qadri and my dear brother Saad.

Around the twentieth of December, my new Mercedes will arrive. I am already preparing to have it fully insured. However, the trip to Austria will be through the University. The amount, going and coming, including staying two weeks in the best hotels, along with insurance against breaking one's legs or arms, is thirty-five pounds, excluding pocket money. Some young men and women from Oxford and Cambridge are accompanying us. I'll return to England before Christmas Day, as I shall spend the remaining half of the holiday studying.

That's all the news I have. I wish you success and good fortune, hoping to receive good news from you. My sincere love to all.

Ever yours with love,
Farouq

Dear Fadwa (God protect her),

I am writing this letter to you at about six o'clock in the morning. I did not go to bed last night as I spent the whole night preparing a term paper entitled, 'What is the Right and What is the Wrong', which I shall deliver in a few hours.

I want you to know that my delay in writing to you wasn't due to laziness or lack of interest in your affairs, but because the information which I want to let you have became available to me only yesterday. Now I need to know your opinion concerning it.

Mrs Moore had sent a letter to my Nablus address, in reply to the letter I had sent her from Nablus. However, that reply of hers arrived after I had left. So Uncle Qadri sent it back to Oxford.

The most important thing in her letter was some addresses of people she recommended me to get in touch with, to see if it would be possible for you to live with one of them. I did, in fact, get touch with the ladies Mrs Moore had recommended. Yesterday I received a letter from a lady named Margaret French, stating that she is prepared to welcome you into her home. In her letter, she says her husband teaches music in Oxford and that her family consists of three children. The two oldest go to school, but the youngest attends school only in the morning. Therefore, she will not be able to entertain you much. She adds that their small town is very quiet and does not contain any places worth visiting. However, it is close to Oxford and to Stratford-upon-Avon, Shakespeare's town. She is prepared to converse with you in English as much as possible, so you can profit from your stay with them. Finally, she says that she will charge the sum of seven pounds, seven shillings a week for room and board, electricity and heat, but excluding private washing (i.e. your clothes).

Yesterday I went to Banbury, Mrs French's town. I found that she lives in an old house in one of the suburbs, but with plenty of amenities. The town is only around thirty kilometres from Oxford.

I suggest you come to Oxford at the end of March, stay with me a couple of weeks or more, then I'll take you to Banbury to stay with this lady for a few weeks, and then we'll see what you decide after that.

At Oxford you will stay in the room next to mine. Fortunately my vacation will begin on 17 March and will last for six weeks.

I hope you will tell me frankly what you think about all this. I swear I am on tenterhooks awaiting your arrival, for I am very sad. Life is no longer sweet to me away from my own country, especially since Father's death, God rest his soul. So having you with me will ease my longing for my country and family. I had never imagined I would arrive at this state of craving and yearning to return. I've had my fill of everything, and am eagerly awaiting the moment when I put my foot on Nablus soil. It is enough that Father's grave is there. His death is the worst misfortune I have ever endured.

Therefore, I sincerely beg you to try to come any day after 17 March.
Ever yours,
Farouq

## 29

For the ambitious person, the journey of life is an uninterrupted progress from one stage to another. Without this reaching forward, there would be no renewal or continuity in life. There is no final goal, no final resting place. Life is motion, forever going forward. A relentless quest for new horizons, even though it may be a hopeless one, is what gives life its richness and fullness.

I left home for England at the end of March 1962, weaving a dream of great and exciting expectations.

On all my journeys by air, Abu al-'Alaa' al-Ma'arri appears

to me through the strange vision he conveyed in his book, *Al-Fusul wa al-Ghayat*:[65]

> If the King [God] so wishes, He brings the one leaving for distant shores near, and makes the distance before him roll up fast, so that the man travels, when the night is close to the red glow of dawn, around the terrestrial globe, in the same time he circumambulates the Kaaba. Then he returns to his bed when night has not yet departed. He makes a greeting in Mecca and his brother would hear him in Syria. He would take the firebrand from Tihama[66] and light with it his fire in Yabreen[67] and the farthest shores.

More than 1,000 years ago, Abu al-'Alaa' al-Ma'arri, with his marvellous imagination, uttered these words, seeing in the vision of a writer and genius of a poet, the aeroplane, radio, electric lighting and other innovations on this age, invented at the peak of human creative power.

Just before sunset, the English countryside began to unfold before my eyes through the plane window: trees, forests and red brick houses. This beauty was offering itself to me and I would know how to take it to my heart.

This was the first time I had travelled alone outside an Arab country. My only previous journey to Europe which had included Holland, Sweden and Russia, as well as the People's Republic of China, was made in the company of a Jordanian delegation to attend a world peace conference, held in Stockholm in 1956. During that trip, other members of the delegation attended to the necessary documents at the various airports, leaving me free from the bother of looking after these things myself.

Farouq was on holiday in Austria, so there was no one to meet me at Heathrow Airport in London. However, I knew that the lady in whose house he lived at Oxford was keeping an empty room for me. The address was in my handbag and everything would be all right.

At Heathrow, everything was done with dazzling efficiency and in awesome silence: no fuss, no shoving with elbows and shoulders. Hundreds of travellers arriving from all parts of the world, some from the developed, others from the developing countries, were standing in line. All were waiting in turn to present their passports in perfect order, in the silence and stillness reigning over that spacious hall, as if it were a Buddhist temple. The officers in charge of entrance visas were all at their posts, attending to their duties. Lifting his eyes from the pages of the passport to the person's face, then, after asking a few questions about the reason for coming, the length of stay, the amount of money in one's possession, the officer hands back the passport and you enter the country.

Descending to ground level, I collected my suitcase from among the hundreds of suitcases, entered the customs and left. Services are rendered automatically and everything proceeds without any difficulty. People at the information desk advise and calmly give you directions. I was directed to the section for hotel reservations and, with one telephone call, a room was reserved in a London hotel, whose address the girl had given me. I would spend a night there, and on the morrow leave by train for Oxford.

I went outside the airport to get a taxi to take me to the hotel. I found myself standing in a queue of waiting travellers, all with suitcases beside them on the pavement. The taxis were crawling along slowly, one after the other, picking up their passengers in turn, then setting off quickly for the big city, leaving their place to the following taxi.

I read the hotel address to the driver, who was silent as the sphinx. The square-shaped, black taxi with its high roof moved off, making its way through the clean wide streets, empty except for a steady stream of cars.

After half an hour or so, London began passing swiftly by me: squares, gardens, fountains, tall buildings, shop windows, automobiles, motorcycles, red double-decker buses and vast throngs of people. A relentless concentration of people, lights and colours. The scene conveyed the rhythm of the dynamic

**139**

life on the evening streets. I felt a strange glow inside, a joy I cannot describe in words. It was as if a hidden hand had suddenly pressed an invisible electric switch inside me, lighting my soul with a dazzling glow I had never before experienced. A mystic illumination cut me off from my whole past, erasing from my heart all traces of other people's crudeness, harshness and cruelty and imbuing me with a sense of confidence and inner peace.

'The world is good. I bless life' (Rimbaud). Farewell to dull despair, farewell to soul-destroying bewilderment and anxiety.

The comfortable hotel room welcomed me. At breakfast in the morning, I asked the waiter whereabouts in the city I was. He told me I was in the heart of London. I went out, on a tour of exploration, into a large crowded square. This square, the famous Piccadilly, was a pageant of people of all races. Thousands of cars poured in like a rushing flood from all four directions. Hustle and bustle and ceaseless motion. Huge classical buildings towered above me; fountains, pouring out water like molten silver, were surrounded by young men and young women in their fancy coloured clothes. I saw a tall statue of a slender, winged young man, whom the sculptor had stood on his left foot with his right foot suspended in the air, holding a bow and arrow that he was on the point of loosing. This, then, was the statue of Eros, the god of love.

This is only one of the features of your face, London; it is not enough to quench my thirst. My desire is to know your real soul. I must stay with you a few months. I shall satisfy this desire in the future.

I went back to the hotel to pick up my suitcase, then got a taxi to Paddington station. Taking my seat on one of the compartments of the Oxford train, I was lost in happy dreams.

## 30

I shall never forget my days in England. The best feeling one can have is that of being at peace with oneself. Time was offering me the hand of reconciliation. A gracious hand, separating me from a past life that was over and done with, and for which I felt no nostalgia. Yearning for the past only becomes a part of life when that past carries happy memories.

There is nothing sweeter than a sense of liberty and freedom from the frustrations that surround one, the grip of whose claws can only be loosened by geographical distance. In England I experienced the same joy as a prisoner at the moment of release. No one but those who have been denied it knows the sweetness of freedom, and the marvel of possessing it. I had not believed that one day I should break through the doors of those dreary relationships and close them behind me. Those were doors behind doors where I had crouched, prey to a despair that was tearing my soul and body to pieces, forever feeling I was the victim of a world over which I had no control.

In a letter to my sister, Adeeba, in Kuwait, I wrote about that rapture welling up, spreading vitality through every atom of my being: 'My life here is unbelievably full and beautiful, unbelievably sweet.

'I once read the following: "Nothing tastes sweet to the mouth used to the taste of honey." And your sister whose mouth is used to nothing but the taste of bitterness now knows the taste of honey and the sweetness of life.'

I remained in Oxford as Farouq's guest for ten days or so, during which he treated me with the greatest hospitality. With him I was able to get to know the features of this ancient city and, more significantly, the splendour of the colleges. The architecture of the university colleges is world famous. One senses the spirit of Oxford alive within the ancient walls, the halls, gardens and passageways of the colleges.

Sometimes he took me out into the country to the small thatched pubs, where we would eat. The restaurants in country pubs are distinguished for their friendly atmosphere.

I was enchanted by Oxfordshire and its great heritage of vast wooded lands with such amazing numbers of beautiful trees. In this green land people have learned to control the cutting down of trees to preserve the forestation of this precious heritage. No tree is cut down before another tree has sprung up and grown beside it.

Before he took me to see his college, New College, I thought, as its name implied, I was going to witness a somewhat modern college. I was surprised to learn that its history goes back six centuries. As Farouq pointed out, a visitor is aware of this blending of the old and new. Standing there, facing the Gothic architecture, was a huge statue of Lazarus sculpted a few years earlier by the famous contemporary sculptor Epstein. Of all the sights, it was this statue, a memorial to the First World War, that moved me most. On it I read the following:

> In memory of the fellows of this college who have entered the heritage of this place, arriving from a foreign country. They then returned to fight and to die for their country in the war of 1914–1918.

These students, victims of the war, whose names were inscribed on the memorial cenotaph, were all Germans who had left the college and died on the battlefield, fighting against England. This, to me, was the ultimate expression of the spirit of this ancient university city.

I was invited with Farouq to a party held by some of his fellow students, where I got to know his friends of both sexes. What struck me most was the quiet of the place, despite the fact that there were no less than thirty present. Conversation was carried on in subdued voices by small groups scattered here and there. This brought to my mind Nietzsche's words: 'As man's mind advances, his desire for noise decreases.'

When I asked Farouq where the university was, I found it strange when he told me there was no university in Oxford in the way there is, for example, in Manchester or Bristol. Oxford is modelled on the same system as Cambridge: a collection of colleges, each with its own independent administration. The university is a governing body for arranging lectures, regulating examinations and assigning marks. Colleges are the real life of Oxford, every college containing students of all disciplines. That is, one would not find all science students in one college and all law students in another. Each college has arts, science, medical and engineering students. Naturally each student pursues an individual course of study, but as the lectures are arranged by the governing body, namely the university, not by the colleges, any student can attend any lecture in any college, since students are members both of their college and of the university. Thus, living with those representing all the other branches of learning allows the student to acquire a broad base of knowledge.

## 31

I settled down temporarily with the French family in Buddicote, a suburb of Banbury. The town was lifeless. But the experience was valuable to me. Mrs French and her husband surrounded me with care and friendship. At the end of each week, I paid the sum of £7.7s, for room, board and service. I was pleased that this amount did not strain my modest income, nor exceed my means.

Saturday and Sunday outings every week were a source of pleasure, enabling me to get to know several midland cities. My visit to Stratford-upon-Avon was the first of these enjoyable outings. On our way to see the house in which the great poet and dramatist was born, on Henley Street in the middle of the town, Mr French remarked: 'Few places have the same attraction as that which draws tourists to Stratford; around 300,000 tourists come here every year from all parts of the world.'

Shakespeare is everywhere there. You accompany him from the house where he was born to the house where he died; from the school in which he studied to the church where he was buried; from the house, Hallscroft, in the old town on the way to the church – the house of his daughter Susanna and her physician husband, John Hall – to the Royal Shakespeare Theatre on the curving River Avon. And finally to the bard's statue, standing on its high pedestal surrounded by statues of four of his main characters, crouching there, watching with him the thousands of visitors crossing the ancient Clapton Bridge that dates back five centuries. Wouldn't it be more suitable for Stratford-upon-Avon to be named Shakespeare-on-Avon? He is its son, its heart, and his presence will ever be there.

The garden behind the house in which he was born runs riot with the trees, grass and flowers Shakespeare mentions in his plays.

We then went on to the small village of Shottery, a mile from Stratford, to visit the cottage of his wife, Anne Hathaway. As the oldest pictures prove, little in the cottage had changed since Shakespeare's day: the old chairs beside the stone fireplace (the bard must have sat on those chairs), the dishes from which he may have eaten, the leather bottle from which Anne poured the ale for him. In that house one feels one is living in the sixteenth century. I stood entranced, listening closely. Nothing remained but that our ears should catch the sound of the bard's footsteps approaching from the narrow entry.

When we left the town in the evening, I was certain I would return more than once. Seeing some of his plays, which are always running, on the stage of the Royal Shakespeare, was a must. But this theatre, which presents only the bard's plays, has not won the admiration of the English for its architecture: they compare it to a gasworks.

Over a period of almost two years I visited most of the historical spots in England and Scotland, including some of the stately homes in rural areas. No longer private property, they had became part of the national legacy, allowing everyone the pleasure of visiting them by paying a small entrance fee.

Despite visiting many resplendently beautiful residences and historical places, I was never as moved as when I stood by the tomb of the world's most renowned poet, that immortal genius who will fascinate people as long as there is life.

Mr French took me on many Sunday trips to the country, with his two sons, twelve-year-old John and ten-year-old

Peter. After parking by the roadside, we would walk for miles. Walking in the English countryside is one of the most wonderful and delightful forms of exercise. The most amazing and eye-catching thing about the English countryside is its expanse and variety: farms, fields, woods, forests and valleys. I discovered that the countryside in all parts of England is never far from a city or town, generously offering its delights for everyone to enjoy. A city-dweller can find relaxation there; and country people love the wonders of nature and protect them. Greenery delights the English. The forests in the countryside are the most important feature of the natural environment and the English make every effort to protect them.

My feelings for nature are acute and strong. From childhood I have identified with nature, feeling myself a part of it. I see it as a living being, sensing its pulse. What extraordinary beauty there is in the English countryside. How can I describe it? Who can describe beauty in words? A pageant of greenness, a cool chrysolite flame of boundless dimension, the silence of the pastures, the stillness of the narrow country paths, the white sheep, the modest cottages set in the natural greenery and merging with it, the clean, fresh air smelling of trees, rain and earth. The soul of the countryside is present in the grass, the cattle, the flowers, the luxuriant woodland plants, and the beauty of it all offers itself to you wherever you turn. However, the most impressive thing about the country is that pervading calmness that soothes the nerves like a lullaby.

Because of his work in Oxford, Mr French left for the city every morning and returned after five. Some days I would accompany him. He would go to his place of work, while I wandered here and there exploring. At noon I would have a sandwich and a cup of coffee in a café, then go to a library and from there to a park if it was sunny. I would read for an hour and meditate for another. At four I would move to the Ashmolean Museum to spend a delightful time with the works of famous artists. The Ashmolean was the first museum of visual arts I had ever seen. From that time on, I have been addicted to visiting museums, whenever I have the opportunity to visit London or any other European capital.

Bt five o'clock I would be standing outside the museum door, awaiting Mr French, to return to Buddicote, completely satisfied.

In order to extend my stay in England, I had to enrol in an educational course so that I could get permission to remain for some time. Such courses were available to everyone, of different levels and ages. Mrs French gave me a pamphlet published by St Clare's College at Oxford, containing information about two summer sessions for the year 1962, the first during July, held at Christ Church, one of the Oxford colleges; and the second held in August in St Clare's College itself. I didn't hesitate for a moment. Here was a golden opportunity. Exchanging letters with the school, I completed my enrolment for the two sesssions.

Beginning to realise what I really wanted, I decided, after the two courses, to enrol in a school for a year, subject to the extension of my stay. I also decided that Oxford would be the right place, while I would make London my chief location later.

Indescribable feelings of rapture and openness of heart overwhelmed me.

The morning of the day of the first session I said farewell to the good lady and her children. Kind and generous as usual, Mr French took me in his car to Oxford. On the stroke of nine o'clock we were at the college door. I introduced myself to the man in charge, who handed me my room key stamped with the number. He asked one of the college servants to take my suitcase and show me to my room; however, Mr French did not leave until he was sure everything was in perfect order. Then, bidding me a brotherly farewell, he wished me all the best.

I went down, back to the quadrangular courtyard enclosed by the college buildings, and which was gradually beginning to resound with the arrival of students enrolled in the course.

146

We were all strangers; no one knew anyone else. Then suddenly spontaneous acquaintances were beginning to form, everyone asking everyone else: 'Where are you from?' The group was becoming acquainted and on familiar terms with each other. Friendly looks and smiles were the common language. Warm feelings in a cordial and expectant atmosphere stimulate feelings of comradeship in human communities, when the individual forgets blind partisanship and the hearts of all are open to each other.

It was time for each student's interview with the examining committee, to decide their appropriate level of study. I was put in the middle section. On the curriculum were: *Animal Farm* by George Orwell, *Room at the Top* by John Braine, and a collection of poems entitled *Metaphysical Poets*.

There were around 400 students from different parts of Europe, Asia and Africa, their ages ranging from eighteen to forty. Naturally the younger ones formed the large majority. The college housed around 200, allotting each one a private room. The college residential buildings were divided into two sections: one for men and one for women. The rest of those enrolled in the session were housed with English families, who gave them room and board.

A few minutes before supper time we started gathering in front of the closed door of the dining-hall, waiting for it to be thrown open. The moment arrived; the crowd poured into the hall which (as we were told) was the largest and most splendid of all the college halls. The walls were hung with oil paintings of great men who had received their university education at Christ Church: the poet, Sir Philip Sidney; William Penn, founder of the Pennsylvania colony in North America; the English politician, Sir Robert Peel; the English preacher, John Wesley, founder of Methodism; John Locke, the English philosopher; William Gladstone, British politician; John Ruskin, English author and critic; Charles Dodgson, writer and mathematical scholar known under his pseudonym, Lewis Carroll and famous for *Alice in Wonderland*, a story told during a river trip to the young daughter of Dodgson's friend, the college dean. We were told that Christ

Church boasts of having given England five prime ministers in one century, in addition to other great men who have graduated from it over its long history.

My seat at the long supper table was next to a German girl of almost the same age. Our conversation was about the excitement of this experience. On such occasions friendships spring up quickly, especially between people of the same age. I learned that she was an English language teacher in her own country. She had enrolled in this summer course in order to improve her knowledge of the language and to spend an enjoyable summer holiday. From that first supper, Ursula and I became companions.

After the substantial evening meal, we strolled around the quadrangle where some water lilies were floating in the large pond covered with water moss. At five minutes past nine we were startled by the sounding of a bell that went on for 101 strokes. Every eye asked the question: what did these strokes mean? What was their significance?

We learned the story:

From Tom Tower, designed by the famous architect Christopher Wren for Christ Church, Great Tom Bell sounds 101 strokes at five minutes past nine every evening to commemorate the 101 students who were in the college at the time of King Henry VIII. The king completed the construction, after the death of its founder, Cardinal Wolsey, in the sixteenth century. The college keeps Wolsey's hat and chair to this day.

I climbed the ancient, narrow staircase to the second floor, where the windows of my room overlooked the quadrangle that lay behind the college church, or rather, the cathedral of the city of Oxford. It is older than the college, dating back twelve centuries.

Looking around the room, I saw that everything in it showed that it belonged to one of the full-time students now spending the summer vacation with their families. I wondered how many students the walls of this silent room, redolent with the odour of time, had seen and known? How many of the feelings and sentiments of those students had it witnessed during their university lives over four centuries? Which of the hopes, ambitions and dreams had been realised and which had not . . . success, failure, happiness, frustration, tears, smiles, love, pain, along with the various sensations, feelings and conflicts of the human soul.

I am deeply sensitive to old places over which the march of time has passed. They bring me face to face with the power of time, our mortal destiny, and the transience of everything in life.

In the morning, I was awakened by two raps on the door and a hoarse voice shouting: 'Half-past seven, half-past seven', the sound of footsteps moving away from the door, and the same hoarse voice accompanied by the two raps on the adjacent doors, one after the other. This was the job of one of the servants: to awaken the students every morning at 7.30 a.m.

The crowd gathered in the dining-hall where the long tables were covered with jugs of coffee and tea, butter, marmalade and toast. After that, the famous English breakfast arrived: fried eggs and bacon. Having little taste for meat, especially red meat, together with a traditional aversion to eating pork, I left the rasher of bacon on the side of my plate. The coffee, toast, butter, marmalade and fried eggs made an excellent and satisfying breakfast.

The next morning, I was sipping my coffee, enjoying its aroma and the presence of my fellow students murmuring to each other: 'Please pass the sugar . . . Be so kind as to pass the salt', when all of a sudden my heart sank at the sound of my name being called out by the red-haired professor supervising the session. Standing up, I looked at him enquiringly. He said: 'Please be so good as to let me see you after breakfast.'

Good Lord, what now? A telegram? A catastrophe? Have mercy, Lord!

When I went to him he said: 'We noticed you did not eat the rasher of bacon yesterday morning. Perhaps you are a Muslim?'

'Yes, a Muslim.'

From that day on, the piece of red meat was missing from

my breakfast plate. The English are blessed with an amazing sense of thrift . . . all the English. It is something we Arabs are scarcely aware of. I noticed this during my stay in England: everything is assessed and accounted for, no matter how small its material value. The word 'waste' is to be found only in the dictionary, in practice it has no place in their lives. The Englishwoman will stand in a grocer's shop, asking for half a cucumber, one peach, one tomato, a quarter of a chicken. She will not buy more than she needs.

Before going to the classrooms, we were asked to assemble in the open courtyard where the headmistress of St Clare's College met us. She was an unmarried woman of middle age, her face bearing signs of a beauty that must have been dazzling once. Her eyes were shadowed with a gentle, hidden sadness.

She was sitting in a wheelchair pushed by a young woman in her thirties. The lower half of her body was covered by a woollen rug which reached down to her feet.

Two or three minutes passed before the silence was broken by the voice of this sensitive crippled lady, welcoming us first, then going on to explain the reasons that led to the setting up of these summer sessions for studying the English language. She talked about the horrors of the Second World War and the tragedies people suffered during that war; about the bomb that had severed her legs in one of the 1941 air raids. She then touched on the importance of nations getting to know and understand each other. It was this that gave her the idea of organising courses that would clearly reflect the spirit of integration that leads to true understanding, building bridges of friendship between people of diverse backgrounds, and helps to put out an end to the curse of war and the feelings of hatred it engenders.

The two courses were crowded with related activities: visits, trips and developing new friendships. As for the classes, the English literature class was the one I found most enjoyable and stimulating. Through it I gained a clear perception of the literary movement of the fifties and early sixties. A literature had appeared, almost solely the creation of the 'Angry Young Men' who had opened their eyes to the eruption of the socialist revolution upon the world, resentment against bourgeois values, and the injustices prevailing in the social system. The movement of the Angry Young Men was an unequivocal rejection of existing society, and was reflected in their rebellion against the prevailing values in literature, art, politics, and sex, and in their lack of concern for the values of empire and the dominance of the Church of England. I, who had grown up under the shadow of British colonialism, so hateful to my country, was amazed and delighted to learn that here there were writers and contemporary authors, poets and artists who did not believe in imperialism, abhorred racial prejudice and ridiculed the monarchic system – writers and artists such as Dylan Thomas, George Orwell and David Hockney, for example. These and others like them who hated monarchism and imperialism, had a predilection for socialism, like most of their contemporaries.

Before reading *Room at the Top*, the professor talked to us about the novel of the anti-hero, or to be more precise, about fiction in which the hero is not heroic, but a very ordinary person. He then went on to talk about the social change that had taken place after the Second World War and how this change was reflected in present-day English narrative and various other art forms. He stated that the focus of young novelists was on social issues such as the life of the working classes, class discrimination, the concern for social change, the emphasis on the value of the individual, and so on.

During this period, one of the Oxford theatres was running John Osborne's play, *Look Back in Anger*, a play that had won its author great fame throughout England and America. By giving fresh and vibrant life to the art of drama after a long stagnation, the play had put the author's name at the top of the roster of contemporary stage writers.

The professor counted the number of those wishing to see the play, and our reserved seats were ready for us at the appointed time. He had lectured to us during the day on the subject of the play to put us in the right mood to appreciate it

151

better. Our attention was glued to the stage from the moment the curtain was raised on the first act until it fell upon the last scene in the last act. The main character personified the revolt, anger and resentment against the values and mores prevailing in English society. Every act of the play throbbed with vitality and action.

From that time on, John Osborne became the focus of my attention. Some years later in London, I went to see his play *West of Suez*, a symbolic representation of a collapsing empire upon which the sun had set. In my poem, 'In the Aging City', there is an allusion to this play.

After these two courses ended, I enrolled in the Swan School on Banbury Road, one of the large main streets in Oxford. I had moved to number 10, Pinton Road, to live with a sedate lady in her seventies, named Mrs Veetham.

At our first meeting we agreed I should pay her £2.10s a week, on condition I be responsible for my own meals and heating. This was a good sum, in keeping with my modest income, as I had to get used to economising on my living expenses. I did not buy more clothes than I needed and discovered a small Chinese restaurant, friendly and very clean, where I could get a hot appetising meal for 4s 6d.

At our first meeting, Mrs Veetham asked me if I liked to help others. When I answered in the affirmative, she said: 'As you see, I'm an old woman, unable to get up in the mornng until I have a cup of hot tea with my breakfast. It would be an act of human kindness on your part if you would make me a cup of tea along with my breakfast and bring it to me in the morning.'

I was happy to comply with the request, realising that this cup of tea would consolidate my relationship with her. And that is precisely what happened. She taught me how to prepare the bacon and every morning I did this for her freely. More than that, I took it upon myself from time to time to buy the vegetables, fruit and meat she needed. She would also ask me to accompany her to church some Sunday mornings, when she felt weak. She would lean on my arm all the way to the nearby church. When, one day, I mentioned to her that the church was empty except for a small number of worshippers, most of whom were elderly, she replied shaking her head regretfully: 'This, my daughter, is the curse of our materialistic civilisation. Religion these days exists only in the church.'

She was amazingly sharp-witted. Her keen mind had not yet been affected by age, in spite of her advanced years. Listening to classical music was her abiding hobby. She considered religious music the highest form of music. She would sit beside the radio, with the sound turned so low it could not be heard beyond the door of the sitting-room, listening with reverent absorption to the orchestral music of Bach or Handel or similar composers. I shall never forget the day I accompanied her to Christ Church Cathedral to hear a famous choir she had read about in the Oxford daily paper. Truly, it is impossible to describe the beauty of that rendition or of the voices. I felt I was not listening to the chanting of human voices, but was soaring in the air with the music of the spheres, unconscious of everything around me.

The year I spent at the Swan School in Oxford was one of the happiest and most satisfying periods of my life. In addition to the educational benefits I acquired there, I was delighted with the friendships I made, some of which have lasted despite geographical distance. Friendship has a sweet, warm flavour which calms the heart. It is one of life's triumphs and probably surpasses love itself; for it lasts longer, even if love takes a stronger hold over the emotions and senses. However, people differ in their human relationships. There are gentle, modest friends, who do not impose upon one in any way and do not insist upon anything; and there are difficult, tiresome friends, whose friendship becomes a heavy burden. But of what use is friendship, and what pleasure can it have, if it does not flow between two hearts as freely as water? However, it is always tragic to discover that there are friends who are disloyal, and whose egoism reaches the point where they can hurt and harm us unawares. There may indeed be a psychological truth in the poet's line: 'Beware of your enemy once, but beware of your friend a thousand times.'

At any rate, if England has been a passion with me ever since that distant time, it is due to the people I got to know and love. If we love a country, we love it through the people we know and care for there. The friendship that developed with the Swan family is one of my most pleasant memories and the bonds of this friendship are still strong as I write these lines. Not very long ago, I received a letter from Mrs Swan, reminding me that I have a family in Oxford. Every time I visit England, I go without fail to see this dear family. I shall never forget the letter I received from her, after the Israeli occupation of the West Bank in 1967, a letter overflowing with expression of concern about me.

One of the nicest letters I received was in 1972, from a member of the teaching staff, Miss Marjorie Morgan, a warmhearted, compassionate woman with a humane and mystical quality. Miss Morgan believes in the presence of good and truth, and in the eventual universality of human fellowship and the possibility of the unity of people, despite the apparent discord and the lack of ties among them. She would sometimes invite me to tea in her house, where she made me feel so comfortably at home that I forgot I was a stranger.

In her letter she said:

You will probably wonder who this is writing to you out of the blue – but I remember so well walking through North Oxford with you one spring evening talking about life and its problems – And now Mrs Eleanor Aitken has just shown me some English translations of your recent poems, and a moment ago on the television screen some pictures of Nablus were shown. So you see you are very much in my thoughts – and I had to write and tell you so. One *has* to make a point of reminding oneself that there is still love and trust and understanding and appreciation of one another, however little this may seem to be true.

What can one say from the warmth and comfort of one's

home to you and your people who seem to be bearing the brunt of the world's agony? Words might seem impudent – but we know, don't we, that every loving thought, every act of mercy, every tolerant consideration of another human being is death to the lie of strife and division which is struggling to survive as if it were a fact.

Oneness is being born to the world, though it is hard to recognise it through the suffering of the birth pangs – but the birth goes on and the 'child' of world unity will be born through the faithfulness and trust and aspirations of people like you.

This brings me to the subject of the impression I gained of the character of the English, and their notoriously strong feelings about individuality and love of privacy. They are very reserved and private, do not talk about themselves, nor do they bring up, in conversation, personal matters that would make you feel close to them. This reserve is not shown only to foreigners, but other English people as well. The saying: 'The Englishman's home is his castle' is one of their favourite proverbs. The English do not allow anyone to enter their homes. The family is tied to the home and they do not like exchanging visits with neighbours. Their interests lie exclusively in their houses, dogs and gardens. You will see neighbours greeting each other across the garden fence, then making a couple of comments on the weather, nothing more. However, country people are somewhat more friendly and spontaneous.

On the other hand, the English are only reserved until they are sure of you. If you become truly acquainted and friendship grows, you become one of the family and the relationship is permanent. The apparent lack of affection and emotion in the English derives, in my opinion, from the fact that they are a race so disciplined that they are incapable of publicly expressing their feelings. That may be rooted in historical and social factors. They deliberately hide their emotions under a mask of pretended coldness.

## 32

The value of travel to me lies not only in my enjoyment of freedom and independence. Feelings of personal inadequacy are the real incentive that drives me to travel: the overwhelming urge for knowledge. One learns so much from travelling; one's horizons are widened; one observes different patterns of life from one country to another. Everywhere one discovers a new human aspect. People do not really differ in their essential nature; each of us is a collection of feelings, desires and inclinations alternating between triumph and defeat.

The English characteristic I liked best was the muted tone in conversation and the general silence in public places such as buses and queues. Doubtless the home is the greatest school, where ethics and civilised behaviour are first taught. Every family I became acquainted with or lived with spoke to their children calmly in a low voice, even when reprimanding or censuring them. In residential areas almost nothing was audible except the sweet songs of the birds. Blowing car horns is prohibited even on the main streets, crowded with pedestrians, unless extreme necessity warrants the use of it, and then only for a moment.

However, love is displayed on the street, in the gardens, in the cinema, everywhere. Kisses between the sexes are easily given and taken, and are rather cheap it seems, as if they were a biological phenomenon as familiar as drinking tea. I remarked to Mr French one day, after seeing a young man and woman in their twenties hugging and kissing on the pavement, heedless and unconcerned about passers-by, that love should have its sacredness and privacy. So why were those young people stripping it of its mystery and scerecy?

He replied: 'Let's leave them to live their life and enjoy it. War taught us a great deal; the conservative puritan countries have changed. It is better for us to make love than to make war.'

I found myself wondering which was the healthier conduct: deprivation and repression that result in personality hang-ups and deviations, or granting freedom so that sex is no longer a problem for the individual and society? It is a question that is difficult to answer, due to the differences between western and eastern thought. Every country has its traditions, concepts, principles and circumstances. 'East is East, and West is West, and never the twain shall meet', as the poet Kipling said.

The shrinking of the empire may have changed England. Today's generation ridicules the expression, 'Great Britain'. They no longer have the arrogance, nurtured by the public school system, which marked the pre-war generations. It was a system that neglected enhancing people's feelings, on the contrary, it purposely leaned towards predisposing people to ruthlessness and cruelty in order to prepare, for the far-flung colonial empire, administrators with hardened hearts and atrophied emotions. I was quite astonished when one of the young professors who was lecturing us on the poets of the First World War, known as the Soldier Poets, ridiculed the extreme patriotic sentiments expressed by the poet in a poem beginning: 'England, England, England'.

I spent Christmas and New Year 1963 with my dear old lady, Mrs Veetham, at the home of her niece, in the Oxford suburb of Ramsden, enjoying the hospitality and sharing in the traditional celebrations under the tinsel-decorated Christmas tree, ablaze with coloured lights. After dining on turkey and pudding, the young daughter of twelve and her brother of nine came over to chat with me, asking very strange questions: 'Do you have chairs in Arab countries? Do you sleep on beds? Do you drink water out of crystal glasses?'

My reply was: 'What do you think?'

I recalled the similar questions of the French children . . . The word 'Arab' portrays nothing to the western mind but images of tents, desert and camels. Opening my handbag, I drew out some photographs taken in our old house. I also had with me some pictures of Nablus taken from various points, showing some tall buildings, the public garden with its towering trees and its many different flowers. They were utterly astounded. The child asked me to draw something in

157

her drawing book, so I drew a house with front steps surrounded by a garden. When the mother saw the drawing, she asked me if we knew about stairs in our country . . . It is indeed strange that the image of the tent and desert sticks in the British mind in this fashion, as if they had not colonised our countries for several decades. The one thing they do know about us is polygamy, something I could not in any way justify.

The English, in general, with the exception of specialists, are uninterested in what goes on outside their own world. The ordinary reader limits his newspaper reading to what is happening in Britain. One of the professors at the Swan School conceded this, when faced with it by some of the European students in the class.

During my stay there, I was an avid reader of the English papers. The papers, along with television and radio, are the best means of keeping one's finger on the pulse of life on different levels: political, social, economic and cultural.

I used to believe that Englishwomen, who had fought for the right to vote and won, had achieved complete equality with men. But I found that the press was full of news of the war of the sexes: women were still seeking equality with men with regard to wages. A woman performs the same work as proficiently as a man, but she receives a smaller pay cheque, simply because she is a woman. The suggestions that a woman's place is in the home, and that a woman must not do anything that would embarrass her husband or hurt his manly pride, are still expressed. Likewise, there are those who believe that the woman is a second-class being revolving in her husband's orbit, or who think that time and money spent on educating a girl are wasted. Despite free education provided by the government, a number of fathers who want their sons to have a good education are obliged to make financial sacrifices. A great deal of money is spent on the boy, while the girl is ignored and expected to look for a husband. It is assumed that this will solve her problems in a world that still hands the other sex privileges as if bestowed by divine right.

I was taken aback to discover these facts. Alongside the conflict between the generations, represented by the wide gap separating the concepts of the sons from those of their fathers, there was the struggle of the angry women. The angry young generation was not limited to men. Women were determined to show what they stood for and what they were against: capital punishment, nuclear testing, racial prejudice, capitalism or communism. These alert women saw that having their say was their right, for they had a share in a country whose passports stated they were citizens. In the prevailing campaign for disarmament, there were a number of women members, working towards a popular movement that could lead to civil disobedience. Fear of nuclear war was rife.

During that term, the school administration arranged, for those students who wished, a visit to see *As You Like It* in the Royal Shakespeare Theatre in Stratford. It chanced that on that day there was a civil disobedience demonstration against nuclear weapons in Trafalgar Square in London, in which thousands of men and women, young and old, participated. There were clergymen, typists, construction workers, students, doctors and university professors. In spite of a bitterly cold spell, Trafalgar Square was packed with people. The demonstrators were surrounded by police, who in turn were surrounded by spectators.

However, in the evening, we made our way to Stratford, and greatly enjoyed watching Vanessa Redgrave play her part in Arden Forest so deftly and light-heartedly, dressed in tight tunic and pantaloons. Later, she became a true friend of the Palestinian cause after the June 1967 War.

The next morning the papers published pictures and news of the demonstration in London. Those of us who had watched Vanessa acting the previous evening were intrigued to read of her participation in civil disobedience, at the risk of exposing herself to arrest and imprisonment, or of catching a cold on the same night as she had an engagement with the

Royal Shakespeare Theatre Company. When the press questioned Vanessa about her participation and the risk she had taken, she replied: 'I knew I bore a responsibility towards the audience, but at the same time I was convinced there was a greater responsibility towards what we were attempting to do in this campaign.'

Both we and the other theatre-goers were fortunate, that day, that the authorities were content with arresting the demonstrators, including Vanessa, then releasing them after charging them.

The British press has a democratic tradition represented by a marvellous freedom of opinion. Not even members of the royal family escape criticism when necessity arises. More surprising is the freedom to express controversial views that touch upon the very essence of religion. This brings to mind a controversy that preoccupied the English throughout the land during my stay there. This was a debate provoked by an outspoken article by the Bishop of Woolwich, Dr Robinson, published in *The Observer*, which stated: 'The God who created this world, who provides it with life and sustains it, has become an encumbrant idol rather than a helper.' Sir Julian Huxley, joining the fray, followed up in a later number of *The Observer*: 'The Bishop's article is a powerful testimony to the intellectual revolution we are struggling for.' In his article, Huxley called for a new religion, one without a God, believing that a reorganisation of religious thought was a necessity and that the system centred upon God must be transformed into a humanistic one based on evolution. In addition he wrote: 'Along with Nietzsche's call for a re-appraisal of values, we shall need a new form of religious expression and new wording for basic religious concepts.'

These radical opinions and others even more so – which I will not discuss here – were published in the established press. What happened after that? The Bishop of Woolwich was neither prosecuted nor imprisoned. Huxley was not accused of blasphemy by the church, the state, or the people. *The Observer* was not shut down for printing these radical

**160**

opinions. Discussion of the subject continued calmly, impartially, and in a relaxed way.

As for the plight of the aged, it is often raised in the press: the lonely, isolated people who are no longer able to work; men and women whose children have grown up and left them. The deep longing for home expressed on the faces of these old people arouses deep sorrow and pity. They fill the reading rooms in the public libraries where many of them return day after day, seeking a warm place to sit. Some turn the pages aimlessly, others stare blankly for a few minutes at the page of a book in their hands, without reading a single line. Some sit looking into empty space, living and breathing on the periphery of life, seeing each other day after day, but with no rapport among them. They are completely cut off from the life to which they once belonged.

It was obvious to me that the homes for the elderly did not get to the root of the problem, as I had imagined. The severing of family ties in the developed countries leaves those in old people's homes completely cut off from the world. When people grow old, others have little time for them and no one bothers about them. The opposite is true in the developing countries, where affection and personal bonds bestow warmth upon those who have entered the winter of old age, thus alleviating their feelings of isolation and alienation.

The problem of old age is not simply one shelter, food and drink: social security and the welfare state are responsible for providing these necessities for the aged. What is tragic is their separation and isolation from the world, their crushing feelings of alienation and aloneness. I have carried a painful, pathetic picture of that in my memory, ever since I went with Mrs Veetham on a visit to a friend of hers who lived in an old people's home. A feeling of coldness and loneliness prevailed throughout the place. The smell of old age and death pervaded the gloomy atmosphere. Mrs Veetham stood at the half-open door of a room, through which I saw the slight body of a woman lying face down on the bedspread. When we entered the room, the woman raised her head and turned questioningly. No sooner did she see her friend than she jumped up and hugged her, then, burying her face in Mrs Veetham's breast, she burst out crying, murmuring as she sobbed: 'Alone, alone, this loneliness is killing me.' Afterwards I happened to read a newspaper report on old people's homes, which concluded that, for the aged, living with the family was much better than living in a home.

## 33

My days in England are unforgettable.

In England I knew pure joy, and in England death dealt me a lightning blow. The source of my joy was a marvellous experience, rich, sweet, dripping with honey. It was as if I had escaped from the limits of time and its confinements, to the place where heartbeats were the true measure of time. Love is the greatest mover. One hour in which the heart drinks from the fountain of bliss can contain a lifetime of joy, open-heartedness and vitality. It is difficult to explain this to those who, no matter what the situation, measure time by the hour, and are incapable of measuring it by their feelings, emotions and heartbeats. Without feeling and emotion, life is of no account. How beautiful its excitements are for us! Don't we want more than just the ability to live life always in neutral?

I knew that in the end separation and pain were inevitable. I often told myself: Tomorrow I'll pick up my suitcase and say: 'Farewell, you evergreen country! And you English summer! How enriching were your evenings, radiant with love! Your long twilit evenings; your nights clinging tenaciously to the curtain of sunset, not letting it fall before ten. I'll leave a part of my life in you. I'll long for you, and it will be painful. But I have been very fortunate. I've been happy and made someone else happy too. I have lived here to the fullness of my existence, even though for a limited time.'

Is our life more than these moments lived to the full?

It was a dazzling experience! Its memory will keep on warming my heart, until this heart burns out in the ashes of death.

A.G. was a brother to my soul, a garden in whose shade I

found peace and quiet. A genial, gentle-hearted person, who banished my persistent feelings of having been cast into a world too powerful for me.

However, a web of gentle sorrow continued to weave itself into my happiness in that earthly paradise. That's the way I am. I can never be perfectly happy. At the height of my joy, a thin thread of anguish creeps in, insinuating its way throughout my whole being – will I be in this paradise tomorrow? If time would only stand still; if I could seize and hang on to the fleeting moments that are dropping one by one into the ocean of time to be dissipated and gone, never to return.

I shall never forget that day in the summer of 1962.

We were walking together along the edge of the woods. The green world around us was clothed in silence . . . the air as clear as crystal . . . birds flitting from tree to tree . . . songs of invisible birds filling space with a taste of sadness . . . The bird song sharpened my senses . . . The melody crept into the depth of my heart full with the tranquil solitude . . . I was enclosed in a mysterious enchanted world.

A.'s voice took me by surprise: 'This bird,' he whispered softly, 'is rarely seen. It prefers hiding in the thick branches. We hear it but don't see it.'

'I'm amazed how many birds there are in England,' I replied. 'The many forests are full of them.'

'Have you heard of the bird artist, John Audubon?' he asked. 'He was passionately fond of birds and it was he who said that a bird and the forest were like a man and his wife.'

Now, as I am writing these lines, the autumn of 1965 comes to mind. In that year I moved from the ancient family residence in the old Nablus market to a small separate house that Jaafar, Ibrahim's son, designed for me, and where I have lived since. The area around the house at the time, situated as it was in an uninhabited area on the eastern edge of Mount Jirzim, was wasteland of rocks, earth and stones, far from the hustle and bustle of the city.

While sitting contemplating one day, the emptiness of the place struck me. The whole area was devoid of birds. There was neither the flutter of wings nor the chirping of song. I had grown up, through childhood and youth, to the noisy chattering of sparrows in the early morning and late evening, for the trees of our home provided them with shelter and protection all year round.

This reminded me of that day with A. along the edge of the woods, and what the bird artist, John Audubon, had said about the birds and forests.

I realised, then, why birds leave arid areas. Where there is a tree, there is a bird.

As soon as the Feast of the Tree came round, I began planting cypress and stone-pine trees around the house. The workman dug and I planted. Then I watched them growing day by day. I would tend them, water them and measure their growth every few weeks. Their quick growth delighted me. During their second year, small flocks of birds found their way to the young trees in the garden which is now a picture of luxuriant greenness, with many different kinds of coloured flowers.

This comment on the relationship between birds and trees later took on a national dimension in my poem, 'The Deluge and the Tree' which I wrote after June 1967. In it I gave special meanings to the words 'bird' and tree', which alluded indirectly to the hope and expectation of freedom and release from the Zionist stranglehold on my homeland.

> When the Tree rises up, the branches
> shall burgeon green and fresh in the sun
> the laughter of the Tree shall leaf
> beneath the sun
> and birds shall return
> Undoubtedly, the birds shall return.
>     The birds shall return.

One weekend I accompanied A. on a short trip to London. Ever since the visit the Swan School in Oxford had arranged for its students, London had become a passion with me. We were told that Greater London had swallowed up the surrounding suburbs and building construction had devoured the countryside. Despite that, London did not appear, to me, to consist merely of huge buildings and streets crowded with department stores. I saw parks, hundreds of acres large, spread in the city centre, and towering trees giving shade to the buildings and alleyways, not to mention the gardens around the houses, and small parks here and there.

We went to Hyde Park. Hand in hand, we made our way towards a bird sanctuary that had been set up in memory of William Hudson (1841–1922), the author of numerous books on nature and the life of birds, in addition to a number of publications for the Royal Society for the Protection of Birds. I remembered that, a few years earlier, my sister Adeeba and I had read *Green Mansions*, by William Hudson, with great interest.

In the aviary, my attention was drawn to a marble monument in the centre of which stood the naked body of a young woman surrounded by a few birds. A. told me she was Rima, the bird woman, one of the characters in *Green Mansions*. The monument reflected the sculptor Jacob Epstein's concept of that character.

In the Tate Gallery, A. stood for a long time in the section containing the works of his favourite contemporary painter, Graham Sutherland. A. was himself an amateur painter. Our first meeting, unplanned and quite unexpectedly, had taken place at an exhibition in Oxford where he was showing two of his canvases. It was to A.G. that I dedicated, that year, my poem, 'A Jordanian-Palestinian in England.'

I have a natural talent for drawing. Doodling faces, houses and trees on the rough copy of a poem is one of my habits when writing poetry. I have not tried to develop this ability to draw, with the exception of some attempts I made while a student in Saint Joseph School in Nablus, where I produced some oil paintings under the tutulage of Sister Zafreen. Poetry continued to be the beginning and the end, the first and last objective of my life. However, I can enjoy and become enthusiastic about the visual arts in their various forms and schools, as much as I can with music. Music, an abstract language that goes beyond the limits of words, can affect us emotionally, and we can then soar in its meaning, without a concrete grasp of what that meaning is.

Sutherland's pictures are unusual. Nature scenes are portrayed in a way that arouses feelings of desolation in the spectator. The painter named the most peculiar of these large canvases, *Origins of the Land*. Whenever I visit London, I always go to the Tate Gallery where I stand before this unusual picture, now hanging on a wall in the sculpture gallery, reliving afresh that profound and sweet savour of paradise.

The opening of the new Coventry Cathedral chanced to be at that time. This was the city destroyed by bombs in the Second World War at the end of 1940. I went with A. to see the new building that was, as I learned from him, one of the most important artistic achievements in England since the war.

With other visitors, we entered the new cathedral standing beside the church tower that alone had remained intact. There was a statue of Saint Michael fighting the devil, which A. told me was the last religious work of Sir Jacob Epstein. The baptistery window bathed the nave of the cathedral in an incandescent flood of colour. Since childhood, colours have bewitched me, affording me great inward joy. One day I told A. how, as a child, I used always to thank God for having created colours for us, because the world would be a dismal place stripped of all colour except for black and white. There would be no blue sky, green trees, coloured butterflies, nor rose mantles covering the horizon at sunrise and sunset, nor . . . nor . . ., etc. A. laughed in wonder, 'at the strange ideas of the child', he said.

The crowds of visitors stood awestruck before an enormous mockado carpet. A. told me it was a Sutherland creation, picturing Christ against a green background, His face overflowing with meekness and peace. It was in great contrast to Sutherland's desolate pictures we had seen in the Tate Gallery.

**166**

I described these and other similar sights in my letters to my sister, Adeeba, and, through these letters, I now see and live again those scenes as I re-record them in these memoirs.

How that wonderful friend enriched those days with joy and the acquisition of knowledge! Everything had a special meaning in my feelings.

But it was all accompanied by a persistent sense of the passage of time and of things slipping through my fingers, since the good gifts that come our way eventually escape, leaving us only with nostalgic memories.

## 34

Weep over a bird that was shot by a youth
Amusing himself. With his arrow he broke his shoulder.
Or who chanced upon a snare that had been erected,
Where he remained as if bound,
He has been out early, seeking his livelihood,
Then at sunrise he was cut and plucked
As though in life he had never alighted
    on a branch to sing or trill.

                    Abu al-'Alaa' al-Ma'arri

At home, a predestined, terrible misfortune was in the making: death was lying in wait for the moment I reached the pinnacle of happiness, to strike me with a bolt of lightning.

A few days before calamity struck, I saw my brother Nimr in a strange dream, his coat-tails flapping in a strong wind, leaving his house in Beirut and going towards a car, where my brother Ibrahim was sitting behind the steering wheel.

After Nimr had sat down beside his brother, the car took off without either uttering a word. In my dream, I screamed in burning anguish: 'Nimr has died.' That's what I sensed in my dream: Nimr's death. My subconscious mind may have retained the common folklore interpretation of dreams as prophecy of the death of living person, if one sees him in a dream going somewhere with a dead person. I woke up immediately, groaning, as if in deep grief.

**167**

Strangely enough, that dream was not at all confused, the way dreams usually are. Had it not been for the appearance of Ibrahim, who had been dead for more than twenty years, the dream would not have been out of the ordinary. The entire picture followed an organised pattern, as if it weren't subject to the inner force of the subconscious to which every dream surrenders.

I lay there in bed, moaning involuntarily at times, and dozing fitfully for short periods, my heart as heavy as lead with grief. I tried convincing myself that it was nothing more than a simple dream and that it was stupid to let myself be influenced by it in this absurd way. But it was no use. I remained frightened and apprehensive during the few days until the tragedy struck at five o'clock in the evening of Friday 15 March 1963. I returned to the house to find a telegram awaiting me. I took it from Mrs Veetham's hand with a beating heart. Mounting the wooden stairs, I entered my room speechless with terror. I sat looking at the telegram for a few minutes before daring to open it. Apprehension had paralysed my fingers.

Suddenly an encouraging thought came to me: why couldn't it contain good news of the coming of one of the family to England? I opened the telegram.

The world outside vanished. Nothing but stupor and numbness; all my senses came to a halt. For the first time in my life, I could not cry. My head was empty, my soul was empty, everything gave way to a mute emptiness. I and everything around me had sunk into a daze. Absolutely nothing was present, all was emptiness. The news was meaningless: it didn't tell me anything.

I descended the stairs like a sleepwalker. I had no sooner done so than I retraced my steps. I opened the window of my room and waves of ice-cold air slapped me in the face. Night had fallen like a black curtain of ice.

Near midnight I began to shudder violently . . . the vacuum was filling with deep sorrow. My right side gave way and pulled me over, so that I involuntarily bent towards the right. I began twisting around, but in no way was I able to sit

168

up straight. This was the same state I had fallen into at the news of Ibrahim's death. Thus I came to understand why poets associate their pain and grief with the heart: 'My heart was broken into pieces.'

Pulling myself together, I crawled over to the bed and threw myself upon it. Then the floodgates opened. I owe you thanks, warm springs of tears. Had you remained unshed, I should have killed myself with grief. Tears flowed without stopping. It was unbelievable. Where did all those tears come from? Three days on end crying continuously. Unbelievable!

In the morning, Mrs Veetham, after knocking on my door, came in wondering why I had not brought her tea: 'Are you all right?'

In her hand she held the *The Daily Telegraph*, on the front page of which was a picture of Emile al-Bustani,[68] with a headline announcing his death, and that of Dr Tuqan, in a fatal accident, when his private plane crashed into the sea in Beirut.

Gazing intently into my face, she saw the distressed state I was in: 'My dear child, what is the matter?'

Quickly making the connection between my condition and the telegram I had received the day before, she leaned over and hugged me compassionately. Then, glancing at the news published in the paper, she asked: 'Is Dr Tuqan . . . ?' I dropped my head on her breast before she finished the question, and she understood everything.

Nimr was a brother, and a very dear friend. He sensed what I had to endure in life; he was sympathetic towards me; and he took an interest in my concerns. He was passionately fond of poetry and music, despite having specialised in pathology and having devoted his working life to writing scientific reports on subjects related to his discipline and to preparing the lectures he gave to his students in the American University of Beirut.

He always urged me to take an interest in world literature. He was the teacher under whom I first began my study of the English language.

At this point, I must mention the literary relationship that existed for a few months between the poet Ali Mahmud Taha and myself.[69]

In 1940, during my stay in Jerusalem with my brother Ibrahim, I read in *al-Ahram* a new poem by Ali Mahmud Taha whose poem, 'The Gondola', set to music and sung, was at the time at the top of the Arabic hit parade. The new poem was an elegy for the captain of the ship *Courageous* which sank during the Second World War, taking its captain with it in sad and dramatic circumstances.

I loved the poem, and memorised it, then began to feel an irresistible desire to write to the author in order to express my great admiration for this touchingly humane poem.

I did not tell Ibrahim about the letter, simply to avoid the feelings of frustration and embarrassment should the poet fail to answer my letter.

Then I was surprised by the unexpected. The poet's reception of my letter was very warm, and he followed it by a copy of his *diwan*,[70] *Layali al-Mallah al-Ta'ih* (*Nights of the Lost Seaman*). My joy at the inscription written in the book knew no bounds.

Delighted by the whole affair, Ibrahim asked me to write a review of the *diwan* and broadcast it over Radio Palestine. I wrote the review with unbounded enthusiasm and sent a copy to the poet along with information about the time of the broadcast.

Some time after the broadcast I received a letter from him, telling me that a select group of Egyptian literary figures, the chief of whom was Professor Ahmad Hasan al-Zayyat, had listened to my talk. He added more words of commendation. His letter was accompanied by clippings from some Egyptian newspapers, *al-Ahram* and *al-Masri*, containing encouraging comments. I was very pleased, afterwards, when unexpectedly I came across the review printed in the May or June 1940 issue of the magazine *al-Risala*.

When I returned to Nablus, immediately after Ibrahim's departure for Baghdad, I was ordered by some members of the household to break off all connections through literary correspondence with the Egyptian poet, despite the fact that everything was above suspicion.

Some years later, my friend, the poet Kamal Nasir, told me about his meeting with Ali Mahmud Taha in Egypt. The Egyptian poet, showing surprise, had asked him why I had broken off communication with him for no apparent reason. I remained silent. At the time, talking about the reality of the wretched situation at home humiliated and shamed me so much that I bluffed my way through these matters, never revealing them to others. Ali Taha passed on to the other world without ever learning the painful truth.

As far as Nimr was concerned, this literary relationship had been a source of joy and pride. He loved Ali Mahmud Taha's poetry. When he returned to spend the summer vacation with us, *Layali al-Mallah* became his constant companion. One day he left it in the office of the family soap factory, when he went off on an errand. He returned to find that the flyleaf, with its inscription, had been cut out of the *diwan* and no trace of it was ever found.

Nimr apologised to me sadly: 'You can do nothing but be patient and bear up. Father doesn't want to stir up trouble with them. He can do nothing about it.'

Immediately after Nimr's death, I experienced a psychological block. I fell prey to a terrible feeling of isolation, not wanting to see anything or anyone. I no longer had any direction in life. I sent a few lines to my friend A. claiming that one of my relatives was arriving and indicating the impossibility of seeing him for some time. I did not want to tell him what had happened. My grief was too deep and too sacred to be divulged, even to the only friend I had there. Who could fathom my sorrow or the extent of my feelings of tragedy? No one. Everyone, in truth, remains alone: everyone is always alone in misery, sorrow and death.

Just as tree roots twist and penetrate deeply into the soil, this great sorrow penetrated my depths and wrapped itself in silence. Possessed by grief and death, I stumbled around the icy streets, while life followed its usual course. People poured from the top and the bottom of Saint Giles Square; the patrons of the coffee shops seemed as light-hearted as if they were in a dance hall. I marvelled at their ability to converse so happily, as if I had never possessed this ability.

One image stuck in my mind: a small plane trying to escape from death. Fifteen minutes spent in a hopeless attempt, while the elements of nature, out of control that morning, tossed the metal plane about as if it were a toy made of paper. No one was able to reach the hands stretched out for aid, to show mercy to the terrified suppliants, to rescue them from their inevitable fate. Was he conscious at the moment of falling into the sea? Was it difficult to face death all alone? How was his leg severed? Did he feel the pain of the severing? Why should he die this senseless death? Is death subject to chance? What sense is there in a person dying at the height of his mental powers, when he has the most to offer?

Nimr was the embodiment of the exuberance of a life driven along its course by what Bergson called vital force. He treasured life, flinging himself into it, not satisfied with surface values, but going to the heart of matters, experiencing them with all the intellectual profundity that marked his unique personality. Why? Why should he die before his time and why should he die in this tragic way?

Life seemed chaotic to me. The world seemed devoid of solace and without purpose.

Ever since Ibrahim's death, fear of Nimr's death had dominated my emotions, for he had been the only substitute for Ibrahim. There had been hidden feelings unconsciously and mercilessly at work within me. Why? Was it because, by nature, I am in a state of constant fear for the safety of those I love? Do I, by nature, perpetually dwell upon the tragedy of human existence, with exaggerated feelings of the problems of life and death?

Approximately two months before the blow fell, I had read, in the literary supplement of *The Times*, a review of a novel entitled *Under the Volcano*, by the English novelist, Malcolm Lowry. The review aroused my curiosity so I bought the book, the introduction to which consisted of a song from one of the choruses in Sophocles' tragedy, *Antigone*.

> Wonders are many, and none is more wonderful than man; the power that crosses the white sea, driven by the stormy south wind, making a path under surges that threaten to engulf him; and Earth the eldest of the gods, the mortal, the unwearied, doth he wear, turning the soil with the offspring of horses, as the ploughs go to and fro from year to year.
>
> And the light-hearted race of birds, and the tribes of savage beasts, and the sea-brood of the deep, he snares in the meshes of his woven tails, he leads captive, man excellent in wit. And he masters by his arts the beast whose lair is in the wilds, who roams the hills; he tames the horse of shaggy mane, he puts the yoke upon its neck, he tames the tireless mountain bull.
>
> And speech, and wind-swift thought, and all the moods that mould a state, hath he taught himself; and how to flee the arrows of the frost, when 'tis hard lodging under the clear sky; and the arrows of the rushing rain; yea, he hath resource for all; without resource he meets nothing that must come: only against Death shall he call for aid in vain; but from baffling maladies he hath devised escapes.

Despite my participation in various school activities, I lived my remaining months in England purely automatically. My intention had been to spend a few weeks in London, before returning home. For that, I had saved a few hundred dollars, a gift from my dear sister's son and my friend, Wa'il Tuqan, who at the time was a member of the Jordanian delegation to the United Nations in New York. However, the psychological inertia I was suffering and my apathetic attitude towards life in general left me cold and indifferent.

I returned to my native land only to leave it a few days later for Doha in Qatar, with my sister Hanan and her two children, to join her husband, Abd al-Rahman Abd al-Hadi, who was employed as assistant director in the Ottoman Bank.

During the nine months I spent there, I found great

consolation in taking care of the two children, Karma and Omar, of whom I was very fond. Nothing delivers us from our pervasive sorrows or takes us out of ourselves like children and their private enchanting world. It is a world of innocence, sincerity and freedom; a world not tinged with spurious affectation; a world in which life has not yet been divided by schisms. The look in a child's eye enthrals me, for whenever I look there I experience a mixture of delight and trepidation: trepidation for the innocence of which the adult world with its ugly confusion will rob it.

# Pages from a Diary
## 1966 –1967

**1**

I sense the absurdity and aimlessness of life as I stand bewildered, lost and weak before the tide of overpowering death.

How time changes us! This heart that lived for years at such a mad pace, whose emotional vitality refused a life of tranquillity, that raced time to collect the greatest number of experiences, where is its life blood gone? Where is its joy buried? Where is the great capacity to love it once possessed? Ah, the capacity to love! What great nobility and glory does this expression epitomise.

How time changes us!

I am no longer the person I once was; I am no longer the person I was a few years ago. It seems that nothing of my past life remains in me but glimpses of images that infrequently flash through my mind. Has my spirit grown old? I feel it has. I know that the laughter I give way to is now counterfeit. It isn't the real me. The searing pain of the open wound in my heart still throbs within me. I try to overcome my sorrow, but fierce, uncontrollable sorrow cannot be overcome. It is the grief of the tragedy of death.

I have come to a standstill. My days slip by imperceptibly. I am lost in the accumulation of years. Who will restore to me my sense of time? Oh God, grant me the power to declare some measure of rebellion against this state.

**176**

I have lost my ability to deal with emotion. My heart that celebrated life, that was a long love poem, that always rose to the excitement of the moment, has now laid down its armour and died. Not like a poet dying with a song on her lips, but silently, from grief at the tragedy of death.

**2**

Opening my eyes upon the feast day, I reached out to switch on the radio for the feast day prayer. Overcome by emotion, I cried. My tears were my prayer.

I do not know where these sentiments came from, for I am not religious. I don't observe any religious rites. My ties to religious matters and books are not very strong. I have my own views about religion. But on occasion I wonder: why don't we either believe completely or doubt completely and so feel at peace with ourselves in either case? Such thoughts keep haunting me, especially on religious occasions.

When some people meet with a private or public catastrophe, the foundations of their faith are sometimes shaken, causing the pillars of their beliefs to come crashing down. But what an appalling existence when the tide of faith suddenly ebbs from the soul; what a frightful life when we lose certainty.

Doubt and misgivings about the rationale of what happens to us; the realities of life, and events that call into question the existence of justice; this eternal longing in the soul for absolute surrender; all this gives rise to dramatic inner feelings and evokes an endless conflict between doubt on the one hand, and the yearning for assurance and for adherence to a lost faith on the other.

When the prayer for the feast day put me into that dilemma of the spirit, I recalled what Carl Jung said about religious feelings. He affirmed that these feelings would always remain in human beings throughout time: 'There are religious sentiments that will remain within people no matter how their religious concepts and views change.'

In the afternoon a friend visited me and I told him how the

feast-day prayer had affected me that same morning. This friend was a true believer, who practised the religious rites assiduously, and was well acquainted with my feeble religious sentiments. Commenting on my remarks, he said: 'It seems to me that the tears flowing from your eyes were nothing but mourning over the word whose light has grown dim in your heart. With the fading of this light, the psychological balance and inward harmony which religious people enjoy has been disturbed. In the light of religion, one can explain every problem, find a meaning for every enigma and an answer to every question.'

'And bear the sins of the universe and the chaos enveloping the world,' I replied. 'Those who inherit their faith along with their household furniture, and never try to depart from their traditional way of thinking, must be happy indeed.'

'My friend,' he said, 'don't allow your mind to wrestle with your heart. The Indian view, that man remains an incomplete being without spiritual knowledge, is truly marvellous.'

## 3

I met my friend, S., after a long absence. Both of us were full of the experiences we had gone through since we last met.

In the course of one of our conversations, she mentioned how tormented she was by the deep emotional and intellectual gap between her and her husband, a businessman. 'To begin with,' I said, 'you shouldn't have accepted such an incompatible husband. You were always aware of the lack of any intellectual or emotional harmony that could unite you in a genuine human relationship.'

'My marriage,' she replied, 'was a flight from the problem of spinsterhood which our society creates for the unmarried girl.'

Her statement astonished me. I told her: 'This problem does not usually arise for a young woman such as yourself who has proved herself and established her place in society as a successful writer and distinguished intellectual.'

In reply she said: 'But others in our country look at the single girl in this way. They look upon her as a failure, worthless, frustrated . . .'

'I don't agree with your ideas on this.' I responded. 'The spinster complex arises only for ordinary girls. What ordinary people say about being single does not apply to one with a strong personality who is socially and economically independent, freed from feelings of subordination, weakness and submission. In addition to that, there are many women who have psychological problems that marriage does not, nor ever will solve. If the problem was there in the beginning, it will continue to trouble the woman whether she is single or married. This is what psychologists say. Moreover, psychological problems are not confined to women. Men are afflicted with them too. If a man grows up in unnatural circumstances, or if his childhood is harsh, problems will continue to govern his conduct and attitudes all his life, and his case will be exactly the same as that of a woman.'

## 4

Yesterday I returned to Nablus after a month's visit to Cairo. When I return after a prolonged absence and open the door of my house, I am met by the peculiar smell of loneliness, of absence, the smell of abandoned, uninhabited places.

The woman whom I send for, periodically, to clean the house, left a few hours ago. I don't like having a servant in the house. Her presence disturbs me. Since I began living by myself I have found there is nothing to housework, although it is dreadfully boring. Whenever a new literary venture makes me mentally and emotionally restless, I live in utter chaos.

I love to travel. Sweden was the first European country I came to know, at the first opportunity granted me, when I received an invitation to attend a world peace conference held in Stockholm in the spring of 1956. The most valuable thing about world peace conferences is the open response of the participants to all that is humanitarian in general. On the same trip, after the conference had ended, we travelled from Moscow to Peking to attend a workers' festival. Everywhere, people show a face that is new, but at the same time basically the same. People are a mass of feelings, inclinations and ambitions, fluctuating between triumphs and defeats, despair and hope. Each is created from the same material, with the same innate nature, descended from one human family tree.

A return to Cairo. How strange the human heart is! Unexpectedly and without prearrangement, I suddenly found myself face to face with someone I had loved more than twenty years ago, and for twenty years we had not once met. I had been crazy abut him. He was my first real love, and had stood in the current of my life like a gigantic boulder obstructing its course, damming it up. The water had grown higher and higher with every new day, until it became a terrible whirlpool, whirling me about and cutting me off from the outside world. At night I would go out and lift my face to the heavens, imploring it to rescue me from this dreadful whirlpool.

We met. To my astonishment, I found myself greeting him with the same neutral feelings I would have greeted anyone to whom I had never had any emotional attachment.

He looked at me in shock. I withdrew my eyes to take a look inside myself. My heart said: 'This is life: every minute one is reborn, leaving behind a personality different from the present one.'

Isn't this what modern philosophy says?

I don't want to philosophise, I simply say that the river of my life goes on and, after that destructive experience, I'll never allow an obstacle to stand in its way.

How strange the heart is! In Cairo I stopped at one of those bookshops that displays their books on the pavement. I was looking over titles and authors in search of something new, when I chanced upon some of my own books.

I am always surprised at the neutral feelings I have towards my books when I see them displayed in a bookshop. When my latest work goes on the market, it becomes a part of my life that no longer concerns me, as if I had not written it with great ambition. My aspirations and concerns are now for what I have not yet written.

## 5

We stood together, she and I, in the shadow of the mountain; silence was our third. Nature was making up her poems all around us, blessing the Creator of beauty!

'This beauty is really affecting me, today,' she remarked in her rather sad voice. 'Have you ever been able to define exactly your feelings towards beauty? I can't. Confronted by it, I can only close my eyes to prevent grief from getting the better of me.'

'You remind me of the artist who lived out his life worshipping at the altar of beauty, to his own ruin,' I replied. 'You remind me of Oscar Wilde, who said, "Beauty makes me cry".'

We resumed our silence, for silence has its own aesthetic genius that bespeaks a thousand thoughts and emotions. But how can two women, who have not seen each other for a long time, patiently maintain this sweet silence for more than five minutes? It was she who broke the stillness: 'Beauty makes me feel a deep sadness mixed with old and new memories, which I try to drive down to the depths of my heart. I think they have slunk away, gone, died, when suddenly, faced with a beautiful sight, I discover them gathering their forces to rush up to the surface of my feelings once more, to torment me and delight me at one and the same time. In my depths, the drama of tears merges with the blessing of suffering, just as if I envy myself for being one of those granted a wealth of experiences. This is enriching to the pain in my soul, for after that I seem to love my pain and value its poetical quality – for I seem only to feel them when I am faced with great beauty.'

I told her I shared her sentiments. Happiness is the child of the moment; it consumes its moment and vanishes with it; but prolonged suffering, although it eventually stops smarting like a live coal, changes into a profound grief where our pain is lulled to sleep until reawakened by a memory or aroused by a beautiful sight.

Despite the warm spring sunshine, grief was casting its shadow over her eyes. On the roof-top of a nearby house, an enormously fat woman was standing, holding a head of lettuce under her arm, breaking off and chewing the leaves one after the other, while trying to catch the warmth of the sun's rays – a profoundly absurd sight!

Hiding a wry smile, I remarked: 'Look over there. Between your suffering and that woman's lettuce lies the remarkable irony that differentiates people.'

I am very relaxed in the company of this friend, with whom I can be perfectly at ease. What attracts me to her most is my confidence in her sincere loyalty. She is a friend who would never act in an underhand way. Anyone who has experienced disastrous friendships and endured treachery from friends, values a friendship that develops on the basis of trust, honesty and confidence. Reservation, apprehension and wariness do not breed true friendship.

## 6

Some of our thinkers believe we Arabs should call a halt to our interest in poetry, history and storytelling to devote all our energies to science and industry, that is to materialistic civilisation.

This idea astonishes me. I do not deny the value of science and industry, nor the fact that they are crucial to the subsistence of a nation in the modern age. However, I don't understand why it should be necessary for us to turn the individual Arab into a soulless tool; into a 'thing', in which we silence one part for the sake of another. Science and art are two separate tendencies, each representing a significant aspect of human enterprise. In general, art in all its branches is one of the vital manifestations of life and its true expression. It is futile to advocate repressing it for it is something that will never die until all life on earth is extinct.

It is wrong for us Arabs to call a halt to literature, ignoring,

182

or ignorant of the fact that future enterprises in any nation are directed and outlined first and foremost by its literature. The way to a conscious revolt and struggle for a free, decent life is paved by literature. Through literature and art, in general, pride is awakened, ambitions are enhanced, and a psychological boost given to the morale of the citizens of a nation.

Tawfiq al-Hakim's novel, *Audat al-Ruh* (*Return of the Soul*) had a very great influence upon Jamal Abd al-Nasser. As he said, it was one of the books that helped awaken his spirit and unleash his psychological strength in his early youth.

A nation whose literature has become dry and sterile cannot determine what is best for itself or for humanity, no matter how high it climbs on the ladder of scientific development.

On the other hand, which one of us, unless greatly lacking in responsiveness of heart and soul, can deny the beauty and aesthetic value art has so lavishly bestowed upon our lives?

## 7

We met, yesterday, quite unexpectedly. A man from a foreign country whom I was meeting for the first time. I rarely accept invitations to cocktail parties, for I don't find people at these gatherings pleasant or entertaining. So what made me accept this time?

He stayed with me most of the time. We talked a great deal about politics. These days my political sentiments are awakening from their slumber in an amazing foashion. My opinions differed radically from the foreigner's. But, by the end of the evening, my emotions were aroused, sending new warmth through me. The sweetest moments in life are those that transcend time and impose themselves on us, with all the life force in them.

I was swept away by an emotional awakening; I realised it was only temporary, but what does it matter? The wonderful emotional experience was enough for me. Wouldn't it put me in the frame of mind to live out a new poem?

**183**

I am unable to spoil the sweetness of the moment with any artifice. When I am full of excitement, I respond to the enchantment of the moment with all my soul and body.

I have never believed that one's emotinal life ends with the end of a particular love affair. Indeed I feel that I am fulfilling the message of Eve. This guarantees a refreshing change of spirit - in particular an inner harmony.

He got in touch with me today and we arranged to meet in Jerusalem.

## 8

I went back to the poem I had written a few days ago. Usually I leave a poem after composing it, and go back to it after it has taken on the perspective of time, when I make either a great many or very few changes in it.

## 9

These days, I feel within me an urge to write. I long for something to disrupt the monotony of my life, to revive it, to recharge it with sunlight. I feel an overwhelming wish to embrace life.

Spring, the breath of youth, sends a driving force through my whole being. I have just returned from a walk. The moon was full, the air laden with a unique fragrance from jasmine, damask roses and *al-naseem* flowers from the gardens of the surrounding houses.

During my walk I stood for a while, getting my fill of the earth, devouring it with my senses, gulping down large draughts of air until my thirst was quenched. Looking up at the mountains, I wished my end would come on the pinnacle of either Mount 'Aibal or Jirzim.

One yearns for death in a place where the body's dust will give life to wild flowers and thyme. How beautiful my country is! Where else would I want to die?

Dear refugees! How cruel for people to die as strangers in a strange land! Only in the land of our ancestors can we have a sense of growth in our humanity and of accord between ourselves and life around us.

While on my walk, the soft, tender voice of Fairuz was borne to me on the breeze, as if coming from an ethereal howdah: 'One day we shall return to our neighbourhood . . .'

Fairuz's voice, in songs that sprang from Palestinian sources, gives me the feeling that our life has stability, that no matter how circumstances scatter us, our ties to this precious stolen country will remain firmly secure. When I hear her songs about my country, my emotions rise and glow. I see my country as more beautiful than it actually is; I love it more than I ever have; I sense the tragedy of its loss as I have never felt it before; I love every face I see in its streets and ancient marketplaces, its shops, schools, factories and fields; I experience the sense of belonging to something even if it has been lost.

When I listen to Fairuz's voice in her Palestinian songs, the sun shines in my heart and I realise that night exists on the outside only.

## 10

I have received a letter from my friend, Nizar Qabbani, informing me that he has finally made up his mind to leave the diplomatic life to devote himself to the literary work that remains our singular and most beautiful destiny. He has decided, he said, to found a publishing house in Beirut to publish the works of those who have been worthy ambassadors of beauty and good will in the Arab world. He asked me to send him my latest collection of unpublished poetry.

I replied, thanking him for his wonderful influence in the literary world, while excusing myself because of the contract I already had with Dr Suhayl Idris, owner of Al-Adab publishing house.

## 11

I returned from Jerusalem after midnight, at half-past one, and woke up around four in the morning, energetic, having slept well. While drinking my coffee in the garden, I looked at everything around me with the eyes of a convalescent. Everything before me was astonishingly new. How could I have been living with this beauty every day without seeing it?

## 12

My friend, L., visited me today. Together we read a poem by Mahmud Darwish, published in *al-Adab*. Having difficulty understanding some of the symbols in his poetry, I remarked: 'We can't take Mahmud Darwish's poetic symbols in isolation from the personal problems in his real life and its experiences and conflict with his environment. But we know very little about Mahmud's life, his circumstances and his psychological make-up.'

'But,' replied my friend, 'a work of art is detached from the personality of its author and his environment.'

'How can we understand this detachment if we don't begin by understanding the poet's personality, circumstances and environment? After that we can comprehend to what extent the poet can become detached from them in his or her art. Perhaps you are influenced by T.S. Eliot's saying, that the artist does not use art as an expression of the self, but to wipe out this self. But later on Eliot renounced this view and corrected it, confessing it was wrong.'

An understanding of the raw experiences that happen to the artist is necessary so we can tell to what extent the poet has succeeded in transferring these experiences to, and exploiting them in, his or her artistic work. As far as Mahmud Darwish is concerned, his life and circumstances are closely linked with his poetry, and the human interest themes in his poetry arise from the depth of his personal experience.

## 13

A vicious attack was launched by the Israeli armed forces on the village of al-Samoua. Houses and the hospital were dynamited. Dozens of people were killed and many were wounded or disabled. The inhabitants of al-Samoua have all been refugees since 1948.

Violent demonstrations have taken place in all the cities of the West Bank, the demonstrators demanding arms and military training in order to fight.[71] A state of emergency is declared and the army intervenes in vain. There are casualties when the army engages with the demonstrators.

The Arab States, with the exception of Saudi Arabia, are filled with anger against King Hussein for his refusal to allow the men of the Palestine Liberation Organisation to operate from a Jordanian base and because his Prime Minister, Wasfi al-Tall, has closed all their offices.

## 14

The power of the Arab reactionaries increases day by day, thanks to the flood of wealth in the arid sands . . . Arab progressivism is still a child, lacking method and organisation.

A world in tumult . . . I search in it for a bright spot, but I hear nothing but the noise of radio broadcasts on every side. It is like a nightmare.

## 15

Oh, these Arab broadcasts! When is this screaming going to end? In this modern age the level of people's manners is measured by their self-restraint. In the modern age, people hide the pain and joy they feel. When they suffer, they suppress their pain, and when they laugh, they subdue the pitch of their laughter.

We still shout when we talk, cry or laugh.

**16**

My foreign friend invited me to dine at his house with some others. Towards the end of the evening we went to sit in an isolated corner of the drawing-room. Our conversation touched on the subject of al-Samoua and politics in general. 'I thought that you were indifferent and stoical about the present situation in the Arab countries', he said to me.

I explained that my reticence and lack of involvement in the political uproar did not mean that I had no sensitivity to it, or did not live under its curse, which hangs constantly over our heads. Like many others, I stood perplexed at the reality around us. With hearts burning from the pain and tragedy we had known, we continued searching, in vain, for a meaning to all that was happening around us. The reality we were living every moment of our lives was one of sheer pain and misery.

**17**

Today I chanced upon a book containing some of the works of the Spanish artist, Goya. Amongst them was a terrifying picture that caught my attention: a grave outlined by the artist in black, with a skeleton hand reaching out from under the cover to touch a black slab upon which its thumb was tracing the Spanish word *nada*, 'nothing'.

Annihilation is, indeed, part of our being, but art is immortal. A sense of the tyranny of annihilation and the ephemeral quality of life always prompts the artist to create something more permanent then the self.

Goya divided humanity into two groups: one deserving mercy and compassion, the other deserving hate and anger. He believed that one person's misery was always created by another.

It appears that war, oppression, moral bankruptcy and all those ugly things that inspired most of Goya's works, were what directed him towards an ethics in art. For him, art was more a means of getting his ideas and fantasies across, than an end in itself.

## 18

I spent the whole day with my foreign friend in Jerusalem. He drove the car through streets I had never seen before. We talked a great deal, and stayed silent much of the time. He asked me about my life and my childhood years. I told him about the misery of those early years, my break with that life, and those unforgettable days, steeped in joy and tears, spent in England. He held me tenderly and lovingly. I nestled to him like a bird without defence.

## 19

The general atmosphere in the Arab countries portends evil. I have no sense of stability nor any confidence in the future. There is already an element of let-down and loss of morale. These are inner sentiments.

The news is announcing Israeli mobilisation on the Syrian border and Abd al-Nasser is signing a joint defence treaty with Syria. The tension increases every day. Abd al-Nasser requests U Thant to remove the United Nations forces from the armistice line. Abd al-Nasser announces the closing of the Straits of Tirân.

Israel will not stand by with folded arms. There is a strange smell in the air.

## 20

Abd al-Nasser holds a news conference in which he says: 'If Israel wants war we say welcome, we are ready.'

Suddenly and unexpectedly King Hussein flies to Cairo. Everyone is in suspense.

## 21

King Hussein adds his signature to that of Egypt and Syria on the joint defence treaty. I am filled with inner despair and fear of a fresh defeat that might rob the Arab people again of their resolution. They lost their self-confidence at the time of the 1948 disaster.

## 22

I had a telephone call summoning me to an immediate, urgent meeting with my 'foreign friend'. I left for Jerusalem at once. He advised me to quit Nablus for Amman or Beirut, as war was inevitable and coming sooner than I imagined.

'I'll die on my doorstep,' I told him. 'rather than flee to another country. Unthinkable!'

'I'm afraid for you,' he replied. 'I respect your stand, but remember you do not own yourself. You belong to others and that is your lot. That's your destiny. You must remain for the others.'

'For me that means escape. And I will never run away!'

In his estimation the carnage was going to be terrible between Nablus resistance fighters and the Israeli army.

I thought to myself: what resistance will there be in a city whose inhabitants have been stripped of arms for nineteen years?

I returned to Nablus, my heart heavy with foreboding. I tried to persuade my sister to leave for Amman, but she refused, declaring: 'I'll live or die with you.'

## 23

The Arab lands have been humiliated . . . We were defeated . . . We lost the war . . . Our grief is insupportable . . . the wind plays with the white flags on our roofs. We have been occupied by the Israeli army . . . The shock has removed us from the realms of reality . . .

I am sick unto death with grief!

## 24

Seven days after the occupation of the city, my foreign friend surprised me with an unexpected visit. I was sick and feverish.

He came to reassure himself about me and ask if I was in need of anything . . . I thanked him with tears in my eyes. His grief was also profound and sincere.

## 25

One month of occupation has gone by. I am unable to write one line of poetry.

## 26

Another month has gone by and I have written nothing . . . Silence . . . continual silence . . . however, it is a conscious silence, aware and vigilant, not a silence of absence and emptiness.

## 27

The chain of silence has been broken; I have written five poems. I feel somewhat at ease.

I shall write, I shall write a lot. I feel I have been for some time living moment by moment in a drama, moved by every act in it. All of a sudden I, myself, am a poem, burning with anguish, dejected, hopeful, looking beyond the horizon!

# Notes

1. The night in which, according to Sura 97, the Quran was revealed. It is celebrated between 26 and 27 Ramadan.
2. Vermicelli prepared with butter and sweetened cheese, then, after baking, drenched with sugar syrup. In some Arab countries it is sometimes made with nuts, but the famous Nablus *kunafa* is prepared with cheese.
3. This is the Persian name for the feast of spring.
4. For another description of this in a Damascus public bath, see 'The women's public bath', by llfat Idilbi, in *Modern Arabic Fiction, An Anthology*, ed. Salma K. Jayyusi, Columbia University Press, forthcoming.
5. A length of cloth wound around the waist to cover the lower part of the body. Also called *meyzar* in some Arab countries.
6. Or loofah.
7. In Palestine, this is the name given to the men's drawing-room. Prominent families have an open *diwan* where men guests come without appointment. Coffee, soft drinks, sweets and often food are served.
8. The Muslim leader who fought and won against Richard the Lionheart in the Crusades.
9. Nablus has been named 'The Mountain of Fire' because of the courageous participation of its young men in the fight against colonialism.
10. See Ihsan al-Nimr, *History of Mount Nablus*, 2nd edn, 1975, Vol. 3. [author's note].

11. The famous university mosque in Cairo, centre of Sunni religious studies.
12. These can be held at any time, usually as a kind of thanksgiving party for some good that has happened to the person or the family, or in anticipation of such good. Religious songs and some Quranic recitals would take place, and sweets and soft drinks would be offered.
13. In Sufism, incessant repetition of certain words and formulas in praise of God, often accompanied by music and dancing.
14. The prayer niche.
15. The glorification exclaiming, 'Allahu Akbar (God is Great).
16. A long, often striped, garment worn by men, open in front and tied with a belt.
17. The exact day of Muslim feast is never pre-set, because it is dependent on the moon calendar and decided by the appearance of the crescent.
18. In a report on the history of school buldings in Nablus, the distinguished Arab educator, Ibrahim Sunaubar says: 'In the Ottoman era the preparatory school for boys, Khan al-Tujjar School, was built, as well as the ground floor of the Ghazzaliyyeh School (formerly the Rushdi) where the boys studied for five years after the preparatory school. However, the girls were in a rented building. Likewise, the building of the Western Rashadiyyeh School was undertaken – named after Sultan Muhammad Rashad – at present the Fatimiyyeh School; as well as the building of the Eastern Rashadiyyeh School, previously the Salahiyyeh. What caught my attention, when I was appointed inspector of education for the district of Samira in 1945, was that the number of government buildings for schools had remained the same, from 1918 to 1945, as it was at the time of Ottoman rule. All expansion in the educational field was being carried out in rented buildings that had been built as houses not schools. The faults of these buildings were that they had not sufficient room or playground space, air or light.

'In 1945 the district governor wanted to write a detailed report on each of the departments in the district of Samira. When he got to the Department of Education he came to a standstill in order to investigate the reality of the situation. After his questioning he was confronted by the following: "It is said that the Turks entered the country in 1517 on ox carts just as they left it in 1918 on ox carts. However, they left behind them in Nablus city four government school buildings, a municipal park, a town clock, and the National hospital. But you have not built one room during 17 years, or from 1918 to this year 1945. The worst part of it is, that you will depart from this country without leaving in it any educational edifice to remind the people of you." These words affected him so deeply he could scarcely believe the information. He said he would write a confidential report to the High Commissioner elucidating this issue. At the same time I was requested to urge the wealthy citizens to undertake the building of schools as is done in England. My answer was that the wealthy of the city did not have wealth of the sort you have in the west. They are wealthy only in contrast to the poor. Thus he was true to his promise and the government immediately allocated, for the first time in its history, a sum for the building of schools in the city, on the condition that the educational committees produce an equal amount for the same purpose.' [author's note]

19. Abu al-Faraj al-Asfahani (987–67), born in Isfahan, was a lineal descendant of Marwan, the last Umayyad Caliph. His *Kitab al-Aghani (Book of Songs)* is a veritable treasury of poetry and literature and an indispensable source for the study of Muslim civilisation. It has been called 'the register of the Arabs'.

    *Al-'Iqd al-Fareed (The Unique Necklace)* was written by Abd Rabbihi of Cordova, a descendant of an enfranchised slave of the Spanish Umayyad Caliph, Hisham b. Abd al-Rahman (788–96). It is a miscellaneous anthology, divided into twenty-five books each bearing the name of a different gem and 'contains something on every subject'.

*Kitab al-Hayawan* (*The Book of Animals*) was written by Abu 'Uthman 'Amr ibn Bahr al-Jahiz (goggle-eyed, C.780–869), a true man of letters who was a representative of the zoological and anthropological sciences. This work is more theological and folkloric than biological. In it the author quotes Aristotle and it contains germs of later theories of evolution, adaptation and animal psychology. Al-Jahiz was a radical theologian who gave his name to one of the Mu'tazilite sects, the Jahiziyya. They believed in intellectual freedom in the search for truth. They admitted the Quran was God's work, produced by a divine inspired prophet, but rejected its deification.

20. The *muwashshah* is a verse form invented in Andalusia (Muslim Spain) at the end of the tenth century A.D. It is dependent on music and shows great variations of metre and composition as compared with the two hemistich, monorhymed *qasida* (ode or poem) written throughout the centuries before. The *muwashshah* is made up of stanzas of identical pattern of metre and rhyme arrangement, the latter often very elaborate.

21. A paste made from sesame seed. Mixed with lemon juice and other ingredients, it makes delicious dips including the now well-known *hummos* and eggplant dip.

22. An Arab stringed instrument resembling the fiddle.

23. Rabab al-Kazimi wrote no known poetry after the death of her famous father in 1935, while Fadwa rose to be a major woman poet.

24. They both had the same wet-nurse.

25. Abu Firas al-Hamadani was a cousin of Sayf al-Dawlah (944–67), ruler of Aleppo who conquered northern Syria from the Ikhshidids and founded the Hamdanid dynasty that lasted until 1003. Abu Firas was a gallant soldier and poet of some mark, noted for his war songs.

26. See Note 19.

27. Al-Mubarrad was a philologist who belonged to the Basra school of grammarians.

28. Al-Qali was a philologist of Baghdad whose book, *al-*

*Amali,* is still studied in Arab lands.
29. See Note 19.
30. See Note 19.
31. Al-Aqqad, Taha Husayn, and Ahmad Amin are modern Egyptian writers of the first half of the twentieth century.
32. Mustafa Sadiq al-Rafi'i (188–1937). Born in Egypt of Lebanese extraction, a leader in the modern Arab literary movement, who founded the Rafi'iyya School, loyal to classical Arabic literature and resembling in style such master authors as al-Jahiz and Abu al-Faraj al-Asfahani.
33. May Ziyada (1886–1941). Born in Nazareth of Lebanese extraction, she later took up residence in Egypt with her parents. A feminist, she was one of the most outstanding literary figures of her day. She especially excelled in the literary essay.

   Along with her renowned scholarship (she was familiar with all the main European literary works in their own languages: French, English, German, Italian, Latin and modern Greek), she was a beautiful, attractive woman. She held a weekly salon, on Tuesdays, which was attended by many of the literary notables of the day.
34. Egyptian professor of Arabic literature, and author of *Modern Arabic Literature.*
35. Ahmad Shawqi (1868–1932) is one of the most out-standing poets and playwrights of modern times; born in Cairo, where he received his secondary education, he then studied law and literature in France. Upon his return to Cairo he gained access to the Khedive and became a member of his entourage. He also furthered his fortunes by marrying into a wealthy high-ranking family. He was exiled with Khedive Abbas during the First World War and returned to Egypt in 1919.
36. Is'af al-Nashashibi was one of the most renowned writers of modern Palestinian literature, history and the Arabic language, and argued vehemently for their preservation, reorganising schools and curricula in Palestine for this purpose. He was editor-in-chief of several Palestinian magazines to which he contributed, as well as to Egyptian

and Syrian papers. He was born in Jerusalem to an old, prominent, wealthy family.

37. Ibn al-Rumi (836–96), poet and philosopher, was born in Baghdad. He received a solid cultural education and his poetic talent showed at an early age. Being a violent Shi'ite and Mu'tazilite closed the door of the court to him, so he sought wealthy patrons outside. His *Diwan* (collected poems) contains 17,000 verses; not all the manuscripts have been published. The greater part of his work is neoclassicist, but alongside the formal poems are a great number of spontaneous, natural poems and hundreds of short poems in which he shows himself to be a society poet.

38. Al-Buhturi and Abu Tammam were distinguished court poets of the ninth century. Their reputation rests upon the anthologies they compiled under the title *Hamasa*.

39. Abu al-Tayyib Ahmad b. Husayn (915–65), known as al-Mutanabbi (the pretender to prophecy), is generally regarded as one of the greatest of Arabian poets, if not the first. The numerous commentaries and critical treatises on his *Diwan* show his popularity. Born at Kufa, he studied in Damascus and spent much time wandering amongst the Bedouin, where he gained his singular knowledge and mastery of Arabic. For nine years he was in favour with Sayf al-Dawlah (see Note 25), whose virtues he extolled in several eulogies.

40. Yahya al-Barmaki was Persian and Harun al-Rasheed's first vizier (minister).

41. These poets are some of the most prominent Romantic poets of the twenties and thirties. Naji (1898–1953) and Taha (1901–49) were Egyptian, Abu 'l-Qasim al-Shabbi (1909–34) was Tunisian, and al-Tijani Yusuf Bashir (1912–37) was Sudanese.

42. Isa al-Sifri, *Arab Palestine between the Mandate and Zionism*, 1937. [author's note]

43. A freelance Iraqi military expert, who became famous in the thirties for his courage and revolutionary zeal. He joined the Palestinian rebellion, becoming a military

leader in high command, and winning for himself great popularity in Palestine at the time.

44. See 'Izzat Darwaza, *About the Modern Arab Movement*, Sidon, 1950, 1951, Vol. 3, p. 201. [author's note]

45. These are the June War of 1967, and the 1970 September siege, in Amman and other Jordanian towns, of Palestinian fighters where many thousands of fighters and civilians were killed.

46. See Emile Touma, *Roots of the Palestinian Question*, 1970, p. 242. [author's note]

47. i.e. the female of Abu Tammam, as Umm means mother and Abu means father. See Note 38.

48. See Note 36.

49. A famous Palestinian writer and educator who wielded great moral and intellectual influence on the rising generations in Palestine between the 1920s and 1948.

50. Later on in the forties, the teachers' training college, which chose its students from amongst the top girl students in the whole of Palestine, was raised to full secondary level.

51. This explanation was merely a rehashing of the explanation contained in the White Paper published in 1922, in which the intentional meaning of the expression. 'The Jewish National Homeland', was elucidated. This explanation denied that the expression meant to impose the Jewish people on the Arabs or deprive the indigenous inhabitants of Palestine of their homes and livelihood. Britain declared that the objective of the Balfour promise was not to make Palestine Jewish. Therefore, although the government of 'His Majesty, the King' regarded these hopes as being impossible to realise, it never, at any time, thought of the subjugation or the extermination of the Arab inhabitants, or the destruction of their language and culture in Palestine. See Emile Touma, *Roots of the Palestine Question*, p. 119. [author's note]

52. See Fadwa Tuqan, *My brother Ibrahim*, Popular Culture Series. [author's note]

53. See Touma, *Roots of the Palestinian Question*, 1970, p. 253. [author's note]

54. The story of Sumaw'al is taught in schools all over the Arab world to illustrate the horror with which the Arabs, before and after Islam, regarded any breach of the solemn covenant between host and guest. 'More loyal than Sumaw'al' is a famous Arab proverb. Sumaw'al, a pre-Islamic poet (fourth century AD), of Arab descent and a Jew by religion, is said to have lived in his castle, al-Ablaq, at Taymaa" north of Medina in the region known now as the Hijaz. The story says that he had a well of sweet water and would entertain the Arabs who stopped beside it, supplying them with provisions. The poet Imru'u al-Qays, the prince of the powerful Kinda tribe in Central Arabia, took refuge with Sumaw'al while fleeing towards Syria from his enemies. Upon his departure, Imru'u al-Qays charged his host with the care of five coats of mail that were family heirlooms. Imru'u al-Qays was killed before reclaiming the coats of mail and the story ends with Sumaw'al sacrificing his son's life, rather than betraying his trust.

55. Maymun ibn Qays, a pre-Islamic professional troubadour, who wandered, harp in hand, singing the praises of those who rewarded him; such was his fame as a satirist that few ventured to withhold the bounty he asked for.

56. 'Abbas ib al-Ahnaf – one of the galaxy of talent Harun al-Rasheed (786–809), the caliph of *A Thousand and One Nights*, gathered under his patronage in Baghdad.

57. In one of my letters to my sister, Adeeba (8 April 1957) I wrote: 'Every Thursday afternoon a lecture is given at the club, after which a discussion is held between the lecturer and the audience. The club frequently invites speakers from outside Nablus. Last Friday evening our speaker was the Prime Minister, al-Sayyid Sulaiman al-Nabulsi. Of course, it was open to the public. A great number of people, of both sexes, crowded into the hall of the Ghazzaliya School that, due to its spaciousness, had been chosen for the occasion. Those standing outnumbered

those who had seats, not to mention the tremendous numbers standing in the street, listening to 'Abu Faris' through the loudspeaker. It was a natural celebration in which the Prime Minister spoke candidly and decisively about the government's stand with regard to America and the Soviet Union. You can imagine the fervour of the shouting and clapping when I relate the most significant thing he said that evening: ''America wants to put us in her back pocket. While we swear, that is the government, that if America told us to forgo our friendship with Russia in exchange for a million, million dollars we would tell her, No!'' Nablus is still talking with pride about Prime Minister Sulaiman's marvellous speech that evening and what a wonderful time it was.' [author's note]

58. See Dr Labeeb Kamhawi, *Palestinian–Arab Relations: A Study of the Political Attitudes and Activities of the Palestinians in the Arab Host-States, 1949–1967* Ph.D. dissertation, University of London. [author's note]

59. Director of the Department of Education of the Relief Agency in the West Bank. [author's note]

60. Ecclesiastes, verses 2–3 (King James Version).

61. Gilgamesh was a traditional hero of Babylon. His story was found in the library of Ashurbanipal, originally on twelve tablets.

62. Al-Ghazzali (AD 1058–1111). In dogmatic theology, there is none to compare with Abu Hamid al-Ghazzali surnamed, 'the Proof of Islam'. A philosopher who spent his life in a search for religious truth, described in his work *Munqidh min al-Dalal (Deliverer from Error)*, which had a momentous influence upon the future history of Muslim thought.

63. Al-Mu'tazila – the Mu'tazilites (Schismatics), a sect in Islam originating in Basra in AD 728. The Mu'tazilite heresy is connected to the doctrine of predestination. As opposed to the orthodox view of fatalism, they believed in free will and intellectual freedom, saying the Quran was God's work in the sense that it was produced by a divinely inspired Prophet, but flatly rejecting its deification.

**201**

64. I hope the reader will forgive me for quoting my cousin's letters from England. When I went back to his letters during the writing of these memoirs, I found myself experiencing the same intoxicating aspirations I had, at that time, concerning my visit to that country. I trust the reader will share this intoxication with me. [author's note]

65. Abu al-'Alaa' al Ma'arri (973–1057), called 'philosopher of poets and poet of philosophers', was born in Syria, in a town south of Aleppo. Blind as a result of smallpox, he developed a prodigious memory. His works express the sceptical and pessimistic sentiments of social decay and political anarchy in Islam. His work *al-Fusul wa al-Ghayat* is a frivolous parody of the sacred Quran. Although not an atheist, he declared that religions were made by people and that there was no divine revelation. His last years were spent in isolation, as a vegetarian.

66. Coastal plain along the south-western and southern shores of the Arabian peninsula.

67. Yabreen is a place near Aleppo, Syria.

68. A famous Lebanese businessman.

69. Ali Mahmud Taha was the most prominent of Egyptian Romantic poets who flourished in the thirties and forties. He died in 1949 at the height of his career.

70. A collection of poems either by a single author or by a number of poets, thus forming an anthology.

71. This refers to the West Bank prior to 1967, when it was in Jordanian hands.

# Afterword

Since completing this book in the late 1970s, Fadwa Tuqan has continued to live in Nablus under the Occupation. She still hopes to complete a further volume of autobiography, but in a sense the *Intifada* has taken over her life, as it has the lives of so many Palestinians.

'It is the villainy of a collective punishment meted out to us by the military which causes the greatest suffering,' she told an interviewer in 1989. 'The *intifada* is the action of our youth, our stone-throwing children of a generation that has broken through the barrier of fear and intimidation and stood proudly in the face of terrible cruelty, from the breaking of bones to actually burying some of the young rebels alive – unbelievable, you might say, but absolutely true!'

She has been able to write little poetry in these troubled years. 'I find that the poem is no longer capable of accommodating the riches of the *intifada* experience in all its aspects. Poetry alludes, but oblique reference does not seem to be enough at the moment. I dream of a bigger work, a work that can accommodate my vision of these great happenings more than the poem can, and I have become haunted with the idea of writing a novel that embraces all aspects of the *intifada*. However, a novel needs time to gestate, to grow before it can be translated into a satisfactory work of art. How I wish I could be confident that that gestation is happening inside me now, unconsciously but surely! And how I wish my life could stretch far enough and my health hold out so that I can realise this dream! But I can't count on much time for work ahead for me.

'However, I have written one poem which totally fits the *intifada*; 'Song of Becoming', printed at the beginning of this translation of my book. I wrote it after the June War in 1967, and you can see how prophetic it is! It describes the *intifada* before it started, which proves how absolutely inevitable it was; it is the essential response to the fact of occupation.'

Fadwa Tuqan thinks a great deal about the situation of young Palestinians now. And when she compares the life of the educated Palestinian woman today with her own early life, she finds joy in the fact that 'the door has been flung open for the young woman to realise her intellectual potential and gain her own economic independence. Contemporary woman has come a long way. She is aware of the importance of education, of joining the workforce, of sharing in building a future society. She sees it as her duty to take part in political and social life. Palestinian men now show considerable respect and admiration for the women, and the women struggle ferociously side by side with the men for the right of the Palestinian people to self-determination.'

But she is not anxious to offer homilies to the young. 'I am not one to stand and give advice to others. I hate the role of the preacher, and cannot volunteer any wise sayings.[1] What I can offer our young women is my life story to contemplate. With all the unhappy experiences I passed through, I have been able to realise my greatest dreams and some of my deepest aspirations. This was possible through sheer perseverance, self-confidence and quiet rejection of the efforts of others, mostly men, to diminish my capabilities and curtail my efforts towards self-realisation. the battle I fought was more heart-rending and severe than a woman needs to face now. However, at the present time, the Palestinian woman faces a double struggle: the struggle to assert her liberation as a woman and the struggle to assert her and everybody else's national liberation. What I am sure about, however, is that once the inevitable national liberation is achieved, our

204

feminist liberation will also prevail and there will be no relapse of the kind that can happen after national revolutions. I know our people and I know that their aspiration to freedom is comprehensive and sincere. And I know our women too, their seriousness, their endurance, their pride in themselves, and their abiding confidence. Let there be no turning from the path of dignity and freedom in all spheres. Human freedom is indivisible. . . Evil forces, either metaphysical, political or social, stand against us, keen to smash us, yet we refuse to surrender, we stand before them face to face, obstinate, determined and proud in spite of our weakness.'

Salma Khadra Jayyusi

## Note

[1] An interesting comment which shows the great difference between the modern Arab poet and his/her classical counterpart. Wise sayings fill the annals of our literature, and the verses which contain wisdom are memorised by millions of Arabs all over the Arab world. However, Fadwa Tuqan is exceptional in her non-didactic attitude. Many modern Arab poets, while avoiding the direct 'wise saying' of classical times, still look at themselves as redeemers, teachers and leaders of other men and women. This attitude has militated against their achieving a truly modernist stance in contemporary poetry. Some younger poets now, however, are completely free of these attitudes and reject all claims to be the redeemers and teachers of the world. Tuqan is a much earlier fore-runner of these.

# Poems

## A Life

My life is tears
and a fond heart
longing, a book of poetry and a lute

My life, my totally sorrowful life,
if its silhouette should vanish tomorrow,
an echo would remain on earth,
my voice repeating:
My life is tears
and a fond heart
longing, a book of poetry and a lute.

On the sad nights
when silence endlessly deepens,
the phantoms of my loved ones pass
before me like wisps of dreams,
poking the fire alive beneath the ashes
and drenching my pillow with tears,
tears of longing
for ones who have died
and lie, folded in the darkness of the grave.

My orphan heart cries,
'Oh Father, look down on us,
from your immortal horizon
Your death has humiliated us!
We have lived trapped between viper and snake,
    exhaled poisons
    and defiant enemies
snagged on this world of ingratitude and denial.'

At night a phantom appears
My father cleaves the curtain of the unknown,
his eyes shadowed by sorrow,
when my tears pour out,
he leans on me, we weep together
    I beg him, 'Come back
    in your lingering absence –
    who'll shelter us?'

On sleepless nights,
    I dream of my brother,
    that fountain of love,
the fuse for my eyes and heart
till the swirl of death
extinguished his torch
    Alone
    without his guiding light
I continue, bewildered.

And here's my youth
    with all its failed dreams . . .
drenched by sorrow
whenever life embraces it with
thousands of braces and chains.
    Pull it back,
    that tortured alien youth
    that prisoner,
    stunted by captivity.

Now I bow my head, desolate.
A lost horizon thunders inside.
Poems alone are my refuge.
In them I describe
my longings
only then can this soul
    find calm.

    Plucking my lute
in time with my lonesome heart
    the throbbing chords
    dissolve my grief.
    With melody and poetry,
I struggle with the grief of a martyred life.

    And here's my song,
    song of my life
leaving echoes behind me:
    My life is tears
    and a fond heart,
longing, a book of poetry, and a lute.

## From the early poetry

She looked with trepidation
at all the pits behind her.
Could she see in them any rays of sunshine?
Perhaps the terrible present
might find consolation in the past,
from the cruelty of the present
yet she saw nothing but hope's wreckage
cast up on the rocks,
and a few torn remnants of dreamy love
tangled with sarcasm.

She looked ahead
to a future wrapped in clouds.
What did she see?
untrammelled desert, bewildering paths
with landmarks confused and scattered
no signs of the road,
and herself wandering tremulously
companioned by loneliness,
and harsh unquenchable thirst,
in a heart swirling after mirage.

## To the Imprisoned Singer
To Kamal Nasir

Your singing soars to us
despite the narrowness of the sky.
Imprisoned bird! Sing forth
from behind the walls of suffering and night.

The iron bars that shape
the sky before your face
will not keep your singing from our ears.
Sing, bird, sing, the road of hope
still stretches, brilliantly lit,
despite the darkness around us!

Your singing, bird, returned me
to the past
when your feet and wings were free,
when the jasmine bower
embraced us, and you sang
the poetry of hope and pride and strength.
Even the stars leaned low
to hear your song. And we
felt as green and fresh
as our pastures
as our mountain slopes
filled with roaring wind
and pride of our mountains' peaks.

Sing, bird, sing!
Despite the chains and darkness
The horizon still offers its rich line of hope
awaiting the sun from behind the smoke.
Glory to sunlight, never despair
and freedom will find victory,
tomorrow, in the homeland of our dreams.
Never say our dreams are lost!

Sing, bird sing, the road of hope
stretches its light forward
though now we are surrounded by night.

## The Rock

See here
   The black rock is tied to my chest
   with oppressive chains
See how they grind my flowers and fruits
My life has been removed, crushed
So leave me
   you won't be able to release me
I'll remain alone
folded inside myself
as long as Fate is my warden
leave me without
   light, future, hope
with the black rock.

I struggle in vain to budge its weight
by forgetting myself
I swim joyously in the sea of life
paddling in all directions
I sing, filling my cup, gulping wildly
almost till I expire
How I deceive my pain and misery
with a life of joy
running away from my sorrows
and dancing with birds
But soon, from the depths of despair
a trembling voice thunders:
'You'll never run away!
I'm here, and you'll never escape!'
The shadow of the black rock
rises, with its ugly face.
In vain I try to push it away
In vain seek escape
There's no way out!

How often I've roamed the land of misery
searching for consolation
for prisoners like me
I entered the hum and press of crowds
where tragedies and tears abound
where whips dance
over the naked backs of humans like me
slaves forever pawned to darkness
I even tried to squeeze consolation
from misery
But there's no escape
The black rock,
a curse born with me
whose shadow will follow mine
see how it has taken root
over my chest?
So leave, you have no power to free me
Forever my spirit will remain locked inside
I'll remain struggling, alone
with this great pain of time and fate
alone,
while this black rock
grinds, grinds, grinds,
and there's no escape!

## I Found It

I found it on a radiant day
after a long drifting.
It was green and blossoming
as the sun over palm trees
scattered golden bouquets;
April was generous that season
with loving and sun.

I found it
after a long wandering.
It was a tender evergreen bough
where birds took shelter,
a bough bending gently under storms
which later was straight again,
rich with sap,
never snapping in the wind's hand.
It stayed supple
as if there were no bad weather,
echoing the brightness of stars,
the gentle breeze,
the dew and the clouds.

I found it
on a vivid summer day
after a long straying,
a tedious search.
It was a quiet lake
where thirsty human wolves
and swirling winds could only briefly
disturb the waters.
then they would clear again like crystal
to be the moon's mirror,
swimming place of light and blue,
bathing pool for the guardian stars.

I found it!
And now when the storms wail
and the face of the sun is masked in clouds,
when my shining fate revolves to dark,
my light will never be extinguished!
Everything that shadowed my life
wrapping it with night after night
has disappeared, laid down
in memory's grave,
since the day
my soul found
my soul.

## A Jordanian-Palestinian in England

To A. Gascoigne

### I

– Our weather is terrible,
the skies are always cloudy.
Where are you from? Are you Spanish?
– No, I'm from . . . from Jordan
– Pardon me, from Jordan? I don't understand!
– I'm from the hills of Jerusalem,
the land of light and sun
– Oh, Oh, you're Jewish!

What a savage stab to my heart!

### II

You ask about a cloud
that's crossed my brow, shrouding
my eyes with gloom . . .
It's you, loving neighbour
who opened the wounds
reminding me I'm
 from the torn land
 the people who've been
 pulled up by their roots, from the roots
 and scattered here and there
 along the pathways of the winds
 with no homeland to claim them
Everything contradicts
that we, like other people,
have a homeland.

But how would *you* know?
In your country fog and smoke
wrap up the view
blotting out light
here the eyes see only
what they are made to see.

## Before the Closed Door
To Salma Khadra Jayyusi

*The King's Will*
The axe hovers at the neck – this is the King's decree.
Do not blaspheme!
It is He who decreed nothing would befall us
except by His order.
The King's wisdom contrives every act.
Do not blaspheme!
All good springs from Him alone,
as well all evil!
This is the royal will,
so hold tight to patience and faith
    and be thankful!
There is no one else, no one else,
to whom you should bow
for all the hideous things in life.

*You Have Altered*
King of men, King of the universe!
Please explain what you do!
My beloved only King,
I frequented no threshold but Yours,
You dwelled in my heart.
I saluted Your countenance each evening,
Your eternal absence, with devotion.
Now I chide You, as if You hear the chiding
    of one whose heart is crushed.
Always You divide Yourself from me,
    rejecting my outstretched hand,
my weakness, my helplessness . . .
Why do You raise the walls so high before me
building layers on layers of darkness
while still remaining far, proud,
    surrounded by silence?

Does my faltering voice frighten You?
Does my calling out make You ashamed
as I lift up my wounded pleadings?
Does my voice startle You after such strong resistance
    to Your continued blows?
Your whips lashing my wound after wound after wound?
Remote You remain, erecting layers of darkness
    on top of themselves.

With love, I beg You to restore my love for You,
to return my child's heart,
and ignite my extinguished lamp.
    You are the One who struck it out
    with bolts of lightning and thunder.
Lift it up! Incline Your countenance toward me
so morning finds You flooding my breast
    with wonder and joy . . .
but You have changed! You have changed!
the columns of the temple are shaken,
the bell towers have collapsed.

*The King Is Dead*
Down it came, the royal throne,
and the King perished in its rubble.
Down with the King! Down with the King!

*After Renunciation*
No shelter, no provisions,
not even a shred of wool to keep me from shivering!
Alone in night's desert, my heart trembling always
with fear as I huddle, always, beneath a half-wrecked
    bridge . . .
The earth beneath my feet shakes and sways,
revolving without axis.
Who can deliver me from this quaking?

*The Return*
Naked of heart, I've returned to You,
proud God of remote abode somewhere near
    the circle of light!
The absence of Your presence encloses me
    in darkness, in the net of the night.

If only You could hear, within Your eternal silence,
my small naked feet stumbling back to You
through overwhelming dark and sorrow . . .
If only You could cleanse my nakedness with rains
and clothe me and make a shelter
    from the light of Your presence
to cover and protect me.

*The Last Knock at the Door*
Won't You open? My fist weakens
as I beat again and again.
I come to beg You for morsels
    of calm or security,
but the door remains closed in my face,
    shrouded by silence.
Lord of the house,
    once this door was open,
    once Your house was a refuge
    for wounded ones and olive trees grew
    high green branches encircling the house.
    Once the oil ignited without struggle
    to guide travellers through the night,
    to give solace to those crushed by the weight
    of this world, or the few who arrived,
        content and calm . . .
Do You hear me, Lord of the house?
After long straying in the wilderness away from You,
    I return,
but the door of Your house is shut in my face
and covered with dust.
If You are in there, open up, do not

veil Your face from me!
Can't You see my solitude and bewilderment
among the ruins of my crumbled world?
On my shoulders I bear
    the grief of living
beneath a tyrannical fate.

*Nothing Here*
In vain – no echo comes, no sound.
Go back, Fadwa, there's nothing here but desolate
    silence,
the shadow of death.

## In the Flux

That evening
faces faded around us
The room was drowned in fog
Nothing lived
but the shining blue of your eyes
and the call in that
shining blue
where my heart
sailed, a ship
driven by the tide
   The tide carried
   us on to a sea
   without shores
   stretching
   limitless current
   and flow
   waves telling the endless
   story of life
   now abridged in one glance
   and the earth drowned in the rushing
   flood of winds and rain

That evening
my garden awoke
The fingers of the wind
unhinged its fences
Grasses swayed, flowers bursting,
fruits ripening
in the blissful dance of wind and rain
Faces faded, all else was a fog
that evening
nothing existed
but the blue shining light in your eyes
and the call in the shining blue
where my heart sailed
like a ship driven by the tide.

221

## A Moment

Love, let's be quiet, don't say
'there was, there will be . . .'
And let's forget yesterday and not
    invade tomorrow!
It's this moment that counts
    only now, nothing before or after,
There's no more value in assigned time
yesterday's just a vanishing shade
while tomorrow's mystery
    stretches far beyond our reach
maybe your dreams and mine
    are different.
But this moment's
unique, radiantly open in our hands
plucked and fruitless
A flower of temporary magnificence
    so let's treasure it before it wilts.

During the first weeks after the June 1967 War, foreign papers and radio stations slanted news in a way that gloated over the misfortune, as if the end of the Arab people had been decided by this relapse. From this situation the following poem was born.

## The Deluge and the Tree

When the hurricane swirled and spread its deluge
of dark evil
on to the good green land
'They' gloated. The western skies
reverberated with joyous accounts:
'The Tree has fallen!
The great trunk is smashed! The hurricane
leaves no life in the Tree!'

Had the Tree really fallen?
Never! Not with our red streams flowing forever,
not while the wine of our torn limbs
fed the thirsty roots,
Arab roots alive
tunnelling deep, deep, into the land!

When the Tree rises up, the branches
shall burgeon green and fresh in the sun
the laughter of the Tree shall leaf
beneath the sun
and birds shall return
Undoubtedly, the birds shall return.
    The birds shall return.

*Fadwa Tuqan with the two Palestinian poets*
*Mahmoud Darwish and Samech al-Qasim*

## I Shall Not Weep
(For the Poets of the Resistance, on our meeting in Haifa)

My loved ones, at the gate of Jaffa,
in the chaos of rubble and thorns,
I stood and spoke to my own eyes:
    Let us cry for those who've abandoned
    their demolished homes.
The houses call for their owners,
announcing their deaths.

The heart said:
    What have the troubles done to you, homes,
    and where are your inhabitants –
    have you received any news of them?
    Here where they used to be, and dream,
    and draw their plans for the morrow –
    Where's the dream and the future now?
    And where have they gone?
The rubble stayed silent.
Nothing spoke but the absence.
    *I shall not weep*
And the silence of silences . . .
    strange flocks of phantom owls
    hovered over the place,
    becoming the new masters.
Oh, how the heart was wrung with grief!

Dear ones!
I wiped the grey cloud of tears off my eyelids
to meet you, eyes shining with love and faith
    in you, in the land, in man
What shame it would be to meet you
    with trembling eyelids,
a dampened heart full of despair.
Now I am here to borrow fire from you,
to borrow from your lit lamps lighting
    the blackness –

a drop of oil for my own.
I stretch my hand to yours
    and raise my brow to the sun beside you.
If you are strong as mountain stones
and fresh as the sweet flowers of our land,
how can a wound destroy me?
And how could I ever cry in front of you?
I make my pledge:
    From this day forward I shall not cry!

Dear ones, our nation's steed has transcended
    yesterday's fall!
Beyond the river, hear the confident neigh
    of the risen stallion,
listen! Shaking off the siege of darkness,
galloping towards his anchor on the sun!
Processions of horsemen gather
    to bless him,
to bid him drink from their crimson blood,
to feed him from their limbs and sinews.
They address the free stallion:
Run towards the eye of the sun!
Run, oh stallion of our people,
visible symbol and banner,
we are the army behind you,
the tide of our anger will not recede.
We shall not rest till
    the shadows are dispelled.

Lamps of the dark night,
    brothers in the wound,
sweet secret of yeast
    and scattered seeds of wheat
that die in your giving . . .
on your road I shall walk.
In the light of your eyes
I collect yesterday's tears
    and wipe them away.

226

Like you, I plant my feet on the land,
   my country,
and fix my eyes, like yours,
   on the road of light and sun.

## Face Lost in the Wilderness

Do not fill postcards with memories.
Between my heart and the luxury of passion
stretches a desert where ropes of fire
blaze and smoulder, where snakes
coil and recoil, swallowing blossoms
with poison and flame.

No! Don't ask me to remember. Love's memory
is dark, the dream clouded;
love is a lost phantom
in a wilderness night.
Friend, the night has slain the moon.
In the mirror of my heart you can find no shelter,
only my country's disfigured face
her face, lovely and mutilated,
her precious face . . .

How did the world revolve in this way?
Our love was young. Did it grow in this horror?
In the night of defeat, black waters
covered my land, blood on the walls
was the only bouquet.
I hallucinated: 'Open your breast,
open your mother's breast for an embrace
priceless are the offerings!'
The jungle beast was toasting in the
tavern of crime; winds of misfortune
howled in the four corners.
He was with me that day.
I didn't realise morning
would remove him.
Our smiles cheated sorrow
as I raved: 'Beloved stranger!
Why did my country become a gateway
to hell? Since when are apples bitter?
When did moonlight stop bathing orchards?

My people used to plant fields and love life
Joyfully they dipped their bread in oil
Fruits and flowers tinted the land
with magnificent hues –
will the seasons ever again
give their gifts to my people?'

Sorrow – Jerusalem's night is silence and smoke.
They imposed a curfew; now nothing beats in the
heart of the City but their bloodied heels
under which Jerusalem trembles
like a raped girl.

Two shadows from a balcony
stared down at the City's night.
In the corner a suitcase of clothes,
souvenirs from the Holy Land –
his blue eyes stretched like sad lakes.
He loved Jerusalem. She was his mystical lover.
On and on I ranted. 'Ah, love! Why did God abandon
my country? Imprisoning light, leaving us
in seas of darkness?'
The world was a mythical dragon standing
at her gate. 'Who will ever solve this mystery,
beloved, the secret of these words?'

Now twenty moons have passed,
twenty moons, and my life continues.
Your absence too continues. Only one memory remaining:
The face of my stricken country filling my heart.

And my life continues –
the wind merges me with my people
on the terrible road of rocks and thorns.
But behind the river, dark forests of spears
sway and swell; the roaring storm
unravels mystery, giving to dragon-silence
the power of words.

A rush and din, flame and sparks
lighting the road –
one group after another
falls embracing, in one lofty death.
The night, no matter how long, will continue
to give birth to star after star
and my life continues,
my life continues.

## Enough For Me

Enough for me to die on her earth
be buried in her
to melt and vanish into her soil
then sprout forth as a flower
played with by a child from my country
Enough for me to remain
in my country's embrace
to be in her close as a handful of dust
    a sprig of grass
      a flower.

## The Sibyl's Prophecy

1

On my twentieth birthday
the eternal soothsayer told me
to shishing winds
and prophesied,
'Evil spell around this house . . .
this house shall stay divided
until a certain horseman arrives . . .
a stately serene man, neither slow nor downhearted.
The winds tell me he shall come
on a road cleaved open by thunder
and lightning.'

Oh Sibyl! Won't you ask the winds
for a time *when* will this horseman arrive?

When rejection becomes
a blazing fire, a Golgotha,
then the womb of the earth shall birth him
But the winds also said,
'Beware of your seven brothers!
Beware
of your seven brothers!'

Under the cracks of this warped ceiling
I stood by the unhinged balcony
waiting for his hooves
listening to the pulse of buried seeds
bursting quietly inside the earth
and the heart of the wheatstalk
Oh, chemistry of life and death,
when would rejection become
a blazing fire, a Golgotha?

2

When he came, his footsteps were bells
echoing in the vaults of darkness.
The wind was the horse running under him,
shaking every ruin he passed.
He pulled me up behind him, saying,
'Dear one, your love protects my naked back,
hold fast, don't fear the night or wolves
Love knows no fear.'

When we mounted our horse
our songs flashed
like glittering daggers
unsheathed against the night!

On the shores of night
the trees grew high
flowers, and fruits ripened.
And the stars:
each time a star plummeted
in hurricane season
our windswept trees sent forth
new constellations.

That day we rode the horse's back
our brows shone radiant with sun
Shimmering vision wreathed our eyes
flowers carpeted the lips of meadows
on lowlands and river bank alike.

   But within me the winds nagged,
   'Beware!
   your seven brothers!
   'Beware!
   your seven brothers!'
   till it became a roar,
   'Beware!
   your seven brothers!'

If only we had spoken softly,
contained our agitation
If we could have continued walking
    slowly, stealthily,
    behind the fences

If only the moon
retired to its quiet cave in the mountains
    drawing its curtains . . .
but I feared the light exposing us, my love.
I feared hounds chasing us on the road,
going mad when the moon's blades gleamed against the dark
– 'Your love protects my naked back,
cling to me, darling, for love is no coward.'

    But the blowing winds chanted
    'Beware your seven brothers,
    Beware your seven brothers!'

3

Cain appears everywhere
knocking at doors
    climbing balconies
    and walls
leaping, crawling, hissing serpent
with a thousand tongues
Cain frolics in squares
swirling with hurricane
blocking paths, flinging open
    the gates of perdition
with his bloodied hands
    he drags the fiery coffins
Cain, the mad god burning Rome
death waxing large
as crystalline red willows
draping across horizons, and the thresholds of houses
Death, a giant growing bigger everywhere,
permeations of death and red Cain.

Sorrowfully, I stretched out my hand
pleading,
'Brothers! don't kill my beloved!
Don't twist the young neck
I beg you, in the name of love, kinship,
compassion,
don't kill him,
don't kill him,
please, don't . . .!'

4

When death reposed
and the branches of silence wove themselves around me
over him I bent, heavy with grief
cleansing his broken chest
with love and tears
collecting his limbs twisted with blood
   and smoke and pebbles
gathering his night black hair
the torn petals of his lips
the jewelled eyes
            (Ah, those eyes once the home
            for visions and dreams!)
            now stitched to the seam of night's jungle!

I gathered him limb by limb,
bouquet of flowers,
and gave him over to the winds
saying, 'Plant the shrapnel of this body
on mountain slopes and summits,
in plains and lowlands and riverbeds
Scatter him across the body of our homeland.'

5

September keeps me pinned to the cracks
   of my divided home

235

Still the Sibyl of winds knocks at my sad door
whenever morning breathes,
repeating,
'The seasons complete their cycle
and the festivals of rain bring him back . . .
March will bring him back
riding a chariot of flowers.'

## In the Aging City*

City streets and pavements receive me
with other people, the human tide rushes
me on. I move in this current, but only on
the surface, remaining by myself.
The tide overflows to sweep
these sidewalks and streets.
Faces, faces, faces rolling on,
dry and grim, they move on the surface,
remaining without human touch.
Here is nearness without being near.
Here is the no-presence in presence.
Here is nothing but the presence of absence!

Traffic light reddens; the tide holds back.
Bats flash across memory:
*a tank passes, as I crossed in the Nablus marketplace,*
*I moved out of its way.*
*How well I've learned not to disturb*
*the path of traffic! How well I've memorised*
*traffic laws!*
*And now here I am, in the London slave market*
*where they sold my parents and people. . .*
*Here I stand, a part of the profitable deal,*
*carrying the brunt of the sin –*
*Mine was that I am a plant*
*grown by the mountains of Palestine.*
*Ah! Those who died yesterday are at rest now.*
*(I suspect that their corpses cursed me*
*as I gave way for a tank to pass,*
*then moved on in the stream.)*
*Aisha's letter is on my desk,*
*Nablus is quiet, life flowing on*
*like river water . . .*

* The Aging City – the poet is speaking here of London, where she was on
a visit.

237

*The prison seal is an eloquent silence*
*(A guard tells her the trees have fallen,*
*the woods are not set ablaze any more.*
*But Aisha insists the forest is thick,*
*trees standing like fortresses. She dreams*
*of the forest she left blazing with fire*
*five years ago. She heard the thunder*
*of wind in her dream, tells the guard:*
*'I don't believe you, you're one of them,*
*and you remain the Prophets of the Lie.'*
*Then she crouches in the darkness of prison, dreaming.*
*Shaded by her standing trees she is joyous at the sound*
*of the far forest rattling with swords of flame.*
*And Aisha dreams and dreams.)*

The traffic light clicks green, the tide drives on.
My memory flits away, bats fall into a deep well.
A shadow changes direction, follows me.
sends out a bridge.
    – Are you a stranger like I am?
Two drops separate from the tide,
sit removed in a corner of the park.
    – Do you like Osborne?
    – Who doesn't?
    – England's elderly and its officers
setting with the sun of Suez . . .
    – Who do you think will plant tomorrow's tree
for this country?
    – The hippie youth.
    – You are sour, very sour.
The hippie tide passes by.
sweeping the city.
London keeps beat with
the toll of Big Ben.
    – Around the corner
    there's a pub and an elegant hotel
    with central heating – will you come?
    – Impossible!

238

A London lady passes, complaining to her dog
of arthritis and a pinched sciatic nerve.
   – Impossible!
   – Aren't you a modern woman?
   – I've grown beyond the days of rashness;
   sorrow has made me a hundred years old. Impossible!
I remove his arm from my shoulders.
   – I'm besieged by loneliness.
   – We're all besieged by loneliness;
   we're all alone, play along with life alone,
   suffer alone, and die by ourselves.
   You will remain alone here, even if a hundred
   women embrace you!
City streets and sidewalks swallow us with others,
a human tide sweeping us away in waves of faces.
We remain on the surface, touching nothing.

## From a Prisoner's Diary in an Unknown Prison

From mountain roads the darkness frowns and flows
  silently
while night sets its vast sail
neither the crawling light of stars
nor the sneaking rays of sun
can find their way to earth
This solid blank night contains no cracks
  for echoes.

Here Time lost its shoes, is stopped in its tracks
seasons seemed inverted
Is it time for sowing,
is it harvest, who knows?
No one will tell
The prison warder stands before us
with stony face and eyes
stealing the sun from us, stealing the moon.

But behind the frontiers of night
the horses of time race, dazzling,
towards the land of dream.
Behind the frontiers of night,
The sun still shines,
and the moon.

240

## Between Ebb and Flow

When words grow jellylike
on people's lying lips,
I shrink into myself,
   I dwindle and recede
avoiding the jellylike leavings on the roads
and all of human sliminess.
Terrified, I retreat
from the wolf's glamorous smile,
holding myself tightly in, lest I slip,
digging my heels deep into slippery ground,
closing my hands, refusing to be deluded
by false smiles
or the gleam of the fox-man.

But when a little child embraces me
touching my tired cheeks
with its velvet face, soft hands
lily fingers lacking claws
when two lovely eyes washed by dawn
and the angels of light
gaze into my life,
my heart softens,
my heart grows large
walls recede
the river of the north pole pours into it
irrigating trees
and the human face
returns from its exile
to dwell inside me.

**Salma Khadra Jayyusi** is a Palestinian poet, critic and anthologist. Born in East Jordan in 1926, she lived in Jerusalem, graduated in Arabic and English literature from the American University of Beirut, and later obtained a Ph.D. from the University of London. She has taught at the Universities of Khartoum, Algiers and Constantine, and in America at the Universities of Utah, Washington and Texas. Her first poetry collection, *Return from the Dreamy Fountain*, was published in 1960. The June 1967 war made her suspend publication of her second diwan, and since then she has founded PROTA (Project of Translation from Arabic), which aims at the dissemination of Arabic culture abroad. So far, Jayyusi has edited more than 30 volumes of prose and poetry, among which are six major anthologies: *Modern Arabic Poetry* (1987); *Literature of Modern Arabic Drama* (1988); *Modern Arabic Fiction*; *Contemporary Arabic Drama* (edited with Roger Allen) and *Anthology of Modern Palestinian Literature*, all three in press. Her anthology *Modern Arabic Short Plays* and a seventh anthology entitled *Poets of the End of the Century* are in preparation.

**Olive Kenny** spent many years in Egypt, where she taught English and studied Arabic at the School of Oriental Studies of the American University of Cairo. She is the translator of many novels, including two of Najib Mahfouz's famous triology *Bayn al-Qasrayn*, the latter translated with her husband Lorne M. Kenny; and the same author's *Wedding Song (Afrah al-Qubba)* Among translations for PROTA are M.Y. al-Qa'id's *War in the Land of Egypt* (1986) and Hanna Mina's *Fragments of Memory* (in press).

**Naomi Shihab Nye** is a poet and musician and translator of poets. Born in St Louis to a Palestinian father and an American mother, she graduated from Trinity University, San Antonio, Texas, then from 1966 to 1967 she lived in Jerusalem. Her publications include *Hugging the Juke Box*, *Different Ways to Pray*, and *Yellow Glove*; and she has co-translated selections from the Tunisian poet, Abu al-Qasim al-Shabbi, and the Syrian poet, Muhammad al-Maghut, as well as other poetry and prose for PROTA's major anthologies: *Modern Arabic Poetry* (1987); *Literature of Modern Arabia* (1988), *Modern Arabic Fiction* and *Anthology of Modern Palestinian Literature*. In 1988 she won the Peter I.B. Lavan Younger Poets Award.

**Fedwa Malti-Douglas** is Professor of Arabic and Director of the Institute for the Study of Literature, Religion and Society in the Contemporary Middle East at the University of Texas. She is the author of numerous studies in Arabic, French and English on classical and modern Arabic literature, including *Structures of Avarice: The Bukhala' in Medieval Arabic Literature* (Leiden, 1985) and *Blindness and Autobiography: Al-Ayyam of Taha Husayn* (Princeton, 1988).